PROTAGORAS,
PHILEBUS,
AND GORGIAS

PROTAGORAS, PHILEBUS, AND GORGIAS

Translated by Benjamin Jowett

PLATO

GREAT BOOKS IN PHILOSOPHY

 **Prometheus Books**

59 John Glenn Drive
Amherst, NewYork 14228-2197

Published 1996 by Prometheus Books

59 John Glenn Drive, Amherst, New York 14228–2197,
716–691–0133. FAX: 716–691–0137.

ISBN 1–57392–062–2

Printed in the United States of America on acid-free paper.

Additional Titles on Ethics in Prometheus's Great Books in Philosophy Series

Aristotle
The Nicomachean Ethics

Marcus Aurelius
Meditations

Jeremy Bentham
The Principles of Morals and Legislation

John Dewey
The Moral Writings of John Dewey, Revised Edition
(edited by James Gouinlock)

Epictetus
Enchiridion

Immanuel Kant
Fundamental Principles of the Metaphysic of Morals

John Stuart Mill
Utilitarianism

George Edward Moore
Principia Ethica

Friedrich Nietzsche
Beyond Good and Evil

Bertrand Russell
Bertrand Russell on Ethics, Sex, and Marriage
(edited by Al Seckel)

Arthur Schopenhauer
The Wisdom of Life and *Counsels and Maxims*

Benedict de Spinoza
Ethics and *The Improvement of the Understanding*

See the back of this volume for a complete list of titles in Prometheus's Great Books in Philosophy and Great Minds series.

PLATO was born about 427 B.C. into the distinguished Athenian family of Ariston and Perictione. Although interested in politics as a young man, he became disenchanted with the cruel and immoral behavior of Athenian rulers. Some small ray of hope emerged when Athens deposed its dictators and established a democracy; however, when the citizens put the philosopher Socrates on trial and later executed him for impiety, Plato left Athens to travel abroad.

In 387 B.C., Plato finally returned to Athens and created the Academy, an intellectual center for philosophy and science that offered scholarly training in such fields as astronomy, biological sciences, mathematics, and political science. From this influential institution emerged Aristotle, Plato's most famous student. Plato dedicated himself to the Academy until his death in about 347 B.C.

During his lifetime Plato wrote a number of supremely important dialogues, which presented and critically analyzed significant philosophical ideas in metaphysics, epistemology, ethics, and social and political philosophy—all of which continue to engage posterity. His better-known dialogues include: *The Apology, Cratylus, Crito, Euthyphro, Gorgias, The Laws, Meno, Parmenides, Phaedo, Phaedrus, Protagoras, The Republic, The Sophist, The Symposium, Theaetetus,* and *Timaeus.*

Contents

PROTAGORAS

PROTAGORAS

PERSONS OF THE DIALOGUE

SOCRATES, *who is the narrator of*   PROTAGORAS, ⎫
the Dialogue to his Companion   HIPPIAS,   ⎬ *Sophists*
HIPPOCRATES   PRODICUS, ⎭
ALCIBIADES   CALLIAS, *a wealthy Athenian*
CRITIAS

SCENE:—*The House of Callias*

Com. WHERE do you come from, Socrates? And yet I need hardly ask the question, for I know that you have been in chase of the fair Alcibiades. I saw him the day before yesterday; and he had got a beard like a man,—and he is a man, as I may tell you in your ear. But I thought that he was still very charming.

Soc. What of his beard? Are you not of Homer's opinion, who says[1]

'Youth is most charming when the beard first appears'?

And that is now the charm of Alcibiades.

Com. Well, and how do matters proceed? Have you been visiting him, and was he gracious to you?

Soc. Yes, I thought that he was very gracious; and especially to-day, for I have just come from him, and he has been helping me in an argument. But shall I tell you a strange thing? I paid no attention to him, and several times I quite forgot that he was present.

Com. What is the meaning of this? Has anything happened between you and him? For surely you cannot have discovered a fairer love than he is; certainly not in this city of Athens.

Soc. Yes, much fairer.

Com. What do you mean—a citizen or a foreigner?

Soc. A foreigner.

The fair Alcibiades.

But there is a fairer still.

[1] Il. xxiv. 348.

3

Prota-
goras

SOCRATES,
COM-
PANION,
HIPPO-
CRATES.

The fairer
is the
wiser, and
the wisest
of all
men is
[310]
Prota-
goras.

He is
actually
in Athens,
and Hip-
pocrates
has come
to bring
the good
news to
Socrates.

Com. Of what country?

Soc. Of Abdera.

Com. And is this stranger really in your opinion a fairer love than the son of Cleinias?

Soc. And is not the wiser always the fairer, sweet friend?

Com. But have you really met, Socrates, with some wise one?

Soc. Say rather, with the wisest of all living men, if you are willing to accord that title to Protagoras.

Com. What! Is Protagoras in Athens?

Soc. Yes; he has been here two days.

Com. And do you just come from an interview with him?

Soc. Yes; and I have heard and said many things.

Com. Then, if you have no engagement, suppose that you sit down and tell me what passed, and my attendant here shall give up his place to you.

Soc. To be sure; and I shall be grateful to you for listening.

Com. Thank you, too, for telling us.

Soc. That is thank you twice over. Listen then:—

Last night, or rather very early this morning, Hippocrates, the son of Apollodorus and the brother of Phason, gave a tremendous thump with his staff at my door; some one opened to him, and he came rushing in and bawled out: Socrates, are you awake or asleep?

I knew his voice, and said: Hippocrates, is that you? and do you bring any news?

Good news, he said; nothing but good.

Delightful, I said; but what is the news? and why have you come hither at this unearthly hour?

He drew nearer to me and said: Protagoras is come.

Yes, I replied; he came two days ago: have you only just heard of his arrival?

Yes, by the gods, he said; but not until yesterday evening.

At the same time he felt for the truckle-bed, and sat down at my feet, and then he said: Yesterday quite late in the evening, on my return from Oenoe whither I had gone in pursuit of my runaway slave Satyrus, as I meant to have told you, if some other matter had not come in the way;—on my return, when we had done supper and were about to retire to rest, my brother said to me: Protagoras is come. I was going to you at once, and then I thought that the night was far spent. But the moment sleep left me after my fatigue, I got up and came hither direct.

I, who knew the very courageous madness of the man, said: What is the matter? Has Protagoras robbed you of anything?

He replied, laughing: Yes, indeed he has, Socrates, of the wisdom which he keeps from me.

But, surely, I said, if you give him money, and make friends with him, he will make you as wise as he is himself.

Would to heaven, he replied, that this were the case! He might take all that I have, and all that my friends, have, if he pleased. But that is why I have come to you now, in order that you may speak to him on my behalf; for I am young, and also I have never seen nor heard him; (when he visited Athens before I was but a child;) and all men praise him, Socrates; he is reputed to be the most accomplished of speakers. There is no reason why we should not go to him at once, and then we shall find him at home. He lodges, as I hear, with Callias the son of Hipponicus: let us start.

I replied: Not yet, my good friend; the hour is too early. But let us rise and take a turn in the court and wait about there until daybreak; when the day breaks, then we will go. For Protagoras is generally at home, and we shall be sure to find him; never fear.

Upon this we got up and walked about in the court, and I thought that I would make trial of the strength of his resolution. So I examined him and put questions to him. Tell me, Hippocrates, I said, as you are going to Protagoras, and will be paying your money to him, what is he to whom you are going? and what will he make of you? If, for example, you had thought of going to Hippocrates of Cos, the Asclepiad, and were about to give him your money, and some one had said to you: You are paying money to your namesake Hippocrates, O Hippocrates; tell me, what is he that you give him money? how would you have answered?

I should say, he replied, that I gave money to him as a physician.

And what will he make of you?

A physician, he said.

And if you were resolved to go to Polycleitus the Argive, or Pheidias the Athenian, and were intending to give them money, and some one had asked you: What are Polycleitus and Pheidias? and why do you give them this money?—how would you have answered?

I should have answered, that they were statuaries.

And what will they make of you?

A statuary, of course.

Well now, I said, you and I are going to Protagoras, and we are ready to pay him money on your behalf. If our own means are sufficient, and we can gain him with these, we shall be only too glad; but if not, then we are to spend the money of your friends as well. Now suppose, that while we are thus enthusiastically pursuing our object some one were to say to us: Tell me, Socrates, and you Hippocrates, what is Protagoras, and why are you going to pay him money,— how should we answer? I know that Pheidias is a sculptor, and that Homer is a poet; but what appellation is given to Protagoras? how is he designated?

They call him a Sophist, Socrates, he replied.

Then we are going to pay our money to him in the character of a Sophist?

Certainly.

312

But suppose a person were to ask this further question: And how about yourself? What will Protagoras make of you, if you go to see him?

**The
breaking
dawn re-
veals a
blush on
the face
of Hippo-
crates as
he replies,
'A
Sophist.'**

He answered, with a blush upon his face (for the day was just beginning to dawn, so that I could see him): Unless this differs in some way from the former instances, I suppose that he will make a Sophist of me.

By the gods, I said, and are you not ashamed at having to appear before the Hellenes in the character of a Sophist?

Indeed, Socrates, to confess the truth, I am.

But you should not assume, Hippocrates, that the instruction of Protagoras is of this nature: may you not learn of him in the same way that you learned the arts of the grammarian, or musician, or trainer, not with the view of making any of them a profession, but only as a part of education, and because a private gentleman and freeman ought to know them?

Just so, he said; and that, in my opinion, is a far truer account of the teaching of Protagoras.

**Do you
know
what you
are doing,
or what is
the nature
of the
Sophist?**

I said: I wonder whether you know what you are doing?

And what am I doing?

You are going to commit your soul to the care of a man whom you call a Sophist. And yet I hardly think that you know what a Sophist is; and if not, then you do not even know to whom you are committing your soul and whether the thing to which you commit yourself be good or evil.

I certainly think that I do know, he replied.

Then tell me, what do you imagine that he is?

I take him to be one who knows wise things, he replied, as his name implies.

And might you not, I said, affirm this of the painter and of the carpenter also: Do not they, too, know wise things? But suppose a person were to ask us: In what are the painters wise? We should answer: In what relates to the making of likenesses, and similarly of other things. And if he were further to ask: What is the wisdom of the Sophist, and what is the manufacture over which he presides?—how should we answer him?

How should we answer him, Socrates? What other answer could there be but that he presides over the art which makes men eloquent?

Yes, I replied, that is very likely true, but not enough; for in the answer a further question is involved: Of what does the Sophist make a man talk eloquently? The player on the lyre may be supposed to make a man talk eloquently about that which he makes him understand, that is about playing the lyre. Is not that true?

Yes.

Then about what does the Sophist make him eloquent? Must not he make him eloquent in that which he understands?

Yes, that may be assumed.

And what is that which the Sophist knows and makes his disciple know?

Indeed, he said, I cannot tell.

Then I proceeded to say: Well, but are you aware of the danger which you are incurring? If you were going to commit your body to some one, who might do good or harm to it, would you not carefully consider and ask the opinion of your friends and kindred, and deliberate many days as to whether you should give him the care of your body? But when the soul is in question, which you hold to be of far more value than the body, and upon the good or evil of which depends the well-being of your all,—about this you never consulted either with your father or with your brother or with any one of us who are your companions. But no sooner does this foreigner appear, than you instantly commit your soul to his keeping. In the evening, as you say, you hear of him, and in the morning you go to him, never deliberating or taking the opinion of any one as to whether you ought to intrust yourself to him or not;—you have quite made up your mind that you will at all hazards be a pupil of Protagoras, and are prepared to expend all the property of yourself and of your friends in carrying out at any price this determination, although, as you admit, you do not know him, and have never spoken with him: and you call him a Sophist, but are manifestly ignorant of what a Sophist is; and yet you are going to commit yourself to his keeping.

When he heard me say this, he replied: No other inference, Socrates, can be drawn from your words.

I proceeded: Is not a Sophist, Hippocrates, one who deals wholesale or retail in the food of the soul? To me that appears to be his nature.

Prota-goras

SOCRATES, HIPPO-CRATES.

He is one who makes men talk eloquently about what he knows.

313
But if you do not know what that is, you cannot safely trust yourself to him.

The Sophist is one who

*Prota-
goras*

SOCRATES,
THE
DOOR-
KEEPER.

sells the
food of
the soul,

314
which
may be
poison.

The
porter of
the house
shows
that he is
not a
friend of
the
Sophists.

And what, Socrates, is the food of the soul?

Surely, I said, knowledge is the food of the soul; and we must take care, my friend, that the Sophist does not deceive us when he praises what he sells, like the dealers wholesale or retail who sell the food of the body; for they praise indiscriminately all their goods, without knowing what are really beneficial or hurtful: neither do their customers know, with the exception of any trainer or physician who may happen to buy of them. In like manner those who carry about the wares of knowledge, and make the round of the cities, and sell or retail them to any customer who is in want of them, praise them all alike; though I should not wonder, O my friend, if many of them were really ignorant of their effect upon the soul; and their customers equally ignorant, unless he who buys of them happens to be a physician of the soul. If, therefore, you have understanding of what is good and evil, you may safely buy knowledge of Protagoras or of any one; but if not, then, O my friend, pause, and do not hazard your dearest interests at a game of chance. For there is far greater peril in buying knowledge than in buying meat and drink: the one you purchase of the wholesale or retail dealer, and carry them away in other vessels, and before you receive them into the body as food, you may deposit them at home and call in any experienced friend who knows what is good to be eaten or drunken, and what not, and how much, and when; and then the danger of purchasing them is not so great. But you cannot buy the wares of knowledge and carry them away in another vessel; when you have paid for them you must receive them into the soul and go your way, either greatly harmed or greatly benefited; and therefore we should deliberate and take counsel with our elders; for we are still young—too young to determine such a matter. And now let us go, as we were intending, and hear Protagoras; and when we have heard what he has to say, we may take counsel of others; for not only is Protagoras at the house of Callias, but there is Hippias of Elis, and, if I am not mistaken, Prodicus of Ceos, and several other wise men.

To this we agreed, and proceeded on our way until we reached the vestibule of the house; and there we stopped in order to conclude a discussion which had arisen between us as we were going along; and we stood talking in the vestibule until we had finished and come to an understanding. And I think that the door-keeper, who was a eunuch, and who was probably annoyed at the great inroad of the Sophists, must have heard us talking. At any rate, when we knocked at the door, and he opened and saw us, he grumbled: They are Sophists—he is not at home; and instantly gave the door a hearty bang with both his hands. Again we knocked, and he answered without opening: Did you not hear me say that he is not at home, fellows? But, my friend, I said, you need not be alarmed; for we are not Sophists, and we are not come to see Callias, but we want to see Protagoras; and I must request you to announce us. At last, after a good deal of difficulty, the man was persuaded to open the door.

When we entered, we found Protagoras taking a walk in the cloister; and next to him, on one side, were walking Callias, the son of Hipponicus, and Paralus, the son of Pericles, who, by the mother's side, is his half-brother, and Charmides, the son of Glaucon. On the other side of him were Xanthippus, the other son of Pericles, Philippides, the son of Philomelus; also Antimoerus of Mende, who of all the disciples of Protagoras is the most famous, and intends to make sophistry his profession. A train of listeners followed him; the greater part of them appeared to be foreigners, whom Protagoras had brought with him out of the various cities visited by him in his journeys, he, like Orpheus, attracting them by his voice, and they following[1]. I should mention also that there were some Athenians in the company. Nothing delighted me more than the precision of their movements: they never got into his way at all; but when he and those who were with him turned back, then the band of listeners parted regularly on either side; he was always in front, and they wheeled round and took their places behind him in perfect order.

After him, as Homer says[2], 'I lifted up my eyes and saw' Hippias the Elean sitting in the opposite cloister on a chair of state, and around him were seated on benches Eryximachus, the son of Acumenus, and Phaedrus the Myrrhinusian, and Andron the son of Androtion, and there were strangers whom he had brought with him from his native city of Elis, and some others: they were putting to Hippias certain physical and astronomical questions, and he, *ex cathedra*, was determining their several questions to them, and discoursing of them.

Also, 'my eyes beheld Tantalus[3];' for Prodicus the Cean was at Athens: he had been lodged in a room which, in the days of Hipponicus, was a storehouse; but, as the house was full, Callias had cleared this out and made the room into a guest-chamber. Now Prodicus was still in bed, wrapped up in sheepskins and bedclothes, of which there seemed to be a great heap; and there was sitting by him on the couches near, Pausanias of the deme of Cerameis, and

Protagoras SOCRATES. Socrates pacifies him.

315

A well-trained band of listeners accompany Protagoras while walking in the cloister.

Hippias is seated in the opposite cloister.

Prodicus in the storehouse, still in bed.

[1] Cp. Rep. x. 600 D.
[2] Od. xi. 601 foll.
[3] Od. xi. 582.

with Pausanias was a youth quite young, who is certainly remarkable for his good looks, and, if I am not mistaken, is also of a fair
and gentle nature. I thought that I heard him called Agathon, and
my suspicion is that he is the beloved of Pausanias. There was this
youth, and also there were the two Adeimantuses, one the son of
Cepis, and the other of Leucolophides, and some others. I was very
anxious to hear what Prodicus was saying, for he seems to me to be
an all-wise and inspired man; but I was not able to get into the
inner circle, and his fine deep voice made an echo in the room which
rendered his words inaudible.

No sooner had we entered than there followed us Alcibiades the
beautiful, as you say, and I believe you; and also Critias the son of
Callaeschrus.

On entering we stopped a little, in order to look about us, and
then walked up to Protagoras, and I said: Protagoras, my friend
Hippocrates and I have come to see you.

Do you wish, he said, to speak with me alone, or in the presence
of the company?

Whichever you please, I said; you shall determine when you have
heard the purpose of our visit.

And what is your purpose? he said.

I must explain, I said, that my friend Hippocrates is a native
Athenian; he is the son of Apollodorus, and of a great and prosper-
ous house, and he is himself in natural ability quite a match for
anybody of his own age. I believe that he aspires to political emi-
nence; and this he thinks that conversation with you is most likely
to procure for him. And now you can determine whether you would
wish to speak to him of your teaching alone or in the presence of the
company.

Thank you, Socrates, for your consideration of me. For certainly
a stranger finding his way into great cities, and persuading the flow-
er of the youth in them to leave the company of their kinsmen or
any other acquaintances, old or young, and live with him, under the
idea that they will be improved by his conversation, ought to be
very cautious; great jealousies are aroused by his proceedings, and
he is the subject of many enmities and conspiracies. Now the art of
the Sophist is, as I believe, of great antiquity; but in ancient times
those who practised it, fearing this odium, veiled and disguised
themselves under various names, some under that of poets, as
Homer, Hesiod, and Simonides, some, of hierophants and prophets,
as Orpheus and Musaeus, and some, as I observe, even under the
name of gymnastic-masters, like Iccus of Tarentum, or the more
recently celebrated Herodicus, now of Selymbria and formerly of

Megara, who is a first-rate Sophist. Your own Agathocles pretended to be a musician, but was really an eminent Sophist; also Pythocleides the Cean; and there were many others; and all of them, as I was saying, adopted these arts as veils or disguises because they were afraid of the odium which they would incur. But that is not my way, for I do not believe that they effected their purpose, which was to deceive the government, who were not blinded by them; and as to the people, they have no understanding, and only repeat what their rulers are pleased to tell them. Now to run away, and to be caught in running away, is the very height of folly, and also greatly increases the exasperation of mankind; for they regard him who runs away as a rogue, in addition to any other objections which they have to him; and therefore I take an entirely opposite course, and acknowledge myself to be a Sophist and instructor of mankind; such an open acknowledgment appears to me to be a better sort of caution than concealment. Nor do I neglect other precautions, and therefore I hope, as I may say, by the favour of heaven that no harm will come of the acknowledgment that I am a Sophist. And I have been now many years in the profession—for all my years when added up are many: there is no one here present of whom I might not be the father. Wherefore I should much prefer conversing with you, if you want to speak with me, in the presence of the company.

As I suspected that he would like to have a little display and glorification in the presence of Prodicus and Hippias, and would gladly show us to them in the light of his admirers, I said: But why should we not summon Prodicus and Hippias and their friends to hear us?

Very good, he said.

Suppose, said Callias, that we hold a council in which you may sit and discuss.—This was agreed upon, and great delight was felt at the prospect of hearing wise men talk; we ourselves took the chairs and benches, and arranged them by Hippias, where the other benches had been already placed. Meanwhile Callias and Alcibiades got Prodicus out of bed and brought in him and his companions.

When we were all seated, Protagoras said: Now that the company are assembled, Socrates, tell me about the young man of whom you were just now speaking.

I replied: I will begin again at the same point, Protagoras, and tell you once more the purport of my visit: this is my friend Hippocrates, who is desirous of making your acquaintance; he would like to know what will happen to him if he associates with you. I have no more to say.

Protagoras answered: Young man, if you associate with me, on

Protagoras

SOCRATES, PROTAGORAS, CALLIAS.
317

poets and musicians, but Protagoras thinks that openness is the best policy.

They agree to hold a council.

318
The question is asked, What will happen to Hippocrates if he be-

*Prota-
goras*

SOCRATES,
PROTA-
GORAS.

comes the
disciple of
Prota-
goras?

Answer:
He will
daily
grow
wiser and
better.

But in
what?

In the
knowl-
edge of
affairs
private
as well as
public.

But such
knowl-

the very first day you will return home a better man than you came, and better on the second day than on the first, and better every day than you were on the day before.

When I heard this, I said: Protagoras, I do not at all wonder at hearing you say this; even at your age, and with all your wisdom, if any one were to teach you what you did not know before, you would become better no doubt: but please to answer in a different way— I will explain how by an example. Let me suppose that Hippocrates, instead of desiring your acquaintance, wished to become acquainted with the young man Zeuxippus of Heraclea, who has lately been in Athens, and he had come to him as he has come to you, and had heard him say, as he has heard you say, that every day he would grow and become better if he associated with him: and then suppose that he were to ask him, 'In what shall I become better, and in what shall I grow?'—Zeuxippus would answer, 'In painting.' And suppose that he went to Orthagoras the Theban, and heard him say the same thing, and asked him, 'In what shall I become better day by day?' he would reply, 'In flute-playing.' Now I want you to make the same sort of answer to this young man and to me, who am asking questions on his account. When you say that on the first day on which he associates with you he will return home a better man, and on every day will grow in like manner,—in what, Protagoras, will he be better? and about what?

When Protagoras heard me say this, he replied: You ask questions fairly, and I like to answer a question which is fairly put. If Hippocrates comes to me he will not experience the sort of drudgery with which other Sophists are in the habit of insulting their pupils; who, when they have just escaped from the arts, are taken and driven back into them by these teachers, and made to learn calculation, and astronomy, and geometry, and music (he gave a look at Hippias as he said this); but if he comes to me, he will learn that which he comes to learn. And this is prudence in affairs private as well as public; he will learn to order his own house in the best manner, and he will be able to speak and act for the best in the affairs of the state.

319   Do I understand you, I said; and is your meaning that you teach the art of politics, and that you promise to make men good citizens? That, Socrates, is exactly the profession which I make.

Then, I said, you do indeed possess a noble art, if there is no mistake about this; for I will freely confess to you, Protagoras, that I have a doubt whether this art is capable of being taught, and yet I know not how to disbelieve your assertion. And I ought to tell you why I am of opinion that this art cannot be taught or communicated by man to man. I say that the Athenians are an understanding people, and indeed they are esteemed to be such by the other Hellenes. Now I observe that when we are met together in the assembly, and the matter in hand relates to building, the builders are summoned as advisers; when the question is one of ship-building, then the ship-wrights; and the like of other arts which they think capable of being taught and learned. And if some person offers to give them advice who is not supposed by them to have any skill in the art, even though he be good-looking, and rich, and noble, they will not listen to him, but laugh and hoot at him, until either he is clamoured down and retires of himself; or if he persist, he is dragged away or put out by the constables at the command of the prytanes. This is their way of behaving about professors of the arts. But when the question is an affair of state, then everybody is free to have a say—carpenter, tinker, cobbler, sailor, passenger; rich and poor, high and low—any one who likes gets up, and no one reproaches him, as in the former case, with not having learned, and having no teacher, and yet giving advice; evidently because they are under the impression that this sort of knowledge cannot be taught. And not only is this true of the state, but of individuals; the best and wisest of our citizens are unable to impart their political wisdom to others: as for example, Pericles, the father of these young men, who gave them excellent instruction in all that could be learned from masters, in his own department of politics neither taught them, nor gave them teachers; but they were allowed to wander at their own free will in a sort of hope that they would light upon virtue of their own accord. Or take another example: there was Cleinias the younger brother of our friend Alcibiades, of whom this very same Pericles was the guardian; and he being in fact under the apprehension that Cleinias would be corrupted by Alcibiades, took him away, and placed him in the house of Ariphron to be educated; but before six months had elapsed, Ariphron sent him back, not knowing what to do with him. And I could mention numberless other instances of persons who were good themselves, and never yet made any one else good, whether friend or stranger. Now I, Protagoras, having these examples before me, am inclined to think that virtue cannot be taught. But then again, when I listen to your words, I waver; and am disposed to think that there must be something in what you say, because I know that you have great experience, and learning, and invention. And I wish that you would, if possible, show me a little more clearly that virtue can be taught. Will you be so good?

That I will, Socrates, and gladly. But what would you like? Shall

*Prota-
goras*

SOCRATES,
PROTA-
GORAS.

edge can-
not be
taught or
communi-
cated by
one man
to an-
other.

320
Pericles
could not
teach his
own sons
politics,
nor his
ward
Cleinias
virtue.

Will Pro-
tagoras be
so good as
to prove
that

*Prota-
goras*

PROTA-
GORAS.

virtue can
be
taught?

Prota-
goras
promises
to do so
in an
apologue.

The cre-
ation of
the brute
animals,
who were
equipped
with the
qualities
[321]
necessary
for their
preserva-
tion,
while men
remained
naked and
defence-
less.

To meet
this need
of theirs
Prome-
theus
stole the
arts of
Athene
and
Hephae-
stus, to-
gether
with fire.

I, as an elder, speak to you as younger men in an apologue or myth, or shall I argue out the question?

To this several of the company answered that he should choose for himself.

Well, then, he said, I think that the myth will be more interesting. Once upon a time there were gods only, and no mortal creatures. But when the time came that these also should be created, the gods fashioned them out of earth and fire and various mixtures of both elements in the interior of the earth; and when they were about to bring them into the light of day, they ordered Prometheus and Epimetheus to equip them, and to distribute to them severally their proper qualities. Epimetheus said to Prometheus: 'Let me distribute, and do you inspect.' This was agreed, and Epimetheus made the distribution. There were some to whom he gave strength without swiftness, while he equipped the weaker with swiftness; some he armed, and others he left unarmed; and devised for the latter some other means of preservation, making some large, and having their size as a protection, and others small, whose nature was to fly in the air or burrow in the ground; this was to be their way of escape. Thus did he compensate them with the view of preventing any race from becoming extinct. And when he had provided against their destruction by one another, he contrived also a means of protecting them against the seasons of heaven; clothing them with close hair and thick skins sufficient to defend them against the winter cold and able to resist the summer heat, so that they might have a natural bed of their own when they wanted to rest; also he furnished them with hoofs and hair and hard and callous skins under their feet. Then he gave them varieties of food,—herb of the soil to some, to others fruits of trees, and to others roots, and to some again he gave other animals as food. And some he made to have few young ones, while those who were their prey were very prolific; and in this manner the race was preserved. Thus did Epimetheus, who, not being very wise, forgot that he had distributed among the brute animals all the qualities which he had to give,—and when he came to man, who was still unprovided, he was terribly perplexed. Now while he was in this perplexity, Prometheus came to inspect the distribution, and he found that the other animals were suitably furnished, but that man alone was naked and shoeless, and had neither bed nor arms of defence. The appointed hour was approaching when man in his turn was to go forth into the light of day; and Prometheus, not knowing how he could devise his salvation, stole the mechanical arts of Hephaestus and Athene, and fire with them (they could neither have been acquired nor used without fire), and gave

them to man. Thus man had the wisdom necessary to the support
of life, but political wisdom he had not; for that was in the keeping
of Zeus, and the power of Prometheus did not extend to entering
into the citadel of heaven, where Zeus dwelt, who moreover had
terrible sentinels; but he did enter by stealth into the common
workshop of Athene and Hephaestus, in which they used to practise
their favourite arts, and carried off Hephaestus' art of working by
fire, and also the art of Athene, and gave them to man. And in this
way man was supplied with the means of life. But Prometheus is
said to have been afterwards prosecuted for theft, owing to the
blunder of Epimetheus.

Now man, having a share of the divine attributes, was at first the
only one of the animals who had any gods, because he alone was of
their kindred; and he would raise altars and images of them. He
was not long in inventing articulate speech and names; and he also
constructed houses and clothes and shoes and beds, and drew suste-
nance from the earth. Thus provided, mankind at first lived dispersed, and there were no cities. But the consequence was that they
were destroyed by the wild beasts, for they were utterly weak in
comparison of them, and their art was only sufficient to provide
them with the means of life, and did not enable them to carry on
war against the animals: food they had, but not as yet the art of
government, of which the art of war is a part. After a while the desire of self-preservation gathered them into cities; but when they
were gathered together, having no art of government, they evil in-
treated one another, and were again in process of dispersion and
destruction. Zeus feared that the entire race would be exterminated,
and so he sent Hermes to them, bearing reverence and justice to be
the ordering principles of cities and the bonds of friendship and con-
ciliation. Hermes asked Zeus how he should impart justice and reverence among men:—Should he distribute them as the arts are distributed; that is to say, to a favoured few only, one skilled individual having enough of medicine or of any other art for many unskilled ones? 'Shall this be the manner in which I am to distribute
justice and reverence among men, or shall I give them to all?' 'To
all,' said Zeus; 'I should like them all to have a share; for cities
cannot exist, if a few only share in the virtues, as in the arts. And
further, make a law by my order, that he who has no part in reverence and justice shall be put to death, for he is a plague of the state.'

And this is the reason, Socrates, why the Athenians and mankind
in general, when the question relates to carpentering or any other
mechanical art, allow but a few to share in their deliberations; and
when any one else interferes, then, as you say, they object, if he be

322
But men
were still
destitute
of politi-
cal wis-
dom, and
were in
danger of
being ex-
termi-
nated by
the wild
beasts.

So to pro-
tect them-
selves
they
gathered
into
cities; but
having no
sense of
right,
they be-
gan to de-
stroy one
another.
Hermes at
the desire
of Zeus
imparted
justice
and re-
verence to
them.

These
virtues
were im-
parted
not, like

323
*Prota-
goras*

PROTA-
GORAS.

the arts,
to a few
only, but
to all.

And cer-
tainly all
men are
expected
to profess
them,

not of the favoured few; which, as I reply, is very natural. But when they meet to deliberate about political virtue, which proceeds only by way of justice and wisdom, they are patient enough of any man who speaks of them, as is also natural, because they think that every man ought to share in this sort of virtue, and that states could not exist if this were otherwise. I have explained to you, Socrates, the reason of this phenomenon.

And that you may not suppose yourself to be deceived in thinking that all men regard every man as having a share of justice or honesty and of every other political virtue, let me give you a further proof, which is this. In other cases, as you are aware, if a man says that he is a good flute-player, or skilful in any other art in which he has no skill, people either laugh at him or are angry with him, and his relations think that he is mad and go and admonish him; but when honesty is in question, or some other political virtue, even if they know that he is dishonest, yet, if the man comes publicly forward and tells the truth about his dishonesty, then, what in the other case was held by them to be good sense, they now deem to be madness. They say that all men ought to profess honesty whether they are honest or not, and that a man is out of his mind who says anything else. Their notion is, that a man must have some degree of honesty; and that if he has none at all he ought not to be in the world.

I have been showing that they are right in admitting every man as a counsellor about this sort of virtue, as they are of opinion that every man is a partaker of it. And I will now endeavour to show further that they do not conceive this virtue to be given by nature, or to grow spontaneously, but to be a thing which may be taught;

and are
punished
for the
want of
them,
which is
a proof
that they
can be
acquired
and
taught.

and which comes to a man by taking pains. No one would instruct, no one would rebuke. or be angry with those whose calamities they suppose to be due to nature or chance; they do not try to punish or to prevent them from being what they are; they do but pity them. Who is so foolish as to chastise or instruct the ugly, or the diminutive, or the feeble? And for this reason. Because he knows that good and evil of this kind is the work of nature and of chance; whereas if a man is wanting in those good qualities which are attained by study and exercise and teaching, and has only the contrary evil qualities, other men are angry with him, and punish and reprove

324

him—of these evil qualities one is impiety, another injustice, and they may be described generally as the very opposite of political virtue. In such cases any man will be angry with another, and reprimand him,—clearly because he thinks that by study and learning, the virtue in which the other is deficient may be acquired. If you will think, Socrates, of the nature of punishment, you will see at once that in the opinion of mankind virtue may be acquired; no one punishes the evil-doer under the notion, or for the reason, that he has done wrong,—only the unreasonable fury of a beast acts in that manner. But he who desires to inflict rational punishment does not retaliate for a past wrong which cannot be undone; he has regard to the future, and is desirous that the man who is punished, and he who sees him punished, may be deterred from doing wrong again. He punishes for the sake of prevention, thereby clearly implying that virtue is capable of being taught. This is the notion of all who retaliate upon others either privately or publicly. And the Athenians, too, your own citizens, like other men, punish and take vengeance on all whom they regard as evil doers; and hence, we may infer them to be of the number of those who think that virtue may be acquired and taught. Thus far, Socrates, I have shown you clearly enough, if I am not mistaken, that your countrymen are right in admitting the tinker and the cobbler to advise about politics, and also that they deem virtue to be capable of being taught and acquired.

There yet remains one difficulty which has been raised by you about the sons of good men. What is the reason why good men teach their sons the knowledge which is gained from teachers, and make them wise in that, but do nothing towards improving them in the virtues which distinguish themselves? And here, Socrates, I will leave the apologue and resume the argument. Please to consider: Is there or is there not some one quality of which all the citizens must be partakers, if there is to be a city at all? In the answer to this question is contained the only solution of your difficulty; there is no other. For if there be any such quality, and this quality or unity is not the art of the carpenter, or the smith, or the potter, but justice and temperance and holiness and, in a word, manly virtue—if this is the quality of which all men must be partakers, and which is the very condition of their learning or doing anything else, and if he who is wanting in this, whether he be a child only or a grown-up man or woman, must be taught and punished, until by punishment he becomes better, and he who rebels against instruction and punishment is either exiled or condemned to death under the idea that he is incurable—if what I am saying be true, good men have their sons taught other things and not this, do consider how extraordinary their conduct would appear to be. For we have shown that they think virtue capable of being taught and cultivated both in private and public; and, notwithstanding, they have their sons taught lesser matters, ignorance of which does not involve the pun-

Prota-goras

PROTA-GORAS.

But why do not good men teach their sons virtue?

325

ishment of death: but greater things, of which the ignorance may cause death and exile to those who have no training or knowledge of them—aye, and confiscation as well as death, and, in a word, may be the ruin of families—those things, I say, they are supposed not to teach them,—not to take the utmost care that they should learn. How improbable is this, Socrates!

They do in fact teach them in all stages of their life by the help of tutors, nurses, teachers, and professors of all sorts.

Education and admonition commence in the first years of childhood, and last to the very end of life. Mother and nurse and father and tutor are vying with one another about the improvement of the child as soon as ever he is able to understand what is being said to him: he cannot say or do anything without their setting forth to him that this is just and that is unjust; this is honourable, that is dishonourable; this is holy, that is unholy; do this and abstain from that. And if he obeys, well and good; if not, he is straightened by threats and blows, like a piece of bent or warped wood. At a later stage they send him to teachers, and enjoin them to see to his manners even more than to his reading and music; and the teachers do as they are desired. And when the boy has learned his letters and is beginning to understand what is written, as before he understood only what was spoken, they put into his hands the works of great poets, which he reads sitting on a bench at school; in these are contained many admonitions, and many tales, and praises, and encomia of ancient famous men, which he is required to learn by heart, in order that he may imitate or emulate them and desire to become like them. Then, again, the teachers of the lyre take similar care that their young disciple is temperate and gets into no mischief; and when they have taught him the use of the lyre, they introduce him to the poems of other excellent poets, who are the lyric poets; and these they set to music, and make their harmonies and rhythms quite familiar to the children's souls, in order that they may learn to be more gentle, and harmonious, and rhythmical, and so more fitted for speech and action; for the life of man in every part has need of harmony and rhythm. Then they send them to the master of gymnastic, in order that their bodies may better minister to the virtuous mind, and that they may not be compelled through bodily weakness to play the coward in war or on any other occasion. This is what is done by those who have the means, and those who have the means are the rich; their children begin to go to school soonest and leave off latest. When they have done with masters, the state again compels them to learn the laws, and live after the pattern which they furnish, and not after their own fancies; and just as in learning to write, the writing-master first draws lines with a style for the use of the young beginner, and gives him the tablet and

When they grow up the laws become their teacher.

326

makes him follow the lines, so the city draws the laws, which were the invention of good lawgivers living in the olden time; these are given to the young man, in order to guide him in his conduct whether he is commanding or obeying; and he who transgresses them is to be corrected, or, in other words, called to account, which is a term used not only in your country, but also in many others, seeing that justice calls men to account. Now when there is all this care about virtue private and public, why, Socrates, do you still wonder and doubt whether virtue can be taught? Cease to wonder, for the opposite would be far more surprising.

But why then do the sons of good fathers often turn out ill? There is nothing very wonderful in this; for, as I have been saying, the existence of a state implies that virtue is not any man's private possession. If so—and nothing can be truer—then I will further ask you to imagine, as an illustration, some other pursuit or branch of knowledge which may be assumed equally to be the condition of the existence of a state. Suppose that there could be no state unless we were all flute-players, as far as each had the capacity, and everybody was freely teaching everybody the art, both in private and public, and reproving the bad player as freely and openly as every man now teaches justice and the laws, not concealing them as he would conceal the other arts, but imparting them—for all of us have a mutual interest in the justice and virtue of one another, and this is the reason why every one is so ready to teach justice and the laws;—suppose, I say, that there were the same readiness and liberality among us in teaching one another flute-playing, do you imagine, Socrates, that the sons of good flute-players would be more likely to be good than the sons of bad ones? I think not. Would not their sons grow up to be distinguished or undistinguished according to their own natural capacities as flute-players, and the son of a good player would often turn out to be a bad one, and the son of a bad player to be a good one, and all flute-players would be good enough in comparison of those who were ignorant and unacquainted with the art of flute-playing? In like manner I would have you consider that he who appears to you to be the worst of those who have been brought up in laws and humanities, would appear to be a just man and a master of justice if he were to be compared with men who had no education, or courts of justice, or laws, or any restraints upon them which compelled them to practise virtue—with the savages, for example, whom the poet Pherecrates exhibited on the stage at the last year's Lenaean festival. If you were living among men such as the man-haters in his Chorus, you would be only too glad to meet with Eurybates and Phrynondas, and you would sorrowfully

Prota-goras

PROTA-GORAS.

Beyond question, then, virtue can be taught.

But the sons of good men are not [327] always good men, any more than the sons of good artists are always good artists.

The worst of civilized men are good enough compared with savages.

Prota-
goras

328
SOCRATES,
PROTA-
GORAS.

All men
are
teachers
of virtue
to a cer-
tain ex-
tent.

long to revisit the rascality of this part of the world. And you,
Socrates, are discontented, and why? Because all men are teachers
of virtue, each one according to his ability; and you say, Where are
the teachers? You might as well ask, Who teaches Greek? For of
that too there will not be any teachers found. Or you might ask,
Who is to teach the sons of our artisans this same art which they
have learned of their fathers? He and his fellow-workmen have
taught them to the best of their ability,—but who will carry them
further in their arts? And you would certainly have a difficulty,
Socrates, in finding a teacher of them; but there would be no difficulty in finding a teacher of those who are wholly ignorant. And
this is true of virtue or of anything else; if a man is better able than
we are to promote virtue ever so little, we must be content with the
result. A teacher of this sort I believe myself to be, and above all
other men to have the knowledge which makes a man noble and
good; and I give my pupils their money's-worth, and even more, as
they themselves confess. And therefore I have introduced the following mode of payment:—When a man has been my pupil, if he
likes he pays my price, but there is no compulsion; and if he does
not like, he has only to go into a temple and take an oath of the
value of the instructions, and he pays no more than he declares to
be their value.

Such is my Apologue, Socrates, and such is the argument by
which I endeavour to show that virtue may be taught, and that this
is the opinion of the Athenians. And I have also attempted to show
that you are not to wonder at good fathers having bad sons, or at
good sons having bad fathers, of which the sons of Polycleitus afford
an example, who are the companions of our friends here, Paralus
and Xanthippus, but are nothing in comparison with their father;
and this is true of the sons of many other artists. As yet I ought not
to say the same of Paralus and Xanthippus themselves, for they are
young and there is still hope of them.

Protagoras ended, and in my ear

'So charming left his voice, that I the while
Thought him still speaking; still stood fixed to hear [1].'

Socrates
is over-
whelmed
by the
eloquence
of Prota-
goras.
But he
would
like to

At length, when the truth dawned upon me, that he had really finished, not without difficulty I began to collect myself, and looking
at Hippocrates, I said to him: O son of Apollodorus, how deeply
grateful I am to you for having brought me hither; I would not have
missed the speech of Protagoras for a great deal. For I used to imagine that no human care could make men good; but I know better

[1] Borrowed by Milton, *Paradise Lost*, viii. 2, 3.

now. Yet I have still one very small difficulty which I am sure that Protagoras will easily explain, as he has already explained so much. If a man were to go and consult Pericles or any of our great speakers about these matters, he might perhaps hear as fine a discourse; but then when one has a question to ask of any of them, like books, they can neither answer nor ask; and if any one challenges the least particular of their speech, they go ringing on in a long harangue, like brazen pots, which when they are struck continue to sound unless some one puts his hand upon them; whereas our friend Protagoras can not only make a good speech, as he has already shown, but when he is asked a question he can answer briefly; and when he asks he will wait and hear the answer; and this is a very rare gift. Now I, Protagoras, want to ask of you a little question, which if you will only answer, I shall be quite satisfied. You were saying that virtue can be taught;—that I will take upon your authority, and there is no one to whom I am more ready to trust. But I marvel at one thing about which I should like to have my mind set at rest. You were speaking of Zeus sending justice and reverence to men; and several times while you were speaking, justice, and temperance, and holiness, and all these qualities, were described by you as if together they made up virtue. Now I want you to tell me truly whether virtue is one whole, of which justice and temperance and holiness are parts; or whether all these are only the names of one and the same thing: that is the doubt which still lingers in my mind.

There is no difficulty, Socrates, in answering that the qualities of which you are speaking are the parts of virtue which is one.

And are they parts, I said, in the same sense in which mouth, nose, and eyes, and ears, are the parts of a face; or are they like the parts of gold, which differ from the whole and from one another only in being larger or smaller?

I should say that they differed, Socrates, in the first way; they are related to one another as the parts of a face are related to the whole face.

And do men have some one part and some another part of virtue? Or if a man has one part, must he also have all the others?

By no means, he said; for many a man is brave and not just, or just and not wise.

You would not deny, then, that courage and wisdom are also parts of virtue?

Most undoubtedly they are, he answered; and wisdom is the noblest of the parts.

And they are all different from one another? I said.

Yes.

Prota-
goras

329
SOCRATES,
PROTA-
GORAS.

put a small question to him:—Are the virtues the parts of a whole or the names of one and the same thing?

They are the parts of a whole differing in the same manner as the parts of a face.

330

*Prota-
goras*

SOCRATES,
PROTA-
GORAS.

Many
men have
one part
of virtue
and not
another.

And has each of them a distinct function like the parts of the face;—the eye, for example, is not like the ear, and has not the same functions; and the other parts are none of them like one another, either in their functions, or in any other way? I want to know whether the comparison holds concerning the parts of virtue. Do they also differ from one another in themselves and in their functions? For that is clearly what the simile would imply.

Yes, Socrates, you are right in supposing that they differ.

Then, I said, no other part of virtue is like knowledge, or like justice, or like courage, or like temperance, or like holiness?

No, he answered.

Well then, I said, suppose that you and I enquire into their natures. And first, you would agree with me that justice is of the nature of a thing, would you not? That is my opinion: would it not be yours also?

Mine also, he said.

And suppose that some one were to ask us, saying, 'O Protagoras, and you, Socrates, what about this thing which you were calling justice, is it just or unjust?'—and I were to answer, just: would you vote with me or against me?

With you, he said.

Thereupon I should answer to him who asked me, that justice is of the nature of the just: would not you?

Yes, he said.

And suppose that he went on to say: 'Well now, is there also such a thing as holiness?'—we should answer, 'Yes,' if I am not mistaken?

Yes, he said.

Which you would also acknowledge to be a thing—should we not say so?

He assented.

'And is this a sort of thing which is of the nature of the holy, or of the nature of the unholy?' I should be angry at his putting such a question, and should say, 'Peace, man; nothing can be holy if holiness is not holy.' What would you say? Would you not answer in the same way?

Certainly, he said.

And then after this suppose that he came and asked us, 'What were you saying just now? Perhaps I may not have heard you rightly, but you seemed to me to be saying that the parts of virtue were not the same as one another.' I should reply, 'You certainly heard that said, but not, as you imagine, by me; for I only asked the question; Protagoras gave the answer.' And suppose that he turned to

331

you and said, 'Is this true, Protagoras? and do you maintain that one part of virtue is unlike another, and is this your position?'— how would you answer him?

I could not help acknowledging the truth of what he said, Socrates.

Well then, Protagoras, we will assume this; and now supposing that he proceeded to say further, 'Then holiness is not of the nature of justice, nor justice of the nature of holiness, but of the nature of unholiness; and holiness is of the nature of the not just, and therefore of the unjust, and the unjust is the unholy:' how shall we answer him? I should certainly answer him on my own behalf that justice is holy, and that holiness is just; and I would say in like manner on your behalf also, if you would allow me, that justice is either the same with holiness, or very nearly the same; and above all I would assert that justice is like holiness and holiness is like justice; and I wish that you would tell me whether I may be permitted to give this answer on your behalf, and whether you would agree with me.

He replied, I cannot simply agree, Socrates, to the proposition that justice is holy and that holiness is just, for there appears to me to be a difference between them. But what matter? if you please I please; and let us assume, if you will, that justice is holy, and that holiness is just.

Pardon me, I replied; I do not want this 'if you wish' or 'if you will' sort of conclusion to be proven, but I want you and me to be proven: I mean to say that the conclusion will be best proven if there be no 'if.'

Well, he said, I admit that justice bears a resemblance to holiness, for there is always some point of view in which everything is like every other thing; white is in a certain way like black, and hard is like soft, and the most extreme opposites have some qualities in common; even the parts of the face which, as we were saying before, are distinct and have different functions, are still in a certain point of view similar, and one of them is like another of them. And you may prove that they are like one another on the same principle that all things are like one another; and yet things which are like in some particular ought not to be called alike, nor things which are unlike in some particular, however slight, unlike.

And do you think, I said in a tone of surprise, that justice and holiness have but a small degree of likeness?

Certainly not; any more than I agree with what I understand to be your view.

Prota-goras

SOCRATES,
PROTA-
GORAS.

The
virtues
differ, yet
many of
them, e. g.
holiness
and
justice,
are very
much
alike.

Prota-
goras
admits
the like-
ness, but
denies the
identity
of the
virtues.

33²
*Prota-
goras*

SOCRATES,
PROTA-
GORAS.

Prota-
goras is
drawn
into
making
the ad-
mission
that
every-
thing has
but one
opposite.

Well, I said, as you appear to have a difficulty about this, let us take another of the examples which you mentioned instead. Do you admit the existence of folly?

I do.

And is not wisdom the very opposite of folly?

That is true, he said.

And when men act rightly and advantageously they seem to you to be temperate?

Yes, he said.

And temperance makes them temperate?

Certainly.

And they who do not act rightly act foolishly, and in acting thus are not temperate?

I agree, he said.

Then to act foolishly is the opposite of acting temperately?

He assented.

And foolish actions are done by folly, and temperate actions by temperance?

He agreed.

And that is done strongly which is done by strength, and that which is weakly done, by weakness?

He assented.

And that which is done with swiftness is done swiftly, and that which is done with slowness, slowly?

He assented again.

And that which is done in the same manner, is done by the same; and that which is done in an opposite manner by the opposite?

He agreed.

Once more, I said, is there anything beautiful?

Yes.

To which the only opposite is the ugly?

There is no other.

And is there anything good?

There is.

To which the only opposite is the evil?

There is no other.

And there is the acute in sound?

True.

To which the only opposite is the grave?

There is no other, he said, but that.

Then every opposite has one opposite only and no more?

He assented.

Then now, I said, let us recapitulate our admissions. First of all we admitted that everything has one opposite and not more than one?

We did so.

And we admitted also that what was done in opposite ways was done by opposites?

Yes.

And that which was done foolishly, as we further admitted, was done in the opposite way to that which was done temperately?

Yes.

And that which was done temperately was done by temperance, and that which was done foolishly by folly?

He agreed.

And that which is done in opposite ways is done by opposites?

Yes.

And one thing is done by temperance, and quite another thing by folly?

Yes.

And in opposite ways?

Certainly.

And therefore by opposites:—then folly is the opposite of temperance?

Clearly.

And do you remember that folly has already been acknowledged by us to be the opposite of wisdom?

He assented.

And we said that everything has only one opposite?

Yes.

Then, Protagoras, which of the two assertions shall we renounce? One says that everything has but one opposite; the other that wisdom is distinct from temperance, and that both of them are parts of virtue; and that they are not only distinct, but dissimilar, both in themselves and in their functions, like the parts of a face. Which of these two assertions shall we renounce? For both of them together are certainly not in harmony; they do not accord or agree: for how can they be said to agree if everything is assumed to have only one opposite and not more than one, and yet folly, which is one, has clearly the two opposites—wisdom and temperance? Is not that true, Protagoras? What else would you say?

He assented, but with great reluctance.

Then temperance and wisdom are the same, as before justice and holiness appeared to us to be nearly the same. And now, Protagoras, I said, we must finish the enquiry, and not faint. Do you think that an unjust man can be temperate in his injustice?

Margin notes:

Prota-goras

Socrates, Prota-goras

Thus, if folly has two opposites, wisdom and temperance, those two opposites must be the same.

333

I should be ashamed, Socrates, he said, to acknowledge this, which nevertheless many may be found to assert.

And shall I argue with them or with you? I replied.

I would rather, he said, that you should argue with the many first, if you will.

Whichever you please, if you will only answer me and say whether you are of their opinion or not. My object is to test the validity of the argument; and yet the result may be that I who ask and you who answer may both be put on our trial.

Protagoras at first made a show of refusing, as he said that the argument was not encouraging; at length, he consented to answer.

Now then, I said, begin at the beginning and answer me. You think that some men are temperate, and yet unjust?

Yes, he said; let that be admitted.

And temperance is good sense?

Yes.

And good sense is good counsel in doing injustice?

Granted.

If they succeed, I said, or if they do not succeed?

If they succeed.

And you would admit the existence of goods?

Yes.

The good
is the ex-
pedient;
yet some
things in-
expedient
are never-
theless
good.

334

And is the good that which is expedient for man?

Yes, indeed, he said: and there are some things which may be inexpedient, and yet I call them good.

I thought that Protagoras was getting ruffled and excited; he seemed to be setting himself in an attitude of war. Seeing this, I minded my business, and gently said:—

When you say, Protagoras, that things inexpedient are good, do you mean inexpedient for man only, or inexpedient altogether? and do you call the latter good?

Certainly not the last, he replied; for I know of many things,— meats, drinks, medicines, and ten thousand other things, which are inexpedient for man, and some which are expedient; and some which are neither expedient nor inexpedient for man, but only for horses; and some for oxen only, and some for dogs; and some for no animals, but only for trees; and some for the roots of trees and not for their branches, as for example, manure, which is a good thing when laid about the roots of a tree, but utterly destructive if thrown upon the shoots and young branches; or I may instance olive oil, which is mischievous to all plants, and generally most injurious to the hair of every animal with the exception of man, but beneficial to human hair and to the human body generally; and even in this application (so various and changeable is the nature of the benefit), that which is the greatest good to the outward parts of a man, is a very great evil to his inward parts: and for this reason physicians always forbid their patients the use of oil in their food, except in very small quantities, just enough to extinguish the disagreeable sensation of smell in meats and sauces.

When he had given this answer, the company cheered him. And I said: Protagoras, I have a wretched memory, and when any one makes a long speech to me I never remember what he is talking about. As then, if I had been deaf, and you were going to converse with me, you would have had to raise your voice; so now, having such a bad memory, I will ask you to cut your answers shorter, if you would take me with you.

What do you mean? he said: how am I to shorten my answers? shall I make them too short?

Certainly not, I said.

But short enough?

Yes, I said.

Shall I answer what appears to me to be short enough, or what appears to you to be short enough?

I have heard, I said, that you can speak and teach others to speak about the same things at such length that words never seemed to fail, or with such brevity that no one could use fewer of them. Please therefore, if you talk with me, to adopt the latter or more compendious method.

Socrates, he replied, many a battle of words have I fought, and if I had followed the method of disputation which my adversaries desired, as you want me to do, I should have been no better than another, and the name of Protagoras would have been nowhere.

I saw that he was not satisfied with his previous answers, and that he would not play the part of answerer any more if he could help; and I considered that there was no call upon me to continue the conversation; so I said: Protagoras, I do not wish to force the conversation upon you if you had rather not, but when you are willing to argue with me in such a way that I can follow you, then I will argue with you. Now you, as is said of you by others and as you say of yourself, are able to have discussions in shorter forms of speech as well as in longer, for you are a master of wisdom; but I cannot manage these long speeches: I only wish that I could. You, on the other hand, who are capable of either, ought to speak shorter as I beg you, and then we might converse. But I see that you are disinclined, and as I have an engagement which will prevent my staying to hear you

Protagoras

SOCRATES, PROTAGORAS.

and is requested by Socrates, who pretends to have a bad memory, to make his answers shorter.

335

As Protagoras declines to adopt his adversary's method, Socrates rises to depart,

Prota-
goras

SOCRATES,
CALLIAS,
ALCIBI-
ADES,
CRITIAS.

but is de-
tained by
Callias.

Socrates
would be
very will-
[336]
ing to
comply
with his
wishes if
he could.

He cannot
run, but
Prota-
goras can
walk.

Yet Pro-
tagoras
may claim
to speak
in his own
manner.

Not so,
says Alci-
biades,
unless he
will admit
his inferi-
ority to
Socrates
in the
shorter
method.

Critias
attempts

at greater length (for I have to be in another place), I will depart; although I should have liked to have heard you.

Thus I spoke, and was rising from my seat, when Callias seized me by the right hand, and in his left hand caught hold of this old cloak of mine. He said: We cannot let you go, Socrates, for if you leave us there will be an end of our discussions: I must therefore beg you to remain, as there is nothing in the world that I should like better than to hear you and Protagoras discourse. Do not deny the company this pleasure.

Now I had got up, and was in the act of departure. Son of Hipponicus, I replied, I have always admired, and do now heartily applaud and love your philosophical spirit, and I would gladly comply with your request, if I could. But the truth is that I cannot. And what you ask is as great an impossibility to me, as if you bade me run a race with Crison of Himera, when in his prime, or with some one of the long or day course runners. To such a request I should reply that I would fain ask the same of my own legs; but they refuse to comply. And therefore if you want to see Crison and me in the same stadium, you must bid him slacken his speed to mine, for I cannot run quickly, and he can run slowly. And in like manner if you want to hear me and Protagoras discoursing, you must ask him to shorten his answers, and keep to the point, as he did at first; if not, how can there be any discussion? For discussion is one thing, and making an oration is quite another, in my humble opinion.

But you see, Socrates, said Callias, that Protagoras may fairly claim to speak in his own way, just as you claim to speak in yours.

Here Alcibiades interposed, and said: That, Callias, is not a true statement of the case. For our friend Socrates admits that he cannot make a speech—in this he yields the palm to Protagoras: but I should be greatly surprised if he yielded to any living man in the power of holding and apprehending an argument. Now if Protagoras will make a similar admission, and confess that he is inferior to Socrates in argumentative skill, that is enough for Socrates; but if he claims a superiority in argument as well, let him ask and answer —not, when a question is asked, slipping away from the point, and instead of answering, making a speech at such length that most of his hearers forget the question at issue (not that Socrates is likely to forget—I will be bound for that, although he may pretend in fun that he has a bad memory). And Socrates appears to me to be more in the right than Protagoras; that is my view, and every man ought to say what he thinks.

When Alcibiades had done speaking, some one—Critias, I believe —went on to say: O Prodicus and Hippias, Callias appears to me to be a partisan of Protagoras: and this led Alcibiades, who loves opposition, to take the other side. But we should not be partisans either of Socrates or of Protagoras; let us rather unite in entreating both of them not to break up the discussion.

Prodicus added: That, Critias, seems to me to be well said, for those who are present at such discussions ought to be impartial hearers of both the speakers; remembering, however, that impartiality is not the same as equality, for both sides should be impartially heard, and yet an equal meed should not be assigned to both of them; but to the wiser a higher meed should be given, and a lower to the less wise. And I as well as Critias would beg you, Protagoras and Socrates, to grant our request, which is, that you will argue with one another and not wrangle; for friends argue with friends out of good-will, but only adversaries and enemies wrangle. And then our meeting will be delightful; for in this way you, who are the speakers, will be most likely to win esteem, and not praise only, among us who are your audience; for esteem is a sincere conviction of the hearers' souls, but praise is often an insincere expression of men uttering falsehoods contrary to their conviction. And thus we who are the hearers will be gratified and not pleased; for gratification is of the mind when receiving wisdom and knowledge, but pleasure is of the body when eating or experiencing some other bodily delight. Thus spoke Prodicus, and many of the company applauded his words.

Hippias the sage spoke next. He said: All of you who are here present I reckon to be kinsmen and friends and fellow-citizens, by nature and not by law; for by nature like is akin to like, whereas law is the tyrant of mankind, and often compels us to do many things which are against nature. How great would be the disgrace then, if we, who know the nature of things, and are the wisest of the Hellenes, and as such are met together in this city, which is the metropolis of wisdom, and in the greatest and most glorious house of this city, should have nothing to show worthy of this height of dignity, but should only quarrel with one another like the meanest of mankind! I do pray and advise you, Protagoras, and you, Socrates, to agree upon a compromise. Let us be your peacemakers. And do not you, Socrates, aim at this precise and extreme brevity in discourse, if Protagoras objects, but loosen and let go the reins of speech, that your words may be grander and more becoming to you[1]. Neither do you, Protagoras, go forth on the gale with every sail set out of sight of land into an ocean of words, but let there be a mean observed by both of you. Do as I say. And let me also persuade you to choose an

[1] Reading ὑμῖν.

Protagoras

PRODICUS,
HIPPIAS.

337

to reconcile Protagoras and Socrates.

Prodicus in a balanced form of words advocates impartiality.

Hippias, in a sententious speech, advocates the appointment of an arbiter

338

Prota-goras

SOCRATES,
CALLIAS,
PROTA-
GORAS.

But there
can be no
arbiter
superior
to Prota-
goras, and
therefore
Socrates
suggests
that Pro-
tagoras
shall ask,
and he
will
answer;
and when
he is tired
of asking,
Socrates
will ask
and Pro-
tagoras
shall
answer.

Prota-
goras re-
luctantly
[339]
assents,
and pro-
poses to
base his
questions
on a pas-
sage in
Simon-
ides.

arbiter or overseer or president; he will keep watch over your words and will prescribe their proper length.

This proposal was received by the company with universal approval; Callias said that he would not let me off, and they begged me to choose an arbiter. But I said that to choose an umpire of discourse would be unseemly; for if the person chosen was inferior, then the inferior or worse ought not to preside over the better; or if he was equal, neither would that be well; for he who is our equal will do as we do, and what will be the use of choosing him? And if you say, 'Let us have a better then,'—to that I answer that you cannot have any one who is wiser than Protagoras. And if you choose another who is not really better, and whom you only say is better, to put another over him as though he were an inferior person would be an unworthy reflection on him; not that, as far as I am concerned, any reflection is of much consequence to me. Let me tell you then what I will do in order that the conversation and discussion may go on as you desire. If Protagoras is not disposed to answer, let him ask and I will answer; and I will endeavour to show at the same time how, as I maintain, he ought to answer: and when I have answered as many questions as he likes to ask, let him in like manner answer me; and if he seems to be not very ready at answering the precise question asked of him, you and I will unite in entreating him, as you entreated me, not to spoil the discussion. And this will require no special arbiter—all of you shall be arbiters.

This was generally approved, and Protagoras, though very much against his will, was obliged to agree that he would ask questions; and when he had put a sufficient number of them, that he would answer in his turn those which he was asked in short replies. He began to put his questions as follows:—

I am of opinion, Socrates, he said, that skill in poetry is the principal part of education; and this I conceive to be the power of knowing what compositions of the poets are correct, and what are not, and how they are to be distinguished, and of explaining when asked the reason of the difference. And I propose to transfer the question which you and I have been discussing to the domain of poetry; we will speak as before of virtue, but in reference to a passage of a poet. Now Simonides says to Scopas the son of Creon the Thessalian:—

'Hardly on the one hand can a man become truly good, built four-square in hands and feet and mind, a work without a flaw.'

Do you know the poem? or shall I repeat the whole?

There is no need, I said; for I am perfectly well acquainted with the ode,—I have made a careful study of it.

Very well, he said. And do you think that the ode is a good composition, and true?

Yes, I said, both good and true.

But if there is a contradiction, can the composition be good or true?

No, not in that case, I replied.

And is there not a contradiction? he asked. Reflect.

Well, my friend, I have reflected.

And does not the poet proceed to say, 'I do not agree with the word of Pittacus, albeit the utterance of a wise man: Hardly can a man be good?' Now you will observe that this is said by the same poet.

I know it.

And do you think, he said, that the two sayings are consistent?

Yes, I said, I think so (at the same time I could not help fearing that there might be something in what he said). And you think otherwise?

Why, he said, how can he be consistent in both? First of all, premising as his own thought, 'Hardly can a man become truly good;' and then a little further on in the poem, forgetting, and blaming Pittacus and refusing to agree with him, when he says, 'Hardly can a man be good,' which is the very same thing. And yet when he blames him who says the same with himself, he blames himself; so that he must be wrong either in his first or his second assertion.

Many of the audience cheered and applauded this. And I felt at first giddy and faint, as if I had received a blow from the hand of an expert boxer, when I heard his words and the sound of the cheering; and to confess the truth, I wanted to get time to think what the meaning of the poet really was. So I turned to Prodicus and called him. Prodicus, I said, Simonides is a countryman of yours, and you ought to come to his aid. I must appeal to you, like the river Scamander in Homer, who, when beleaguered by Achilles, summons the Simoïs to aid him, saying:

'Brother dear, let us both together stay the force of the hero [1].'

And I summon you, for I am afraid that Protagoras will make an end of Simonides. Now is the time to rehabilitate Simonides, by the application of your philosophy of synonyms, which enables you to distinguish 'will' and 'wish,' and make other charming distinctions like those which you drew just now. And I should like to know whether you would agree with me; for I am of opinion that there is no contradiction in the words of Simonides. And first of all I wish

[1] Il. xxi. 308.

Prota-
goras

SOCRATES,
PRODICUS,
PROTA-
GORAS.

one; for
'being' is
not the
same as
'becom-
ing.'

that you would say whether, in your opinion, Prodicus, 'being' is the same as 'becoming.'

Not the same, certainly, replied Prodicus.

Did not Simonides first set forth, as his own view, that 'Hardly can a man become truly good'?

Quite right, said Prodicus.

And then he blames Pittacus, not, as Protagoras imagines, for repeating that which he says himself, but for saying something different from himself. Pittacus does not say as Simonides says, that hardly can a man become good, but hardly can a man be good: and our friend Prodicus would maintain that being, Protagoras, is not the same as becoming; and if they are not the same, then Simonides is not inconsistent with himself. I dare say that Prodicus and many others would say, as Hesiod says,

> 'On the one hand, hardly can a man become good,
> For the gods have made virtue the reward of toil;
> But on the other hand, when you have climbed the height,
> Then, to retain virtue, however difficult the acquisition, is easy [1].'

Simoni-
des could
never
have
meant to
say that
virtue can
be easily
possessed.

Prodicus heard and approved; but Protagoras said: Your correction, Socrates, involves a greater error than is contained in the sentence which you are correcting.

Alas! I said, Protagoras; then I am a sorry physician, and do but aggravate a disorder which I am seeking to cure.

Such is the fact, he said.

How so? I asked.

The poet, he replied, could never have made such a mistake as to say that virtue, which in the opinion of all men is the hardest of all things, can be easily retained.

Socrates
has
learned
from Pro-
[341]
dicus that
'hard'
means
'evil.'

Well, I said, and how fortunate are we in having Prodicus among us, at the right moment; for he has a wisdom, Protagoras, which, as I imagine, is more than human and of very ancient date, and may be as old as Simonides or even older. Learned as you are in many things, you appear to know nothing of this; but I know, for I am a disciple of his. And now, if I am not mistaken, you do not understand the word 'hard' (χαλεπόν) in the sense which Simonides intended; and I must correct you, as Prodicus corrects me when I use the word 'awful' (δεινόν) as a term of praise. If I say that Protagoras or any one else is an 'awfully' wise man, he asks me if I am not ashamed of calling that which is good 'awful'; and then he explains to me that the term 'awful' is always taken in a bad sense, and that no one speaks of being 'awfully' healthy or

---

[1] Works and Days, 264 foll.

wealthy, or 'awful' peace, but of 'awful' disease, 'awful' war, 'awful' poverty, meaning by the term 'awful,' evil. And I think that Simonides and his countrymen the Ceans, when they spoke of 'hard' meant 'evil,' or something which you do not understand. Let us ask Prodicus, for he ought to be able to answer questions about the dialect of Simonides. What did he mean, Prodicus, by the term 'hard'?

Evil, said Prodicus.

And therefore, I said, Prodicus, he blames Pittacus for saying, 'Hard is the good,' just as if that were equivalent to saying, Evil is the good.

Yes, he said, that was certainly his meaning; and he is twitting Pittacus with ignorance of the use of terms, which in a Lesbian, who has been accustomed to speak a barbarous language, is natural.

Do you hear, Protagoras, I asked, what our friend Prodicus is saying? And have you an answer for him?

You are entirely mistaken, Prodicus, said Protagoras; and I know very well that Simonides in using the word 'hard' meant what all of us mean, not evil, but that which is not easy—that which takes a great deal of trouble: of this I am positive.

I said: I also incline to believe, Protagoras, that this was the meaning of Simonides, of which our friend Prodicus was very well aware, but he thought that he would make fun, and try if you could maintain your thesis; for that Simonides could never have meant the other is clearly proved by the context, in which he says that God only has this gift. Now he cannot surely mean to say that to be good is evil, when he afterwards proceeds to say that God only has this gift, and that this is the attribute of him and of no other. For if this be his meaning, Prodicus would impute to Simonides a character of recklessness which is very unlike his countrymen. And I should like to tell you, I said, what I imagine to be the real meaning of Simonides in this poem, if you will test what, in your way of speaking, would be called my skill in poetry; or if you would rather, I will be the listener.

To this proposal Protagoras replied: As you please;—and Hippias, Prodicus, and the others told me by all means to do as I proposed.

Then now, I said, I will endeavour to explain to you my opinion about this poem of Simonides. There is a very ancient philosophy which is more cultivated in Crete and Lacedaemon than in any other part of Hellas, and there are more philosophers in those countries than anywhere else in the world. This, however, is a secret which the Lacedaemonians deny; and they pretend to be ignorant,

Protagoras

SOCRATES, PRODICUS, PROTAGORAS.

Nonsense, says Protagoras.

We were only making trial of you, replies Socrates; but as you are not to be taken in, shall I [342] offer an interpretation?

The true ancient philosophy is to be found, not in the long dis-

Prota-
goras

SOCRATES.

courses of
the
Sophists,

just because they do not wish to have it thought that they rule the
world by wisdom, like the Sophists of whom Protagoras was speaking, and not by valour of arms; considering that if the reason of
their superiority were disclosed, all men would be practising their
wisdom. And this secret of theirs has never been discovered by the
imitators of Lacedaemonian fashions in other cities, who go about
with their ears bruised in imitation of them, and have the caestus
bound on their arms, and are always in training, and wear short
cloaks; for they imagine that these are the practices which have en-
abled the Lacedaemonians to conquer the other Hellenes. Now
when the Lacedaemonians want to unbend and hold free conversation with their wise men, and are no longer satisfied with mere secret
intercourse, they drive out all these laconizers, and any other foreigners who may happen to be in their country, and they hold a

but in the
pregnant
brevity of
the Lace-
daemo-
nians.

philosophical *séance* unknown to strangers; and they themselves
forbid their young men to go out into other cities—in this they are
like the Cretans—in order that they may not unlearn the lessons
which they have taught them. And in Lacedaemon and Crete not
only men but also women have a pride in their high cultivation. And
hereby you may know that I am right in attributing to the Lacedaemonians this excellence in philosophy and speculation: If a man
converses with the most ordinary Lacedaemonian, he will find him
seldom good for much in general conversation, but at any point in
the discourse he will be darting out some notable saying, terse and
full of meaning, with unerring aim; and the person with whom he is
talking seems to be like a child in his hands. And many of our own
age and of former ages have noted that the true Lacedaemonian
type of character has the love of philosophy even stronger than the
love of gymnastics; they are conscious that only a perfectly edu-

cated man is capable of uttering such expressions. Such were Thales
of Miletus, and Pittacus of Mitylene, and Bias of Priene, and our
own Solon, and Cleobulus the Lindian, and Myson the Chenian;
and seventh in the catalogue of wise men was the Lacedaemonian
Chilo. All these were lovers and emulators and disciples of the cul-
ture of the Lacedaemonians, and any one may perceive that their
wisdom was of this character; consisting of short memorable sen-
tences, which they severally uttered. And they met together and
dedicated in the temple of Apollo at Delphi, as the first-fruits of
their wisdom, the far-famed inscriptions, which are in all men's
mouths,—'Know thyself,' and 'Nothing too much.'

Why do I say all this? I am explaining that this Lacedaemonian
brevity was the style of primitive philosophy. Now there was a saying of Pittacus which was privately circulated and received the ap-

probation of the wise, 'Hard is it to be good.' And Simonides, who was ambitious of the fame of wisdom, was aware that if he could overthrow this saying, then, as if he had won a victory over some famous athlete, he would carry off the palm among his contemporaries. And if I am not mistaken, he composed the entire poem with the secret intention of damaging Pittacus and his saying.

Let us all unite in examining his words, and see whether I am speaking the truth. Simonides must have been a lunatic, if, in the very first words of the poem, wanting to say only that to become good is hard, he inserted μέν, 'on the one hand' ['on the one hand to become good is hard']; there would be no reason for the introduction of μέν, unless you suppose him to speak with a hostile reference to the words of Pittacus. Pittacus is saying 'Hard is it to be good,' and he, in refutation of this thesis, rejoins that the truly hard thing, Pittacus, is to become good, not joining 'truly' with 'good,' but with 'hard.' Not, that the hard thing is to be truly good, as though there were some truly good men, and there were others who were good but not truly good (this would be a very simple observation, and quite unworthy of Simonides); but you must suppose him to make a trajection of the word 'truly' (ἀλαθέως), construing the saying of Pittacus thus (and let us imagine Pittacus to be speaking and Simonides answering him): 'O my friends,' says Pittacus, 'hard is it to be good,' and Simonides answers, 'In that, Pittacus, you are mistaken; the difficulty is not to be good, but on the one hand, to become good, four-square in hands and feet and mind, without a flaw—that is hard truly.' This way of reading the passage accounts for the insertion of μέν, 'on the one hand,' and for the position at the end of the clause of the word 'truly,' and all that follows shows this to be the meaning. A great deal might be said in praise of the details of the poem, which is a charming piece of workmanship, and very finished, but such minutiae would be tedious. I should like, however, to point out the general intention of the poem, which is certainly designed in every part to be a refutation of the saying of Pittacus. For he speaks in what follows a little further on as if he meant to argue that although there is a difficulty in becoming good, yet this is possible for a time, and only for a time. But having become good, to remain in a good state and be good, as you, Pittacus, affirm, is not possible, and is not granted to man; God only has this blessing; 'but man cannot help being bad when the force of circumstances overpowers him.' Now whom does the force of circumstance overpower in the command of a vessel?—not the private individual, for he is always overpowered; and as one who is already prostrate cannot

Protagoras

SOCRATES.

Socrates
proposes
an explanation,
ingenious
rather
than true
of the
verses of
Simonides.

344

He seems
to be
adopting
the Sophists'
arts of
interpretation.

Prota-
goras

SOCRATES.

Socrates
by the
help of
logic and
rhetoric
strives to
elicit the
meaning
of Si-
monides.

be overthrown, and only he who is standing upright but not he who is prostrate can be laid prostrate, so the force of circumstances can only overpower him who, at some time or other, has resources, and not him who is at all times helpless. The descent of a great storm may make the pilot helpless, or the severity of the season the husbandman or the physician; for the good may become bad, as another poet witnesses:—

'The good are sometimes good and sometimes bad.'

But the bad does not become bad; he is always bad. So that when the force of circumstances overpowers the man of resources and skill and virtue, then he cannot help being bad. And you, Pittacus, are saying, 'Hard is it to be good.' Now there is a difficulty in becoming good; and yet this is possible: but to be good is an impossibility—

'For he who does well is the good man, and he who does ill is the bad.'

345　But what sort of doing is good in letters? and what sort of doing makes a man good in letters? Clearly the knowing of them. And what sort of well-doing makes a man a good physician? Clearly the knowledge of the art of healing the sick. 'But he who does ill is the bad.' Now who becomes a bad physician? Clearly he who is in the first place a physician, and in the second place a good physician; for he may become a bad one also: but none of us unskilled individuals can by any amount of doing ill become physicians, any more than we can become carpenters or anything of that sort; and he who by doing ill cannot become a physician at all, clearly cannot become a bad physician. In like manner the good may become deteriorated by time, or toil, or disease, or other accident (the only real doing ill is to be deprived of knowledge), but the bad man will never become bad, for he is always bad; and if he were to become bad, he must previously have been good. Thus the words of the poem tend to show that on the one hand a man cannot be continuously good, but that he may become good and may also become bad; and again that

'They are the best for the longest time whom the gods love.'

All this relates to Pittacus, as is further proved by the sequel. For he adds:—

The entire
poem is
really a
polemic
against
Pittacus.

'Therefore I will not throw away my span of life to no purpose in searching after the impossible, hoping in vain to find a perfectly faultless man among those who partake of the fruit of the broad-bosomed earth: if I find him, I will send you word.'

(this is the vehement way in which he pursues his attack upon Pittacus throughout the whole poem):

'But him who does no evil, voluntarily I praise and love;—not even the gods war against necessity.'

All this has a similar drift, for Simonides was not so ignorant as to say that he praised those who did no evil voluntarily, as though there were some who did evil voluntarily. For no wise man, as I believe, will allow that any human being errs voluntarily, or voluntarily does evil and dishonourable actions; but they are very well aware that all who do evil and dishonourable things do them against their will. And Simonides never says that he praises him who does no evil voluntarily; the word 'voluntarily' applies to himself. For he was under the impression that a good man might often compel himself to love and praise another[1], and to be tne friend and approver of another; and that there might be an involuntary love, such as a man might feel to an unnatural father or mother, or country, or the like. Now bad men, when their parents or country have any defects, look on them with malignant joy, and find fault with them and expose and denounce them to others, under the idea that the rest of mankind will be less likely to take themselves to task and accuse them of neglect; and they blame their defects far more than they deserve, in order that the odium which is necessarily incurred by them may be increased: but the good man dissembles his feelings, and constrains himself to praise them; and if they have wronged him and he is angry, he pacifies his anger and is reconciled, and compels himself to love and praise his own flesh and blood. And Simonides, as is probable, considered that he himself had often had to praise and magnify a tyrant or the like, much against his will, and he also wishes to imply to Pittacus that he does not censure him because he is censorious.

'For I am satisfied,' he says, 'when a man is neither bad nor very stupid; and when he knows justice (which is the health of states), and is of sound mind, I will find no fault with him, for I am not given to finding fault, and there are innumerable fools'

(implying that if he delighted in censure he might have abundant opportunity of finding fault).

'All things are good with which evil is unmingled.'

In these latter words he does not mean to say that all things are good which have no evil in them, as you might say 'All things are white which have no black in them,' for that would be ridiculous; but he means to say that he accepts and finds no fault with the moderate or intermediate state.

---

[1] Reading φιλεῖν καὶ ἐπαινεῖν καὶ φίλον τιν' κ.τ.λ.

*Prota-
goras*

SOCRATES,
HIPPIAS,
ALCIBI-
ADES.

['I do not hope,' he says, 'to find a perfectly blameless man among those who partake of the fruits of the broad-bosomed earth (if I find him, I will send you word); in this sense I praise no man. But he who is moderately good, and does no evil, is good enough for me, who love and approve every one']

(and here observe that he uses a Lesbian word, ἐπαίνημι (approve), because he is addressing Pittacus,—

'Who love and *approve* every one *voluntarily*, who does no evil:'

and that the stop should be put after 'voluntarily'); 'but there are some whom I involuntarily praise and love. And you, Pittacus, I would never have blamed, if you had spoken what was moderately good and true; but I do blame you because, putting on the appearance of truth, you are speaking falsely about the highest matters.'— And this, I said, Prodicus and Protagoras, I take to be the meaning of Simonides in this poem.

347

Hippias
thinks
this an
excellent
interpre-
tation of
the poem;
but he has
a still
better one
of his
own.

Hippias said: I think, Socrates, that you have given a very good explanation of the poem; but I have also an excellent interpretation of my own which I will propound to you, if you will allow me.

Nay, Hippias, said Alcibiades; not now, but at some other time. At present we must abide by the compact which was made between Socrates and Protagoras, to the effect that as long as Protagoras is willing to ask, Socrates should answer; or that if he would rather answer, then that Socrates should ask.

He is pre-
vented
from in-
terrupting
by Alcibi-
ades.
Socrates
would
rather
have done
with the
poets and
return to
the argu-
ment.

I said: I wish Protagoras either to ask or answer as he is inclined; but I would rather have done with poems and odes, if he does not object, and come back to the question about which I was asking you at first, Protagoras, and by your help make an end of that. The talk about the poets seems to me like a commonplace entertainment to which a vulgar company have recourse; who, because they are not able to converse or amuse one another, while they are drinking, with the sound of their own voices and conversation, by reason of their stupidity, raise the price of flute-girls in the market, hiring for a great sum the voice of a flute instead of their own breath, to be the medium of intercourse among them: but where the company are real gentlemen and men of education, you will see no flute-girls, nor dancing-girls, nor harp-girls; and they have no nonsense or games, but are contented with one another's conversation, of which their own voices are the medium, and which they carry on by turns and in an orderly manner, even though they are very liberal in their potations. And a company like this of ours, and men such as we profess to be, do not require the help of another's voice, or of the poets whom you cannot interrogate about the meaning of what they are saying; people who cite them declaring, some that the poet has one meaning, and others that he has another, and the point which is in dispute can never be decided. This sort of entertainment they decline, and prefer to talk with one another, and put one another to the proof in conversation. And these are the models which I desire that you and I should imitate. Leaving the poets, and keeping to ourselves, let us try the mettle of one another and make proof of the truth in conversation. If you have a mind to ask, I am ready to answer; or if you would rather, do you answer, and give me the opportunity of resuming and completing our unfinished argument.

I made these and some similar observations; but Protagoras would not distinctly say which he would do. Thereupon Alcibiades turned to Callias, and said:—Do you think, Callias, that Protagoras is fair in refusing to say whether he will or will not answer? for I certainly think that he is unfair; he ought either to proceed with the argument, or distinctly to refuse to proceed, that we may know his intention; and then Socrates will be able to discourse with some one else, and the rest of the company will be free to talk with one another.

I think that Protagoras was really made ashamed by these words of Alcibiades, and when the prayers of Callias and the company were superadded, he was at last induced to argue, and said that I might ask and he would answer.

So I said: Do not imagine, Protagoras, that I have any other interest in asking questions of you but that of clearing up my own difficulties. For I think that Homer was very right in saying that

'When two go together, one sees before the other [1],'

for all men who have a companion are readier in deed, word, or thought; but if a man

'Sees a thing when he is alone,'

he goes about straightway seeking until he finds some one to whom he may show his discoveries, and who may confirm him in them. And I would rather hold discourse with you than with any one, because I think that no man has a better understanding of most things which a good man may be expected to understand, and in particular of virtue. For who is there, but you?—who not only claim to be a good man and a gentleman, for many are this, and yet have not the power of making others good—whereas you are not only good yourself, but also the cause of goodness in others. Moreover such confidence have you in yourself, that although other Sophists conceal their profession, you proclaim in the face of Hellas that you are a

[1] Il. x. 224.

Margin notes:

Protagoras

348
SOCRATES,
ALCIBI-
ADES.

Protagoras is compelled to resume the argument.

Half ironical eulogium of Protagoras.

349
*Prota-
goras*

SOCRATES,
PROTA-
GORAS.

To the
old ques-
tion,—
'Are the
virtues
one or
many?'
—the old
answer is
returned
that four
out of five
are to
some
extent
similar,
but the
fifth,
courage,
is very
different
from the
other
four.

And the
courage-
ous are
the confi-
dent; but
not all
the confi-
dent are
truly
coura-
geous.

350

Sophist or teacher of virtue and education, and are the first who demanded pay in return. How then can I do otherwise than invite you to the examination of these subjects, and ask questions and consult with you? I must, indeed. And I should like once more to have my memory refreshed by you about the questions which I was asking you at first, and also to have your help in considering them. If I am not mistaken the question was this: Are wisdom and temperance and courage and justice and holiness five names of the same thing? or has each of the names a separate underlying essence and corresponding thing having a peculiar function, no one of them being like any other of them? And you replied that the five names were not the names of the same thing, but that each of them had a separate object, and that all these objects were parts of virtue, not in the same way that the parts of gold are like each other and the whole of which they are parts, but as the parts of the face are unlike the whole of which they are parts and one another, and have each of them a distinct function. I should like to know whether this is still your opinion; or if not, I will ask you to define your meaning, and I shall not take you to task if you now make a different statement. For I dare say that you may have said what you did only in order to make trial of me.

I answer, Socrates, he said, that all these qualities are parts of virtue, and that four out of the five are to some extent similar, and that the fifth of them, which is courage, is very different from the other four, as I prove in this way: You may observe that many men are utterly unrighteous, unholy, intemperate, ignorant, who are nevertheless remarkable for their courage.

Stop, I said; I should like to think about that. When you speak of brave men, do you mean the confident, or another sort of nature?

Yes, he said; I mean the impetuous, ready to go at that which others are afraid to approach.

In the next place, you would affirm virtue to be a good thing, of which good thing you assert yourself to be a teacher.

Yes, he said; I should say the best of all things, if I am in my right mind.

And is it partly good and partly bad, I said, or wholly good?

Wholly good, and in the highest degree.

Tell me then; who are they who have confidence when diving into a well?

I should say, the divers.

And the reason of this is that they have knowledge?

Yes, that is the reason.

And who have confidence when fighting on horseback—the skilled horseman or the unskilled?

The skilled.

And who when fighting with light shields—the peltasts or the nonpeltasts?

The peltasts. And that is true of all other things, he said, if that is your point: those who have knowledge are more confident than those who have no knowledge, and they are more confident after they have learned than before.

And have you not seen persons utterly ignorant, I said, of these things, and yet confident about them?

Yes, he said, I have seen such persons far too confident.

And are not these confident persons also courageous?

In that case, he replied, courage would be a base thing, for the men of whom we are speaking are surely madmen.

Then who are the courageous? Are they not the confident?

Yes, he said; to that statement I adhere.

And those, I said, who are thus confident without knowledge are really not courageous, but mad; and in that case the wisest are also the most confident, and being the most confident are also the bravest, and upon that view again wisdom will be courage.

Nay, Socrates, he replied, you are mistaken in your remembrance of what was said by me. When you asked me, I certainly did say that the courageous are the confident; but I was never asked whether the confident are the courageous; if you had asked me, I should have answered 'Not all of them:' and what I did answer you have not proved to be false, although you proceeded to show that those who have knowledge are more courageous than they were before they had knowledge, and more courageous than others who have no knowledge, and were then led on to think that courage is the same as wisdom. But in this way of arguing you might come to imagine that strength is wisdom. You might begin by asking whether the strong are able, and I should say 'Yes;' and then whether those who know how to wrestle are not more able to wrestle than those who do not know how to wrestle, and more able after than before they had learned, and I should assent. And when I had admitted this, you might use my admissions in such a way as to prove that upon my view wisdom is strength; whereas in that case I should not have admitted, any more than in the other, that the able are strong, although I have admitted that the strong are able. For there is a difference between ability and strength; the former is given by knowledge as well as by madness or rage, but strength comes from

Prota-
goras
complains
that
Socrates
has mis-
represent-
ed him.

351

nature and a healthy state of the body. And in like manner I say of confidence and courage, that they are not the same; and I argue that the courageous are confident, but not all the confident courageous. For confidence may be given to men by art, and also, like ability, by madness and rage; but courage comes to them from nature and the healthy state of the soul.

I said: You would admit, Protagoras, that some men live well and others ill?

He assented.

And do you think that a man lives well who lives in pain and grief?

He does not.

But if he lives pleasantly to the end of his life, will he not in that case have lived well?

He will.

Then to live pleasantly is a good, and to live unpleasantly an evil?

Yes, he said, if the pleasure be good and honourable.

And do you, Protagoras, like the rest of the world, call some pleasant things evil and some painful things good?—for I am rather disposed to say that things are good in as far as they are pleasant, if they have no consequences of another sort, and in as far as they are painful they are bad.

I do not know, Socrates, he said, whether I can venture to assert in that unqualified manner that the pleasant is the good and the painful the evil. Having regard not only to my present answer, but also to the whole of my life, I shall be safer, if I am not mistaken, in saying that there are some pleasant things which are not good, and that there are some painful things which are good, and some which are not good, and that there are some which are neither good nor evil.

And you would call pleasant, I said, the things which participate in pleasure or create pleasure?

Certainly, he said.

Then my meaning is, that in as far as they are pleasant they are good; and my question would imply that pleasure is a good in itself.

According to your favourite mode of speech, Socrates, 'let us reflect about this,' he said; and if the reflection is to the point, and the result proves that pleasure and good are really the same, then we will agree; but if not, then we will argue.

And would you wish to begin the enquiry? I said; or shall I begin?

You ought to take the lead, he said; for you are the author of the discussion.

May I employ an illustration? I said. Suppose some one who is enquiring into the health or some other bodily quality of another:— he looks at his face and at the tips of his fingers, and then he says, Uncover your chest and back to me that I may have a better view: —that is the sort of thing which I desire in this speculation. Having seen what your opinion is about good and pleasure, I am minded to say to you: Uncover your mind to me, Protagoras, and reveal your opinion about knowledge, that I may know whether you agree with the rest of the world. Now the rest of the world are of opinion that knowledge is a principle not of strength, or of rule, or of command: their notion is that a man may have knowledge, and yet that the knowledge which is in him may be overmastered by anger, or pleasure, or pain, or love, or perhaps by fear,—just as if knowledge were a slave, and might be dragged about anyhow. Now is that your view? or do you think that knowledge is a noble and commanding thing, which cannot be overcome, and will not allow a man, if he only knows the difference of good and evil, to do anything which is contrary to knowledge, but that wisdom will have strength to help him?

I agree with you, Socrates, said Protagoras; and not only so, but I, above all other men, am bound to say that wisdom and knowledge are the highest of human things.

Good, I said, and true. But are you aware that the majority of the world are of another mind; and that men are commonly supposed to know the things which are best, and not to do them when they might? And most persons whom I have asked the reason of this have said that when men act contrary to knowledge they are overcome by pain, or pleasure, or some of those affections which I was just now mentioning.

Yes, Socrates, he replied; and that is not the only point about which mankind are in error.

Suppose, then, that you and I endeavour to instruct and inform them what is the nature of this affection which they call 'being overcome by pleasure,' and which they affirm to be the reason why they do not always do what is best. When we say to them: Friends, you are mistaken, and are saying what is not true, they would probably reply: Socrates and Protagoras, if this affection of the soul is not to be called 'being overcome by pleasure,' pray, what is it, and by what name would you describe it?

But why, Socrates, should we trouble ourselves about the opinion of the many, who just say anything that happens to occur to them?

I believe, I said, that they may be of use in helping us to discover how courage is related to the other parts of virtue. If you are disposed to abide by our agreement, that I should show the way in

Protagoras

Socrates, Protagoras.

Let Protagoras reveal to us his mind about knowledge.

Is not knowledge the strongest of all things? Protagoras agrees, but the world will not agree about this and many other things which are true, nevertheless.
353

Prota-
goras

SOCRATES,
PROTA-
GORAS.

which, as I think, our recent difficulty is most likely to be cleared up, do you follow; but if not, never mind.

You are quite right, he said; and I would have you proceed as you have begun.

Well then, I said, let me suppose that they repeat their question, What account do you give of that which, in our way of speaking, is termed being overcome by pleasure? I should answer thus: Listen, and Protagoras and I will endeavour to show you. When men are overcome by eating and drinking and other sensual desires which are pleasant, and they, knowing them to be evil, nevertheless indulge in them, would you not say that they were overcome by pleasure? They will not deny this. And suppose that you and I were to go on and ask them again: 'In what way do you say that they are evil,—in that they are pleasant and give pleasure at the moment, or because they cause disease and poverty and other like evils in the future? Would they still be evil, if they had no attendant evil consequences, simply because they give the consciousness of pleasure of whatever nature?'—Would they not answer that they are not evil on account of the pleasure which is immediately given by them, but on account of the after consequences—diseases and the like?

I believe, said Protagoras, that the world in general would answer as you do.

Pleasure
is evil
when it
deprives
us of
some
other
pleasure.

And in causing diseases do they not cause pain? and in causing poverty do they not cause pain;—they would agree to that also, if I am not mistaken?

Protagoras assented.

Then I should say to them, in my name and yours: Do you think them evil for any other reason, except because they end in pain and rob us of other pleasures:—there again they would agree?

354

Goods are
painful
which are
remedial,
and,
though
they occa-
sion im-
mediate
suffering,
bring
good in
the
future.

We both of us thought that they would.

And then I should take the question from the opposite point of view, and say: 'Friends, when you speak of goods being painful, do you not mean remedial goods, such as gymnastic exercises, and military service, and the physician's use of burning, cutting, drugging, and starving? Are these the things which are good but painful?'—they would assent to me?

He agreed.

'And do you call them good because they occasion the greatest immediate suffering and pain; or because, afterwards, they bring health and improvement of the bodily condition and the salvation of states and power over others and wealth?'—they would agree to the latter alternative, if I am not mistaken?

He assented.

'Are these things good for any other reason except that they end in pleasure, and get rid of and avert pain? Are you looking to any other standard but pleasure and pain when you call them good?'— they would acknowledge that they were not?

I think so, said Protagoras.

'And do you not pursue after pleasure as a good, and avoid pain as an evil?'

He assented.

'Then you think that pain is an evil and pleasure is a good: and even pleasure you deem an evil, when it robs you of greater pleasures than it gives, or causes pains greater than the pleasure. If, however, you call pleasure an evil in relation to some other end or standard, you will be able to show us that standard. But you have none to show.'

I do not think that they have, said Protagoras.

'And have you not a similar way of speaking about pain? You call pain a good when it takes away greater pains than those which it has, or gives pleasures greater than the pains: then if you have some standard other than pleasure and pain to which you refer when you call actual pain a good, you can show what that is. But you cannot.'

True, said Protagoras.

Suppose again, I said, that the world says to me: 'Why do you spend many words and speak in many ways on this subject?' Excuse me, friends, I should reply; but in the first place there is a difficulty in explaining the meaning of the expression 'overcome by pleasure;' and the whole argument turns upon this. And even now, if you see any possible way in which evil can be explained as other than pain, or good as other than pleasure, you may still retract. Are you satisfied, then, at having a life of pleasure which is without pain? If you are, and if you are unable to show any good or evil which does not end in pleasure and pain, hear the consequences:— If what you say is true, then the argument is absurd which affirms that a man often does evil knowingly, when he might abstain, because he is seduced and overpowered by pleasure; or again, when you say that a man knowingly refuses to do what is good because he is overcome at the moment by pleasure. And that this is ridiculous will be evident if only we give up the use of various names, such as pleasant and painful, and good and evil. As there are two things, let us call them by two names—first, good and evil, and then pleasant and painful. Assuming this, let us go on to say that a man does evil knowing that he does evil. But some one will ask, Why? Because he is overcome, is the first answer. And by what is he overcome? the enquirer will proceed to ask. And we shall not be able to reply 'By pleasure,' for the name of pleasure has been exchanged for that of good. In our answer, then, we shall only say that he is overcome. 'By what?' he will reiterate. By the good, we shall have to reply; indeed we shall. Nay, but our questioner will rejoin with a laugh, if he be one of the swaggering sort, 'That is too ridiculous, that a man should do what he knows to be evil when he ought not, because he is overcome by good. Is that, he will ask, because the good was worthy or not worthy of conquering the evil'? And in answer to that we shall clearly reply, Because it was not worthy; for if it had been worthy, then he who, as we say, was overcome by pleasure, would not have been wrong. 'But how,' he will reply, 'can the good be unworthy of the evil, or the evil of the good'? Is not the real explanation that they are out of proportion to one another, either as greater and smaller, or more and fewer? This we cannot deny. And when you speak of being overcome—'what do you mean,' he will say, 'but that you choose the greater evil in exchange for the lesser good'? Admitted. And now substitute the names of pleasure and pain for good and evil, and say, not as before, that a man does what is evil knowingly, but that he does what is painful knowingly, and because he is overcome by pleasure, which is unworthy to overcome. What measure is there of the relations of pleasure to pain other than excess and defect, which means that they become greater and smaller, and more and fewer, and differ in degree? For if any one says: 'Yes, Socrates, but immediate pleasure differs widely from future pleasure and pain'—To that I should reply: And do they differ in anything but in pleasure and pain? There can be no other measure of them. And do you, like a skilful weigher, put into the balance the pleasures and the pains, and their nearness and distance, and weigh them, and then say which outweighs the other. If you weigh pleasures against pleasures, you of course take the more and greater; or if you weigh pains against pains, you take the fewer and the less; or if pleasures against pains, then you choose that course of action in which the painful is exceeded by the pleasant, whether the distant by the near or the near by the distant; and you avoid that course of action in which the pleasant is exceeded by the painful. Would you not admit, my friends, that this is true? I am confident that they cannot deny this.

He agreed with me.

Well then, I shall say, if you agree so far, be so good as to answer me a question: Do not the same magnitudes appear larger to your sight when near, and smaller when at a distance? They will acknowledge that. And the same holds of thickness and number; also

*Whether
we speak
of
pleasure
and pain,
or of good
and evil,
the result
is the
same.*

sounds, which are in themselves equal, are greater when near, and lesser when at a distance. They will grant that also. Now suppose happiness to consist in doing or choosing the greater, and in not doing or in avoiding the less, what would be the saving principle of human life? Would not the art of measuring be the saving principle; or would the power of appearance? Is not the latter that deceiving art which makes us wander up and down and take the things at one time of which we repent at another, both in our actions and in our choice of things great and small? But the art of measurement would do away with the effect of appearances, and, showing the truth, would fain teach the soul at last to find rest in the truth, and would thus save our life. Would not mankind generally acknowledge that the art which accomplishes this result is the art of measurement?

Yes, he said, the art of measurement.

Suppose, again, the salvation of human life to depend on the choice of odd and even, and on the knowledge of when a man ought to choose the greater or less, either in reference to themselves or to each other, and whether near or at a distance; what would be the saving principle of our lives? Would not knowledge? —a knowledge of measuring, when the question is one of excess and defect, and a knowledge of number, when the question is of odd and even? The world will assent, will they not?

Protagoras himself thought that they would.

Well then, my friends, I say to them; seeing that the salvation of human life has been found to consist in the right choice of pleasures and pains,—in the choice of the more and the fewer, and the greater and the less, and the nearer and remoter, must not this measuring be a consideration of their excess and defect and equality in relation to each other?

This is undeniably true.

And this, as possessing measure, must undeniably also be an art and science?

They will agree, he said.

The nature of that art or science will be a matter of future consideration; but the existence of such a science furnishes a demonstrative answer to the question which you asked of me and Protagoras. At the time when you asked the question, if you remember, both of us were agreeing that there was nothing mightier than knowledge, and that knowledge, in whatever existing, must have the advantage over pleasure and all other things; and then you said that pleasure often got the advantage even over a man who has knowledge; and we refused to allow this, and you rejoined: O Protagoras and Socrates, what is the meaning of being overcome by

*Prota-
goras*

SOCRATES,
PROTA-
GORAS.

greater or
less by
distance;
that is,
they ap-
pear to be
greater.

The art of
measuring
contrast-
ed with
the power
of ap-
pearance

The num-
[357]
bering
principle
and the
measuring
principle
are the
laws of
human
life.

Thus we
arrive at
the con-
clusion
that men
err in
their
choice of
good and
evil
through
ignorance,
and yet

*Prota-
goras*

SOCRATES,
PROTA-
GORAS.

the world
refuses to
be taught
by the
Sophists
who are
the phy-
sicians of
ignorance.

pleasure if not this?—tell us what you call such a state:—if we had immediately and at the time answered 'Ignorance,' you would have laughed at us. But now, in laughing at us, you will be laughing at yourselves: for you also admitted that men err in their choice of pleasures and pains; that is, in their choice of good and evil, from defect of knowledge; and you admitted further, that they err, not only from defect of knowledge in general, but of that particular knowledge which is called measuring. And you are also aware that the erring act which is done without knowledge is done in ingorance. This, therefore, is the meaning of being overcome by pleasure;— ignorance, and that the greatest. And our friends Protagoras and Prodicus and Hippias declare that they are the physicians of igno- rance; but you, who are under the mistaken impression that igno- rance is not the cause, and that the art of which I am speaking cannot be taught, neither go yourselves, nor send your children, to the Sophists, who are the teachers of these things—you take care of your money and give them none; and the result is, that you are the worse off both in public and private life:—Let us suppose this to be our answer to the world in general: And now I should like to ask

358   you, Hippias, and you, Prodicus, as well as Protagoras (for the ar- gument is to be yours as well as ours), whether you think that I am speaking the truth or not?

They all thought that what I said was entirely true.

Then you agree, I said, that the pleasant is the good, and the painful evil. And here I would beg my friend Prodicus not to intro- duce his distinction of names, whether he is disposed to say pleasur- able, delightful, joyful. However, by whatever name he prefers to call them, I will ask you, most excellent Prodicus, to answer in my sense of the words.

Prodicus laughed and assented, as did the others.

Then, my friends, what do you say to this? Are not all actions honourable and useful, of which the tendency is to make life painless and pleasant? The honourable work is also useful and good?

This was admitted.

Then, I said, if the pleasant is the good, nobody does anything under the idea or conviction that some other thing would be better and is also attainable, when he might do the better. And this inferi- ority of a man to himself is merely ignorance, as the superiority of a man to himself is wisdom.

They all assented.

And is not ignorance the having a false opinion and being de- ceived about important matters?

To this also they unanimously assented.

Then, I said, no man voluntarily pursues evil, or that which he thinks to be evil. To prefer evil to good is not in human nature; and when a man is compelled to choose one of two evils, no one will choose the greater when he may have the less.

All of us agreed to every word of this.

Well, I said, there is a certain thing called fear or terror; and here, Prodicus, I should particularly like to know whether you would agree with me in defining this fear or terror as expectation of evil.

Protagoras and Hippias agreed, but Prodicus said that this was fear and not terror.

Never mind, Prodicus, I said; but let me ask whether, if our former assertions are true, a man will pursue that which he fears when he is not compelled? Would not this be in flat contradiction to the admission which has been already made, that he thinks the things which he fears to be evil; and no one will pursue or voluntarily accept that which he thinks to be evil?

That also was universally admitted.

Then, I said, these, Hippias and Prodicus, are our premisses; and I would beg Protagoras to explain to us how he can be right in what he said at first. I do not mean in what he said quite at first, for his first statement, as you may remember, was that whereas there were five parts of virtue none of them was like any other of them; each of them had a separate function. To this, however, I am not referring, but to the assertion which he afterwards made that of the five virtues four were nearly akin to each other, but that the fifth, which was courage, differed greatly from the others. And of this he gave me the following proof. He said: You will find, Socrates, that some of the most impious, and unrighteous, and intemperate, and ignorant of men are among the most courageous; which proves that courage is very different from the other parts of virtue. I was surprised at his saying this at the time, and I am still more surprised now that I have discussed the matter with you. So I asked him whether by the brave he meant the confident. Yes, he replied, and the impetuous or goers. (You may remember, Protagoras, that this was your answer.)

He assented.

Well then, I said, tell us against what are the courageous ready to go—against the same dangers as the cowards?

No, he answered.

Then against something different?

Yes, he said.

Then do cowards go where there is safety, and the courageous where there is danger?

*Prota-
goras*

SOCRATES,
PROTA-
GORAS.

No man
volun-
tarily
pursues
evil

Then will
a man
pursue
that
which he
fears, al-
though he
need not ?
359

Prota-
goras

SOCRATES,
PROTA-
GORAS.

The cou-
rageous
pursue
dangers,
but not in
the belief
that they
are dan
gers.

The cou-
rageous
and the
cowardly
alike go to
meet dan-
gers, but
they have
different
uotions of
what con-
stitutes
danger.

360

Yes, Socrates, so men say.

Very true, I said. But I want to know against what do you say that the courageous are ready to go—against dangers, believing them to be dangers, or not against dangers?

No, said he; the former case has been proved by you in the previous argument to be impossible.

That, again, I replied, is quite true. And if this has been rightly proven, then no one goes to meet what he thinks to be dangers, since the want of self-control, which makes men rush into dangers, has been shown to be ignorance.

He assented.

And yet the courageous man and the coward alike go to meet that about which they are confident; so that, in this point of view, the cowardly and the courageous go to meet the same things.

And yet, Socrates, said Protagoras, that to which the coward goes is the opposite of that to which the courageous goes; the one, for example, is ready to go to battle, and the other is not ready.

And is going to battle honourable or disgraceful? I said.

Honourable, he replied.

And if honourable, then already admitted by us to be good; for all honourable actions we have admitted to be good.

That is true; and to that opinion I shall always adhere.

True, I said. But which of the two are they who, as you say, are unwilling to go to war, which is a good and honourable thing?

The cowards, he replied.

And what is good and honourable, I said, is also pleasant?

It has certainly been acknowledged to be so, he replied.

And do the cowards knowingly refuse to go to the nobler, and pleasanter, and better?

The admission of that, he replied, would belie our former admissions.

But does not the courageous man also go to meet the better, and pleasanter, and nobler?

That must be admitted.

And the courageous man has no base fear or base confidence?

True, he replied.

And if not base, then honourable?

He admitted this.

And if honourable, then good?

Yes.

But the fear and confidence of the coward or foolhardy or madman, on the contrary, are base?

He assented.

And these base fears and confidences originate in ignorance and uninstructedness?

True, he said.

Then as to the motive from which the cowards act, do you call it cowardice or courage?

I should say cowardice, he replied.

And have they not been shown to be cowards through their ignorance of dangers?

Assuredly, he said.

And because of that ignorance they are cowards?

He assented.

And the reason why they are cowards is admitted by you to be cowardice?

He again assented.

Then the ignorance of what is and is not dangerous is cowardice?

He nodded assent.

But surely courage, I said, is opposed to cowardice?

Yes.

Then the wisdom which knows what are and are not dangers is opposed to the ignorance of them?

To that again he nodded assent.

And the ignorance of them is cowardice?

To that he very reluctantly nodded assent.

And the knowledge of that which is and is not dangerous is courage, and is opposed to the ignorance of these things?

At this point he would no longer nod assent, but was silent.

And why, I said, do you neither assent nor dissent, Protagoras?

Finish the argument by yourself, he said.

I only want to ask one more question, I said. I want to know whether you still think that there are men who are most ignorant and yet most courageous?

You seem to have a great ambition to make me answer, Socrates, and therefore I will gratify you, and say, that this appears to me to be impossible consistently with the argument.

My only object, I said, in continuing the discussion, has been the desire to ascertain the nature and relations of virtue; for if this were clear, I am very sure that the other controversy which has been carried on at great length by both of us—you affirming and I denying that virtue can be taught—would also become clear. The result of our discussion appears to me to be singular. For if the argument had a human voice, that voice would be heard laughing at us and saying: 'Protagoras and Socrates, you are strange beings; there are you, Socrates, who were saying that virtue cannot be taught, contradict-

Prota-goras

SOCRATES, PROTA-GORAS.

They have somehow both of them changed their position in the course of the argument.

ing yourself now by your attempt to prove that all things are knowledge, including justice, and temperance, and courage,—which tends to show that virtue can certainly be taught; for if virtue were other than knowledge, as Protagoras attempted to prove, then clearly virtue cannot be taught; but if virtue is entirely knowledge, as you are seeking to show, then I cannot but suppose that virtue is capable of being taught. Protagoras, on the other hand, who started by saying that it might be taught, is now eager to prove it to be anything rather than knowledge; and if this is true, it must be quite incapable of being taught.' Now I, Protagoras, perceiving this terrible confusion of our ideas, have a great desire that they should be cleared up. And I should like to carry on the discussion until we ascertain what virtue is, and whether capable of being taught or not, lest haply Epimetheus should trip us up and deceive us in the argument, as he forgot us in the story; I prefer your Prometheus to your Epimetheus, for of him I make use, whenever I am busy about these questions, in Promethean care of my own life. And if you have no objection, as I said at first, I should like to have your help in the enquiry.

Protagoras replied: Socrates, I am not of a base nature, and I am the last man in the world to be envious. I cannot but applaud your energy and your conduct of an argument. As I have often said, I admire you above all men whom I know, and far above all men of your age; and I believe that you will become very eminent in philosophy. Let us come back to the subject at some future time; at present we had better turn to something else.

By all means, I said, if that is your wish; for I too ought long since to have kept the engagement of which I spoke before, and only tarried because I could not refuse the request of the noble Callias. So the conversation ended, and we went our way.

PHILEBUS

PHILEBUS

PERSONS OF THE DIALOGUE

SOCRATES   PROTARCHUS   PHILEBUS

Socrates. Observe, Protarchus, the nature of the position which you are now going to take from Philebus, and what the other position is which I maintain, and which, if you do not approve of it, is to be controverted by you. Shall you and I sum up the two sides?

Protarchus. By all means.

Soc. Philebus was saying that enjoyment and pleasure and delight, and the class of feelings akin to them, are a good to every living being, whereas I contend, that not these, but wisdom and intelligence and memory, and their kindred, right opinion and true reasoning, are better and more desirable than pleasure for all who are able to partake of them, and that to all such who are or ever will be they are the most advantageous of all things. Have I not given, Philebus, a fair statement of the two sides of the argument?

Philebus. Nothing could be fairer, Socrates.

Soc. And do you, Protarchus, accept the position which is assigned to you?

Pro. I cannot do otherwise, since our excellent Philebus has left the field.

Soc. Surely the truth about these matters ought, by all means, to be ascertained.

Pro. Certainly.

Soc. Shall we further agree —

Pro. To what?

Soc. That you and I must now try to indicate some state and disposition of the soul which has the property of making all men happy.

Pro. Yes, by all means.

Soc. And you say that pleasure, and I say that wisdom, is such a state?

Pro. True.

Soc. And what if there be a third state, which is better than ei-

Steph.
11
SOCRATES
PROTAR-
CHUS,
PHILE-
BUS.

Philebus, who is now to be succeeded by Protarchus, maintains that pleasure is the good; Socrates prefers wisdom.

Which of these two positions is the truer?

55

Philebus

ther? Then both of us are vanquished—are we not? But if this life, which really has the power of making men happy, turn out to be more akin to pleasure than to wisdom, the life of pleasure may still have the advantage over the life of wisdom.

Pro. True.

Soc. Or suppose that the better life is more nearly allied to wisdom, then wisdom conquers, and pleasure is defeated;—do you agree?

Pro. Certainly.

Soc. And what do you say, Philebus?

Phi. I say, and shall always say, that pleasure is easily the conqueror; but you must decide for yourself, Protarchus.

Pro. You, Philebus, have handed over the argument to me, and have no longer a voice in the matter?

Phi. True enough. Nevertheless I would clear myself and deliver my soul of you; and I call the goddess herself to witness that I now do so.

Pro. You may appeal to us; we too will be the witnesses of your words. And now, Socrates, whether Philebus is pleased or displeased, we will proceed with the argument.

Soc. Then let us begin with the goddess herself, of whom Philebus says that she is called Aphrodite, but that her real name is Pleasure.

Pro. Very good.

Soc. The awe which I always feel, Protarchus, about the names of the gods is more than human—it exceeds all other fears. And now I would not sin against Aphrodite by naming her amiss; let her be called what she pleases. But Pleasure I know to be manifold, and with her, as I was just now saying, we must begin, and consider what her nature is. She has one name, and therefore you would imagine that she is one; and yet surely she takes the most varied and even unlike forms. For do we not say that the intemperate has pleasure, and that the temperate has pleasure in his very temperance,—that the fool is pleased when he is full of foolish fancies and hopes, and that the wise man has pleasure in his wisdom? and how foolish would any one be who affirmed that all these opposite pleasures are severally alike!

Pro. Why, Socrates, they are opposed in so far as they spring from opposite sources, but they are not in themselves opposite. For must not pleasure be of all things most absolutely like pleasure,—that is, like itself?

Soc. Yes, my good friend, just as colour is like colour;—in so far as colours are colours, there is no difference between them; and yet

12

SOCRATES, PROTARCHUS, PHILEBUS.

In the course of our enquiry something superior both to pleasure and to wisdom may appear. In that case, if pleasure be more akin to this superior nature, pleasure must be adjudged conqueror: but if wisdom, wisdom.

We will begin with pleasure, which is one, but also has many varieties, some of them being mutually opposed.

Pleasures are opposed when

we all know that black is not only unlike, but even absolutely opposed to white: or again, as figure is like figure, for all figures are comprehended under one class; and yet particular figures may be absolutely opposed to one another, and there is an infinite diversity of them. And we might find similar examples in many other things; therefore do not rely upon this argument, which would go to prove the unity of the most extreme opposites. And I suspect that we shall find a similar opposition among pleasures.

Pro. Very likely; but how will this invalidate the argument?

Soc. Why, I shall reply, that dissimilar as they are, you apply to them a new predicate, for you say that all pleasant things are good; now although no one can argue that pleasure is not pleasure, he may argue, as we are doing, that pleasures are oftener bad than good; but you call them all good, and at the same time are compelled, if you are pressed, to acknowledge that they are unlike. And so you must tell us what is the identical quality existing alike in good and bad pleasures, which makes you designate all of them as good.

Pro. What do you mean, Socrates? Do you think that any one who asserts pleasure to be the good, will tolerate the notion that some pleasures are good and others bad?

Soc. And yet you will acknowledge that they are different from one another, and sometimes opposed?

Pro. Not in so far as they are pleasures.

Soc. That is a return to the old position, Protarchus, and so we are to say (are we?) that there is no difference in pleasures, but that they are all alike; and the examples which have just been cited do not pierce our dull minds, but we go on arguing all the same, like the weakest and most inexperienced reasoners?[1]

Pro. What do you mean?

Soc. Why, I mean to say, that in self-defence I may, if I like, follow your example, and assert boldly that the two things most unlike are most absolutely alike; and the result will be that you and I will prove ourselves to be very tyros in the art of disputing; and the argument will be blown away and lost. Suppose that we put back, and return to the old position; then perhaps we may come to an understanding with one another.

Pro. How do you mean?

Soc. Shall I, Protarchus, have my own question asked of me by you?

Pro. What question?

Soc. Ask me whether wisdom and science and mind, and those

[1] Probably corrupt.

Philebus

13
SOCRATES,
PROTAR-
CHUS.

springing
from
opposite
sources:
in them-
selves
they are
all alike.

But this
proves
only that
all
pleasures
are plea-
sures, and
not that
all
pleasures
are good.

We shall
not be
able to
proceed,
if obvious
facts are
ignored.

58 Dialectic and eristic

Philebus

SOCRATES,
PROTAR-
CHUS.

To say
that there
are no
[14]
differ-
ences
between
pleasures,
is as ab-
surd as to
say that
there are
no differ-
ences
between
sciences.

We have
lighted
upon the
old prob-
lem of the
One and
Many.

The co-
existence
of the
One and
Many in
concrete
objects
presents
no diffi-
culty.

other qualities which I, when asked by you at first what is the nature of the good, affirmed to be good, are not in the same case with the pleasures of which you spoke.

Pro. What do you mean?

Soc. The sciences are a numerous class, and will be found to present great differences. But even admitting that, like the pleasures, they are opposite as well as different, should I be worthy of the name of dialectician if, in order to avoid this difficulty, I were to say (as you are saying of pleasure) that there is no difference between one science and another;—would not the argument founder and disappear like an idle tale, although we might ourselves escape drowning by clinging to a fallacy?

Pro. May none of this befall us, except the deliverance! Yet I like the even-handed justice which is applied to both our arguments. Let us assume, then, that there are many and diverse pleasures, and many and different sciences.

Soc. And let us have no concealment, Protarchus, of the differences between my good and yours; but let us bring them to the light in the hope that, in the process of testing them, they may show whether pleasure is to be called the good, or wisdom, or some third quality; for surely we are not now simply contending in order that my view or that yours may prevail, but I presume that we ought both of us to be fighting for the truth.

Pro. Certainly we ought.

Soc. Then let us have a more definite understanding and establish the principle on which the argument rests.

Pro. What principle?

Soc. A principle about which all men are always in a difficulty, and some men sometimes against their will.

Pro. Speak plainer.

Soc. The principle which has just turned up, which is a marvel of nature; for that one should be many or many one, are wonderful propositions; and he who affirms either is very open to attack.

Pro. Do you mean, when a person says that I, Protarchus, am by nature one and also many, dividing the single 'me' into many 'me's,' and even opposing them as great and small, light and heavy, and in ten thousand other ways?

Soc. Those, Protarchus, are the common and acknowledged paradoxes about the one and many, which I may say that everybody has by this time agreed to dismiss as childish and obvious and detrimental to the true course of thought; and no more favour is shown to that other puzzle, in which a person proves the members and parts of anything to be divided, and then confessing that they are all one, says laughingly in disproof of his own words: Why, here is a miracle, the one is many and infinite, and the many are only one.

Pro. But what, Socrates, are those other marvels connected with this subject which, as you imply, have not yet become common and acknowledged?

Soc. When, my boy, the one does not belong to the class of things that are born and perish, as in the instances which we were giving, for in those cases, and when unity is of this concrete nature, there is, as I was saying, a universal consent that no refutation is needed; but when the assertion is made that man is one, or ox is one, or beauty one, or the good one, then the interest which attaches to these and similar unities and the attempt which is made to divide them gives birth to a controversy.

Pro. Of what nature?

Soc. In the first place, as to whether these unities have a real existence; and then how each individual unity, being always the same, and incapable either of generation or of destruction, but retaining a permanent individuality, can be conceived either as dispersed and multiplied in the infinity of the world of generation, or as still entire and yet divided from itself, which latter would seem to be the greatest impossibility of all, for how can one and the same thing be at the same time in one and in many things? These, Protarchus, are the real difficulties, and this is the one and many to which they relate; they are the source of great perplexity if ill decided, and the right determination of them is very helpful.

Pro. Then, Socrates, let us begin by clearing up these questions.

Soc. That is what I should wish.

Pro. And I am sure that all my other friends will be glad to hear them discussed; Philebus, fortunately for us, is not disposed to move, and we had better not stir him up with questions.

Soc. Good; and where shall we begin this great and multifarious battle, in which such various points are at issue? Shall we begin thus?

Pro. How?

Soc. We say that the one and many become identified by thought, and that now, as in time past, they run about together, in and out of every word which is uttered, and that this union of them will never cease, and is not now beginning, but is, as I believe, an everlasting quality of thought itself, which never grows old. Any young man, when he first tastes these subtleties, is delighted, and fancies that he has found a treasure of wisdom; in the first enthusiasm of his joy he leaves no stone, or rather no thought unturned,

Philebus

SOCRATES, PROTARCHUS.

15

Our troubles begin with abstract unities.

What is the relation of ideas and phenomena?

The co-existence of one and many is a consequence of thought. —The enthusiasm of young

Philebus

16
SOCRATES,
PROTAR-
CHUS.

men when
they first
discover
the
puzzle.

What we
want is to
find a
path to
the truth.

Socrates'
favourite
method is
to pro-
ceed from
unity to
infinity,
from the
one to the
many, by
regular
steps,
omitting
none of
the inter-
mediate
species.

We must
go on
defining
while
anything
remains
to be de-
fined.

now rolling up the many into the one, and kneading them together, now unfolding and dividing them; he puzzles himself first and above all, and then he proceeds to puzzle his neighbours, whether they are older or younger, or of his own age—that makes no difference; neither father nor mother does he spare; no human being who has ears is safe from him, hardly even his dog, and a barbarian would have no chance of escaping him, if an interpreter could only be found.

Pro. Considering, Socrates, how many we are, and that all of us are young men, is there not a danger that we and Philebus may all set upon you, if you abuse us? We understand what you mean; but is there no charm by which we may dispel all this confusion, no more excellent way of arriving at the truth? If there is, we hope that you will guide us into that way, and we will do our best to follow, for the enquiry in which we are engaged, Socrates, is not unimportant.

Soc. The reverse of unimportant, my boys, as Philebus calls you, and there neither is nor ever will be a better than my own favourite way, which has nevertheless already often deserted me and left me helpless in the hour of need.

Pro. Tell us what that is.

Soc. One which may be easily pointed out, but is by no means easy of application; it is the parent of all the discoveries in the arts.

Pro. Tell us what it is.

Soc. A gift of heaven, which, as I conceive, the gods tossed among men by the hands of a new Prometheus, and therewith a blaze of light; and the ancients, who were our betters and nearer the gods than we are, handed down the tradition, that whatever things are said to be are composed of one and many, and have the finite and infinite implanted in them: seeing, then, that such is the order of the world, we too ought in every enquiry to begin by laying down one idea of that which is the subject of enquiry; this unity we shall find in everything. Having found it, we may next proceed to look for two, if there be two, or, if not, then for three or some other number, subdividing each of these units, until at last the unity with which we began is seen not only to be one and many and infinite, but also a definite number; the infinite must not be suffered to approach the many until the entire number of the species intermediate between unity and infinity has been discovered,—then, and not till then, we may rest from division, and without further troubling ourselves about the endless individuals may allow them to drop into infinity. This, as I was saying, is the way of considering and learning and teaching one another, which the gods have handed down to us. But the wise men of our time are either too quick or too slow in conceiving plurality in unity. Having no method, they make their one and many anyhow, and from unity pass at once to infinity; the intermediate steps never occur to them. And this, I repeat, is what makes the difference between the mere art of disputation and true dialectic.

Pro. I think that I partly understand you, Socrates, but I should like to have a clearer notion of what you are saying.

Soc. I may illustrate my meaning by the letters of the alphabet, Protarchus, which you were made to learn as a child.

Pro. How do they afford an illustration?

Soc. The sound which passes through the lips whether of an individual or of all men is one and yet infinite.

Pro. Very true.

Soc. And yet not by knowing either that sound is one or that sound is infinite are we perfect in the art of speech, but the knowledge of the number and nature of sounds is what makes a man a grammarian.

Pro. Very true.

Soc. And the knowledge which makes a man a musician is of the same kind.

Pro. How so?

Soc. Sound is one in music as well as in grammar?

Pro. Certainly.

Soc. And there is a higher note and a lower note, and a note of equal pitch:—may we affirm so much?

Pro. Yes.

Soc. But you would not be a real musician if this was all that you knew; though if you did not know this you would know almost nothing of music.

Pro. Nothing.

Soc. But when you have learned what sounds are high and what low, and the number and nature of the intervals and their limits or proportions, and the systems compounded out of them, which our fathers discovered, and have handed down to us who are their descendants under the name of harmonies; and the affections corresponding to them in the movements of the human body, which when measured by numbers ought, as they say, to be called rhythms and measures; and they tell us that the same principle should be applied to every one and many;—when, I say, you have learned all this, then, my dear friend, you are perfect; and you may be said to understand any other subject, when you have a similar grasp of it. But the infinity of kinds and the infinity of individuals

17
Philebus
SOCRATES,
PROTAR-
CHUS.

The true
method
applied to
grammar,

and to
music.

which there is in each of them, when not classified, creates in every one of us a state of infinite ignorance; and he who never looks for number in anything, will not himself be looked for in the number of famous men.

18

SOCRATES,
PROTAR-
CHUS,
PHILE-
BUS.

If a man
has to
start with
infinity,
he should
not jump
at once to
unity, but
should
proceed
first to
some
definite
quantity.
—An il-
lustration
of this
process
taken
from
grammar.

Pro. I think that what Socrates is now saying is excellent, Philebus.

Phi. I think so too, but how do his words bear upon us and upon the argument?

Soc. Philebus is right in asking that question of us, Protarchus.

Pro. Indeed he is, and you must answer him.

Soc. I will; but you must let me make one little remark first about these matters; I was saying, that he who begins with any individual unity, should proceed from that, not to infinity, but to a definite number, and now I say conversely, that he who has to begin with infinity should not jump to unity, but he should look about for some number representing a certain quantity, and thus out of all end in one. And now let us return for an illustration of our principle to the case of letters.

Pro. What do you mean?

Soc. Some god or divine man, who in the Egyptian legend is said to have been Theuth, observing that the human voice was infinite, first distinguished in this infinity a certain number of vowels, and then other letters which had sound, but were not pure vowels (i. e. the semivowels); these too exist in a definite number; and lastly, he distinguished a third class of letters which we now call mutes, without voice and without sound, and divided these, and likewise the two other classes of vowels and semivowels, into the individual sounds, and told the number of them, and gave to each and all of them the name of letters; and observing that none of us could learn any one of them and not learn them all, and in consideration of this common bond which in a manner united them, he assigned to them all a single art, and this he called the art of grammar or letters.

Phi. The illustration, Protarchus, has assisted me in understanding the original statement, but I still feel the defect of which I just now complained.

Soc. Are you going to ask, Philebus, what this has to do with the argument?

Phi. Yes, that is a question which Protarchus and I have been long asking.

Soc. Assuredly you have already arrived at the answer to the question which, as you say, you have been so long asking?

Phi. How so?

Soc. Did we not begin by enquiring into the comparative eligibility of pleasure and wisdom?

Phi. Certainly.

Soc. And we maintain that they are each of them one?

Phi. True.

Soc. And the precise question to which the previous discussion desires an answer is, how they are one and also many [i. e. how they have one genus and many species], and are not at once infinite, and what number of species is to be assigned to either of them before they pass into infinity[1].

Pro. That is a very serious question, Philebus, to which Socrates has ingeniously brought us round, and please to consider which of us shall answer him; there may be something ridiculous in my being unable to answer, and therefore imposing the task upon you, when I have undertaken the whole charge of the argument, but if neither of us were able to answer, the result methinks would be still more ridiculous. Let us consider, then, what we are to do:— Socrates, if I understood him rightly, is asking whether there are not kinds of pleasure, and what is the number and nature of them, and the same of wisdom.

Soc. Most true, O son of Callias; and the previous argument showed that if we are not able to tell the kinds of everything that has unity, likeness, sameness, or their opposites, none of us will be of the smallest use in any enquiry.

Pro. That seems to be very near the truth, Socrates. Happy would the wise man be if he knew all things, and the next best thing for him is that he should know himself. Why do I say so at this moment? I will tell you. You, Socrates, have granted us this opportunity of conversing with you, and are ready to assist us in determining what is the best of human goods. For when Philebus said that pleasure and delight and enjoyment and the like were the chief good, you answered—No, not those, but another class of goods; and we are constantly reminding ourselves of what you said, and very properly, in order that we may not forget to examine and compare the two. And these goods, which in your opinion are to be designated as superior to pleasure, and are the true objects of pursuit, are mind and knowledge and understanding and art, and the like. There was a dispute about which were the best, and we playfully threatened that you should not be allowed to go home until the question was settled; and you agreed, and placed yourself at our disposal. And now, as children say, what has been

Philebus

SOCRATES,
PROTAR-
CHUS,
PHILE-
BUS.

We wish
to compare
pleasure
and
wisdom.
[19]
If then
we would
follow the
true
method of
investigation, we
must seek
to discover the
number
and
nature of
their
kinds.

---

[1] i. e. into the infinite number of individuals.

fairly given cannot be taken back; cease then to fight against us in this way.

Soc. In what way?

Phi. Do not perplex us, and keep asking questions of us to which we have not as yet any sufficient answer to give; let us not imagine that a general puzzling of us all is to be the end of our discussion, but if we are unable to answer, do you answer, as you have promised. Consider, then, whether you will divide pleasure and knowledge according to their kinds; or you may let the matter drop, if you are able and willing to find some other mode of clearing up our controversy.

Soc. If you say that, I have nothing to apprehend, for the words 'if you are willing' dispel all my fear; and, moreover, a god seems to have recalled something to my mind.

Phi. What is that?

Soc. I remember to have heard long ago certain discussions about pleasure and wisdom, whether awake or in a dream I cannot tell; they were to the effect that neither the one nor the other of them was the good, but some third thing, which was different from them, and better than either. If this be clearly established, then pleasure will lose the victory, for the good will cease to be identified with her:—Am I not right?

Pro. Yes.

Soc. And there will cease to be any need of distinguishing the kinds of pleasures, as I am inclined to think, but this will appear more clearly as we proceed.

Pro. Capital, Socrates; pray go on as you propose.

Soc. But, let us first agree on some little points.

Pro. What are they?

Soc. Is the good perfect or imperfect?

Pro. The most perfect, Socrates, of all things.

Soc. And is the good sufficient?

Pro. Yes, certainly, and in a degree surpassing all other things.

Soc. And no one can deny that all percipient beings desire and hunt after good, and are eager to catch and have the good about them, and care not for the attainment of anything which is not accompanied by good.

Pro. That is undeniable.

Soc. Now let us part off the life of pleasure from the life of wisdom, and pass them in review.

Pro. How do you mean?

Soc. Let there be no wisdom in the life of pleasure, nor any

Philebus and Protarchus confess themselves incapable of doing this. They therefore ask help of Socrates.

Socrates has heard some one say that neither pleasure nor wisdom is the good, but some third thing. If this be brought to light, there will be no need to distinguish the kinds of pleasure and wisdom.

Let us first admit that the good is perfect, and sufficient, and pleasure in the life of wisdom, for if either of them is the chief good, it cannot be supposed to want anything, but if either is shown to want anything, then it cannot really be the chief good.

Pro. Impossible.

Soc. And will you help us to test these two lives?

Pro. Certainly.

Soc. Then answer.

Pro. Ask.

Soc. Would you choose, Protarchus, to live all your life long in the enjoyment of the greatest pleasures?

Pro. Certainly I should.

Soc. Would you consider that there was still anything wanting to you if you had perfect pleasure?

Pro. Certainly not.

Soc. Reflect; would you not want wisdom and intelligence and forethought, and similar qualities? would you not at any rate want sight?

Pro. Why should I? Having pleasure I should have all things.

Soc. Living thus, you would always throughout your life enjoy the greatest pleasures?

Pro. I should.

Soc. But if you had neither mind, nor memory, nor knowledge, nor true opinion, you would in the first place be utterly ignorant of whether you were pleased or not, because you would be entirely devoid of intelligence.

Pro. Certainly.

Soc. And similarly, if you had no memory you would not recollect that you had ever been pleased, nor would the slightest recollection of the pleasure which you feel at any moment remain with you; and if you had no true opinion you would not think that you were pleased when you were; and if you had no power of calculation you would not be able to calculate on future pleasure, and your life would be the life, not of a man, but of an oyster or 'pulmo marinus.' Could this be otherwise?

Pro. No.

Soc. But is such a life eligible?

Pro. I cannot answer you, Socrates; the argument has taken away from me the power of speech.

Soc. We must keep up our spirits;—let us now take the life of mind and examine it in turn.

Pro. And what is this life of mind?

Soc. I want to know whether any one of us would consent to

Philebus

21

SOCRATES,
PROTAR-
CHUS.

above all
things to
be de-
sired.

Next let
us separ-
ate the
life of
pleasure
from the
life of
wisdom,
and
examine
each
apart.

Pleasure
without
knowl-
edge is
pleasure
of which
we are
uncon-
scious,—
the life of
an oyster.

Philebus

SOCRATES,
PROTAR-
CHUS,
PHILE-
BUS.

live, having wisdom and mind and knowledge and memory of all things, but having no sense of pleasure or pain, and wholly unaffected by these and the like feelings?

Pro. Neither life, Socrates, appears eligible to me, or is likely, as I should imagine, to be chosen by any one else.

22

Soc. What would you say, Protarchus, to both of these in one, or to one that was made out of the union of the two?

Pro. Out of the union, that is, of pleasure with mind and wisdom?

Soc. Yes, that is the life which I mean.

Pro. There can be no difference of opinion; not some but all would surely choose this third rather than either of the other two, and in addition to them.

Soc. But do you see the consequence?

Pro. To be sure I do. The consequence is, that two out of the three lives which have been proposed are neither sufficient nor eligible for man or for animal.

Soc. Then now there can be no doubt that neither of them has the good, for the one which had would certainly have been sufficient and perfect and eligible for every living creature or thing that was able to live such a life; and if any of us had chosen any other, he would have chosen contrary to the nature of the truly eligible, and not of his own free will, but either through ignorance or from some unhappy necessity.

Pro. Certainly that seems to be true.

Soc. And now have I not sufficiently shown that Philebus' goddess is not to be regarded as identical with the good?

Phi. Neither is your 'mind' the good, Socrates, for that will be open to the same objections.

Soc. Perhaps, Philebus, you may be right in saying so of my 'mind'; but of the true, which is also the divine mind, far otherwise. However, I will not at present claim the first place for mind as against the mixed life; but we must come to some understanding about the second place. For you might affirm pleasure and I mind to be the cause of the mixed life; and in that case although neither of them would be the good, one of them might be imagined to be the cause of the good. And I might proceed further to argue in opposition to Philebus, that the element which makes this mixed life eligible and good, is more akin and more similar to mind than to pleasure. And if this is true, pleasure cannot be truly said to share either in the first or second place, and does not, if I may trust my own mind, attain even to the third.

Pro. Truly, Socrates, pleasure appears to me to have had a fall;

And knowledge, without pleasure, is equally undesirable.

The mixed life of pleasure and wisdom is to be preferred.

'And so pleasure,' says Socrates, 'is not the same with the good.' —'Nor your mind', rejoins Philebus. —'Not my mind, certainly, but the divine, yes. And I might add that the excellence of the mixed life is due in fighting for the palm, she has been smitten by the argument, and is laid low. I must say that mind would have fallen too, and may therefore be thought to show discretion in not putting forward a similar claim. And if pleasure were deprived not only of the first but of the second place, she would be terribly damaged in the eyes of her admirers, for not even to them would she still appear as fair as before.

Soc. Well, but had we not better leave her now, and not pain her by applying the crucial test, and finally detecting her?

Pro. Nonsense, Socrates.

Soc. Why? because I said that we had better not pain pleasure, which is an impossibility?

Pro. Yes, and more than that, because you do not seem to be aware that none of us will let you go home until you have finished the argument.

Soc. Heavens! Protarchus, that will be a tedious business, and just at present not at all an easy one. For in going to war in the cause of mind, who is aspiring to the second prize, I ought to have weapons of another make from those which I used before; some, however, of the old ones may do again. And must I then finish the argument?

Pro. Of course you must.

Soc. Let us be very careful in laying the foundation.

Pro. What do you mean?

Soc. Let us divide all existing things into two, or rather, if you do not object, into three classes.

Pro. Upon what principle would you make the division?

Soc. Let us take some of our newly-found notions.

Pro. Which of them?

Soc. Were we not saying that God revealed a finite element of existence, and also an infinite?

Pro. Certainly.

Soc. Let us assume these two principles, and also a third, which is compounded out of them; but I fear that I am ridiculously clumsy at these processes of division and enumeration.

Pro. What do you mean, my good friend?

Soc. I say that a fourth class is still wanted.

Pro. What will that be?

Soc. Find the cause of the third or compound, and add this as a fourth class to the three others.

Pro. And would you like to have a fifth class or cause of resolution as well as a cause of composition?

23
Philebus

SOCRATES,
PROTAR-
CHUS.

rather to
wisdom
than to
pleasure.'

In sup-
porting
the claims
of mind
to the
second
place,
some new
weapons
will be
required.

All things
may be
divided
into three
or four
classes:
(1) the
finite,
(2) the
infinite,
(3) the
union of
the two,
and
(4) the
cause of
the union.

Soc. Not, I think, at present; but if I want a fifth at some future time you shall allow me to have it.

Pro. Certainly.

Soc. Let us begin with the first three; and as we find two out of the three greatly divided and dispersed, let us endeavour to reunite them, and see how in each of them there is a one and many.

24   *Pro.* If you would explain to me a little more about them, perhaps I might be able to follow you.

Soc. Well, the two classes are the same which I mentioned before, one the finite, and the other the infinite; I will first show that the infinite is in a certain sense many, and the finite may be hereafter discussed.

Pro. I agree.

The class
of the
infinite
contains
all things
into
which the
more and
the less
enter; for
the more
and the
less are
without
limit and
measure.

Soc. And now consider well; for the question to which I invite your attention is difficult and controverted. When you speak of hotter and colder, can you conceive any limit in those qualities? Does not the more and less, which dwells in their very nature, prevent their having any end? for if they had an end, the more and less would themselves have an end.

Pro. That is most true.

Soc. Ever, as we say, into the hotter and the colder there enters a more and a less.

Pro. Yes.

Soc. Then, says the argument, there is never any end of them, and being endless they must also be infinite.

Pro. Yes, Socrates, that is exceedingly true.

Soc. Yes, my dear Protarchus, and your answer reminds me that such an expression as 'exceedingly,' which you have just uttered, and also the term 'gently,' have the same significance as more or less; for whenever they occur they do not allow of the existence of quantity—they are always introducing degrees into actions, instituting a comparison of a more or a less excessive or a more or a less gentle, and at each creation of more or less, quantity disappears. For, as I was just now saying, if quantity and measure did not disappear, but were allowed to intrude in the sphere of more and less and the other comparatives, these last would be driven out of their own domain. When definite quantity is once admitted, there can be no longer a 'hotter' or a 'colder' (for these are always progressing, and are never in one stay); but definite quantity is at rest, and has ceased to progress. Which proves that comparatives, such as the hotter and the colder, are to be ranked in the class of the infinite.

Pro. Your remark certainly has the look of truth, Socrates; but these subjects, as you were saying, are difficult to follow at first. I think, however, that if I could hear the argument repeated by you once or twice, there would be a substantial agreement between us.

Soc. Yes, and I will try to meet your wish; but, as I would rather not waste time in the enumeration of endless particulars, let me know whether I may not assume as a note of the infinite—

Pro. What?

Soc. I want to know whether such things as appear to us to admit of more or less, or are denoted by the words 'exceedingly,' 'gently,' 'extremely,' and the like, may not be referred to the class of the infinite, which is their unity, for, as was asserted in the previous argument, all things that were divided and dispersed should be brought together, and have the mark or seal of some one nature, if possible, set upon them—do you remember?

Pro. Yes.

Soc. And all things which do not admit of more or less, but admit their opposites, that is to say, first of all, equality, and the equal, or again, the double, or any other ratio of number and measure—all these may, I think, be rightly reckoned by us in the class of the limited or finite; what do you say?

Pro. Excellent, Socrates.

Soc. And now what nature shall we ascribe to the third or compound kind?

Pro. You, I think, will have to tell me that.

Soc. Rather God will tell you, if there be any God who will listen to my prayers.

Pro. Offer up a prayer, then, and think.

Soc. I am thinking, Protarchus, and I believe that some God has befriended us.

Pro. What do you mean, and what proof have you to offer of what you are saying?

Soc. I will tell you, and do you listen to my words.

Pro. Proceed.

Soc. Were we not speaking just now of hotter and colder?

Pro. True.

Soc. Add to them drier, wetter, more, less, swifter, slower, greater, smaller, and all that in the preceding argument we placed under the unity of more and less.

Pro. In the class of the infinite, you mean?

Soc. Yes; and now mingle this with the other.

Pro. What is the other?

Soc. The class of the finite which we ought to have brought to-

The union
of finite
and infi-
nite gives
rise to the
third
class,

gether as we did the infinite; but, perhaps, it will come to the same thing if we do so now;—when the two are combined, a third will appear.

Pro. What do you mean by the class of the finite?

Soc. The class of the equal and the double, and any class which puts an end to difference and opposition, and by introducing number creates harmony and proportion among the different elements.

Pro. I understand; you seem to me to mean that the various opposites, when you mingle with them the class of the finite, takes certain forms.

Soc. Yes, that is my meaning.

Pro. Proceed.

under
which are
included
health
[26]
and har-
mony and
beauty
and the
seasons
and every
sort of
good.

Soc. Does not the right participation in the finite give health—in disease, for instance?

Pro. Certainly.

Soc. And whereas the high and low, the swift and the slow are infinite or unlimited, does not the addition of the principles aforesaid introduce a l'mit, and perfect the whole frame of music?

Pro. Yes, certainly.

Soc. Or, again, when cold and heat prevail, does not the introduction of them take away excess and indefiniteness, and infuse moderation and harmony?

Pro. Certainly.

Soc. And from a like admixture of the finite and infinite come the seasons, and all the del'ghts of life?

Pro. Most true.

Soc. I omit ten thousand other things, such as beauty and health and strength, and the many beauties and high perfections of the soul: O my beautiful Philebus, the goddess, methinks, seeing the universal wantonness and wickedness of all things, and that there was in them no limit to pleasures and self-indulgence, devised the limit of law and order, whereby, as you say, Philebus, she torments, or as I maintain, delivers the soul.—What think you, Protarchus?

Pro. Her ways are much to my mind, Socrates.

Soc. You will observe that I have spoken of three classes?

Pro. Yes, I think that I understand you: you mean to say that the infinite is one class, and that the finite is a second class of existences; but what you would make the third I am not so certain.

The third
class
takes an
amazing
variety
of forms,

Soc. That is because the amazing variety of the third class is too much for you, my dear friend; but there was not this difficulty with the infinite, which also comprehended many classes, for all of them were sealed with the note of more and less, and therefore appeared one.

Pro. True.

Soc. And the finite or limit had not many divisions, and we readily acknowledged it to be by nature one?

Pro. Yes.

Soc. Yes, indeed; and when I speak of the third class, understand me to mean any offspring of these, being a birth into true being, effected by the measure which the limit introduces.

Pro. I understand.

Soc. Still there was, as we said, a fourth class to be investigated, and you must assist in the investigation; for does not everything which comes into being, of necessity come into being through a cause?

Pro. Yes, certainly; for how can there be anything which has no cause?

Soc. And is not the agent the same as the cause in all except name; the agent and the cause may be rightly called one?

Pro. Very true.

Soc. And the same may be said of the patient, or effect; we shall find that they too differ, as I was saying, only in name—shall we not?

Pro. We shall.

Soc. The agent or cause always naturally leads, and the patient or effect naturally follows it?

Pro. Certainly.

Soc. Then the cause and what is subordinate to it in generation are not the same, but different?

Pro. True.

Soc. Did not the things which were generated, and the things out of which they were generated, furnish all the three classes?

Pro. Yes.

Soc. And the creator or cause of them has been satisfactorily proven to be distinct from them—and may therefore be called a fourth principle?

Pro. So let us call it.

Soc. Quite right; but now, having distinguished the four, I think that we had better refresh our memories by recapitulating each of them in order.

Pro. By all means.

Soc. Then the first I will call the infinite or unlimited, and the second the finite or limited; then follows the third, an essence compound and generated; and I do not think that I shall be far wrong in speaking of the cause of mixture and generation as the fourth.

Pro. Certainly not.

and is therefore more difficult to conceive than the two first classes.

The fourth class is the cause of the union of finite and infinite.

27

Order of the classes: (1) the infinite; (2) the finite;

Philebus

SOCRATES,
PROTAR-
CHUS.
PHILE-
BUS.

(3) the
union of
these;
(4) the
cause of
the union.

To the
third be-
longs the
mixed
life of
pleasure
and
wisdom.

Pleasure
and also
pain be-
long to
the first
class.

Soc. And now what is the next question, and how came we hither? Were we not enquiring whether the second place belonged to pleasure or wisdom?

Pro. We were.

Soc. And now, having determined these points, shall we not be better able to decide about the first and second place, which was the original subject of dispute?

Pro. I dare say.

Soc. We said, if you remember, that the mixed life of pleasure and wisdom was the conqueror—did we not?

Pro. True.

Soc. And we see what is the place and nature of this life and to what class it is to be assigned?

Pro. Beyond a doubt.

Soc. This is evidently comprehended in the third or mixed class; which is not composed of any two particular ingredients, but of all the elements of infinity, bound down by the finite, and may therefore be truly said to comprehend the conqueror life.

Pro. Most true.

Soc. And what shall we say, Philebus, of your life which is all sweetness; and in which of the aforesaid classes is that to be placed? Perhaps you will allow me to ask you a question before you answer?

Phi. Let me hear.

Soc. Have pleasure and pain a limit, or do they belong to the class which admits of more and less?

Phi. They belong to the class which admits of more, Socrates; for pleasure would not be perfectly good if she were not infinite in quantity and degree.

28

To which
does mind
belong?

Soc. Nor would pain, Philebus, be perfectly evil. And therefore the infinite cannot be that element which imparts to pleasure some degree of good. But now—admitting, if you like, that pleasure is of the nature of the infinite—in which of the aforesaid classes, O Protarchus and Philebus, can we without irreverence place wisdom and knowledge and mind? And let us be careful, for I think that the danger will be very serious if we err on this point.

Phi. You magnify, Socrates, the importance of your favourite god.

Soc. And you, my friend, are also magnifying your favourite goddess; but still I must beg you to answer the question.

Pro. Socrates is quite right, Philebus, and we must submit to him.

Phi. And did not you, Protarchus, propose to answer in my place?

Pro. Certainly I did; but I am now in a great strait, and I must entreat you, Socrates, to be our spokesman, and then we shall not say anything wrong or disrespectful of your favourite.

Soc. I must obey you, Protarchus; nor is the task which you impose a difficult one; but did I really, as Philebus implies, disconcert you with my playful solemnity, when I asked the question to what class mind and knowledge belong?

Pro. You did, indeed, Socrates.

Soc. Yet the answer is easy, since all philosophers assert with one voice that mind is the king of heaven and earth—in reality they are magnifying themselves. And perhaps they are right. But still I should like to consider the class of mind, if you do not object, a little more fully.

Phi. Take your own course, Socrates, and never mind length; we shall not tire of you.

Soc. Very good; let us begin then, Protarchus, by asking a question.

Pro. What question?

Soc. Whether all this which they call the universe is left to the guidance of unreason and chance medley, or, on the contrary, as our fathers have declared, ordered and governed by a marvellous intelligence and wisdom.

Pro. Wide asunder are the two assertions, illustrious Socrates, for that which you were just now saying to me appears to be blasphemy; but the other assertion, that mind orders all things, is worthy of the aspect of the world, and of the sun, and of the moon, and of the stars and of the whole circle of the heavens; and never will I say or think otherwise.

Soc. Shall we then[1] agree with them of old time in maintaining[1] this doctrine,—not merely reasserting the notions of others, without risk to ourselves,—but shall we share in the danger, and take our part of the reproach which will await us, when an ingenious individual declares that all is disorder?

Pro. That would certainly be my wish.

Soc. Then now please to consider the next stage of the argument.

Pro. Let me hear.

Soc. We see that the elements which enter into the nature of the bodies of all animals, fire, water, air, and, as the storm-tossed sailor cries, 'land' [i. e. earth], reappear in the constitution of the world.

Pro. The proverb may be applied to us; for truly the storm gathers over us, and we are at our wit's end.

Marginal notes:

Philebus

SOCRATES, PROTARCHUS, PHILEBUS.

To the highest, as philosophers declare. But they are interested witnesses, and therefore further proof is needed.

First, we agree that the world is governed by mind, and not by chance.

29

Next, our bodies are dependent on the body of the

---

[1] Or, 'maintain in accordance with our previous statements:' but cf. supra 28 D, and infra 30 D.

Philebus

SOCRATES,
PROTAR-
CHUS.

universe,
whence
the ele-
ments,
which
compose
them,
are de-
rived.

Soc. There is something to be remarked about each of these elements.

Pro. What is it?

Soc. Only a small fraction of any one of them exists in us, and that of a mean sort, and not in any way pure, or having any power worthy of its nature. One instance will prove this of all of them; there is fire within us, and in the universe.

Pro. True.

Soc. And is not our fire small and weak and mean? But the fire in the universe is wonderful in quantity and beauty, and in every power that fire has.

Pro. Most true.

Soc. And is the fire in the universe nourished and generated and ruled by the fire in us, or is the fire in you and me, and in other animals, dependent on the universal fire?

Pro. That is a question which does not deserve an answer.

Soc. Right; and you would say the same, if I am not mistaken, of the earth which is in animals and the earth which is in the universe, and you would give a similar reply about all the other elements?

Pro. Why, how could any man who gave any other be deemed in his senses?

Soc. I do not think that he could—but now go on to the next step. When we saw those elements of which we have been speaking gathered up in one, did we not call them a body?

Pro. We did.

Soc. And the same may be said of the cosmos, which for the same reason may be considered to be a body, because made up of the same elements.

Pro. Very true.

Soc. But is our body nourished wholly by this body, or is this body nourished by our body, thence deriving and having the qualities of which we were just now speaking?

Pro. That again, Socrates, is a question which does not deserve to be asked.

30

Soc. Well, tell me, is this question worth asking?

Pro. What question?

And,
following
out the
analogy,
we must
conclude
that our
souls and

Soc. May our body be said to have a soul?

Pro. Clearly.

Soc. And whence comes that soul, my dear Protarchus, unless the body of the universe, which contains elements like those in our bodies but in every way fairer, had also a soul? Can there be another source?

Pro. Clearly, Socrates, that is the only source.

Soc. Why, yes, Protarchus; for surely we cannot imagine that of the four classes, the finite, the infinite, the composition of the two, and the cause, the fourth, which enters into all things, giving to our bodies souls, and the art of self-management, and of healing disease, and operating in other ways to heal and organize, having too all the attributes of wisdom;—we cannot, I say, imagine that whereas the self-same elements exist, both in the entire heaven and in great provinces of the heaven, only fairer and purer, this last should not also in that higher sphere have designed the noblest and fairest things?

Pro. Such a supposition is quite unreasonable.

Soc. Then if this be denied, should we not be wise in adopting the other view and maintaining that there is in the universe a mighty infinite and an adequate limit, of which we have often spoken, as well as a presiding cause of no mean power, which orders and arranges years and seasons and months, and may be justly called wisdom and mind?

Pro. Most justly.

Soc. And wisdom and mind cannot exist without soul?

Pro. Certainly not.

Soc. And in the divine nature of Zeus would you not say that there is the soul and mind of a king, because there is in him the power of the cause? And other gods have other attributes, by which they are pleased to be called.

Pro. Very true.

Soc. Do not then suppose that these words are rashly spoken by us, O Protarchus, for they are in harmony with the testimony of those who said of old time that mind rules the universe.

Pro. True.

Soc. And they furnish an answer to my enquiry (cp. 28 A); for they imply that mind is the parent of that class of the four which we called the cause of all; and I think that you now have my answer.

Pro. I have indeed, and yet I did not observe that you had answered.

Soc. A jest is sometimes refreshing, Protarchus, when it interrupts earnest.

Pro. Very true.

Soc. I think, friend, that we have now pretty clearly set forth the class to which mind belongs and what is the power of mind.

Pro. True.

Soc. And the class to which pleasure belongs has also been long ago discovered?

Pro. Yes.

Soc. And let us remember, too, of both of them, (1) that mind was akin to the cause and of this family; and (2) that pleasure is infinite and belongs to the class which neither has, nor ever will have in itself, a beginning, middle, or end of its own.

Pro. I shall be sure to remember.

Soc. We must next examine what is their place and under what conditions they are generated. And we will begin with pleasure, since her class was first examined; and yet pleasure cannot be rightly tested apart from pain.

Pro. If this is the road, let us take it.

Soc. I wonder whether you would agree with me about the origin of pleasure and pain.

Pro. What do you mean?

Soc. I mean to say that their natural seat is in the mixed class.

Pro. And would you tell me again, sweet Socrates, which of the aforesaid classes is the mixed one?

Soc. I will, my fine fellow, to the best of my ability.

Pro. Very good.

Soc. Let us then understand the mixed class to be that which we placed third in the list of four.

Pro. That which followed the infinite and the finite; and in which you ranked health, and, if I am not mistaken, harmony.

Soc. Capital; and now will you please to give me your best attention?

Pro. Proceed; I am attending.

In the
body they
arise
through
the res-
toration
and dis-
solution
of the
harmony
of finite
and in-
finite.

Soc. I say that when the harmony in animals is dissolved, there is also a dissolution of nature and a generation of pain.

Pro. That is very probable.

Soc. And the restoration of harmony and return to nature is the source of pleasure, if I may be allowed to speak in the fewest and shortest words about matters of the greatest moment.

Pro. I believe that you are right, Socrates; but will you try to be a little plainer?

Soc. Do not obvious and every-day phenomena furnish the simplest illustration?

Pro. What phenomena do you mean?

Soc. Hunger, for example, is a dissolution and a pain.

Pro. True.

Soc. Whereas eating is a replenishment and a pleasure?

Pro. Yes.

Soc. Thirst again is a destruction and a pain, but the effect of moisture replenishing the dry place is a pleasure: once more, the unnatural separation and dissolution caused by heat is painful, and the natural restoration and refrigeration is pleasant.

Pro. Very true.

Soc. And the unnatural freezing of the moisture in an animal is pain, and the natural process of resolution and return of the elements to their original state is pleasure. And would not the general proposition seem to you to hold, that the destroying of the natural union of the finite and infinite, which, as I was observing before, make up the class of living beings, is pain, and that the process of return of all things to their own nature is pleasure?

Pro. Granted; what you say has a general truth.

Soc. Here then is one kind of pleasures and pains originating severally in the two processes which we have described?

Pro. Good.

Soc. Let us next assume that in the soul herself there is an antecedent hope of pleasure which is sweet and refreshing, and an expectation of pain, fearful and anxious.

Pro. Yes; this is another class of pleasures and pains, which is of the soul only, apart from the body, and is produced by expectation.

Soc. Right; for in the analysis of these, pure, as I suppose them to be, the pleasures being unalloyed with pain and the pains with pleasure, methinks that we shall see clearly whether the whole class of pleasure is to be desired, or whether this quality of entire desirableness is not rather to be attributed to another of the classes which have been mentioned; and whether pleasure and pain, like heat and cold, and other things of the same kind, are not sometimes to be desired and sometimes not to be desired, as being not in themselves good, but only sometimes and in some instances admitting of the nature of good.

Pro. You say most truly that this is the track which the investigation should pursue.

Soc. Well, then, assuming that pain ensues on the dissolution, and pleasure on the restoration of the harmony, let us now ask what will be the condition of animated beings who are neither in process of restoration nor of dissolution. And mind what you say: I ask whether any animal who is in that condition can possibly have any feeling of pleasure or pain, great or small?

Pro. Certainly not.

Soc. Then here we have a third state, over and above that of pleasure and of pain?

Pro. Very true.

In the soul there are pleasures and pains of expectation corresponding to these.

But besides dissolution and restoration, there is a neutral state of the body,

33

Soc. And do not forget that there is such a state; it will make a great difference in our judgment of pleasure, whether we remember this or not. And I should like to say a few words about it.

Pro. What have you to say?

Soc. Why, you know that if a man chooses the life of wisdom, there is no reason why he should not live in this neutral state.

Pro. You mean that he may live neither rejoicing nor sorrowing?

in which,
if he
pleases,
the man
who
chooses
the life
of wis-
dom may
live, like
the gods,
having
neither
joy nor
sorrow.

Soc. Yes; and if I remember rightly, when the lives were compared, no degree of pleasure, whether great or small, was thought to be necessary to him who chose the life of thought and wisdom.

Pro. Yes, certainly, we said so.

Soc. Then he will live without pleasure; and who knows whether this may not be the most divine of all lives?

Pro. If so, the gods, at any rate, cannot be supposed to have either joy or sorrow.

Soc. Certainly not—there would be a great impropriety in the assumption of either alternative. But whether the gods are or are not indifferent to pleasure is a point which may be considered hereafter if in any way relevant to the argument, and whatever is the conclusion we will place it to the account of mind in her contest for the second place, should she have to resign the first.

Pro. Just so.

Soc. The other class of pleasures, which as we were saying is purely mental, is entirely derived from memory.

Pro. What do you mean?

Soc. I must first of all analyze memory, or rather perception which is prior to memory, if the subject of our discussion is ever to be properly cleared up.

Pro. How will you proceed?

Some
affections
of the
body do
not reach
the soul;
those
which do
are con-
scious
affections.

Soc. Let us imagine affections of the body which are extinguished before they reach the soul, and leave her unaffected; and again, other affections which vibrate through both soul and body, and impart a shock to both and to each of them.

Pro. Granted.

Soc. And the soul may be truly said to be oblivious of the first but not of the second?

Pro. Quite true.

Soc. When I say oblivious, do not suppose that I mean forgetfulness in a literal sense; for forgetfulness is the exit of memory, which in this case has not yet entered; and to speak of the loss of that which is not yet in existence, and never has been, is a contradiction; do you see?

Pro. Yes.

Soc. Then just be so good as to change the terms.

Pro. How shall I change them?

Soc. Instead of the oblivion of the soul, when you are describing the state in which she is unaffected by the shocks of the body, say unconsciousness.

Pro. I see.

Soc. And the union or communion of soul and body in one feeling and motion would be properly called consciousness?

Pro. Most true.

Soc. Then now we know the meaning of the word?

Pro. Yes.

Soc. And memory may, I think, be rightly described as the preservation of consciousness?

Pro. Right.

Soc. But do we not distinguish memory from recollection?

Pro. I think so.

Soc. And do we not mean by recollection the power which the soul has of recovering, when by herself, some feeling which she experienced when in company with the body?

Pro. Certainly.

Soc. And when she recovers of herself the lost recollection of some consciousness or knowledge, the recovery is termed recollection and reminiscence?

Pro. Very true.

Soc. There is a reason why I say all this.

Pro. What is it?

Soc. I want to attain the plainest possible notion of pleasure and desire, as they exist in the mind only, apart from the body; and the previous analysis helps to show the nature of both.

Pro. Then now, Socrates, let us proceed to the next point.

Soc. There are certainly many things to be considered in discussing the generation and whole complexion of pleasure. At the outset we must determine the nature and seat of desire.

Pro. Ay; let us enquire into that, for we shall lose nothing.

Soc. Nay, Protarchus, we shall surely lose the puzzle if we find the answer.

Pro. A fair retort; but let us proceed.

Soc. Did we not place hunger, thirst, and the like, in the class of desires?

Pro. Certainly.

Soc. And yet they are very different; what common nature have we in view when we call them by a single name?

Philebus

34
SOCRATES,
PROTAR-
CHUS.

Memory
is the
preserva-
tion of
conscious
affec-
tions; re-
collection
is the re-
covery
of them.

These
prelimi-
nary
remarks
will help
us to
under-
stand the
nature of
pleasure
and
desire.

What is
desire?—
The wish
for re-
plenish-
ment.

Philebus

SOCRATES,
PROTAR-
CHUS.

Pro. By heavens, Socrates, that is a question which is not easily answered; but it must be answered.

Soc. Then let us go back to our examples.

Pro. Where shall we begin?

Soc. Do we mean anything when we say 'a man thirsts'?

Pro. Yes.

Soc. We mean to say that he 'is empty'?

Pro. Of course.

Soc. And is not thirst desire?

Pro. Yes, of drink.

35

Soc. Would you say of drink, or of replenishment with drink?

Pro. I should say, of replenishment with drink.

Soc. Then he who is empty desires, as would appear, the opposite of what he experiences; for he is empty and desires to be full?

Pro. Clearly so.

But how
can a
man,
when first
empty,
desire
replenish-
ment of
which he
has no ex-
perience?

Yet he
does de-
sire it,
not how-
ever with
his body,
but with
his mind
by the
help of
memory.

Soc. But how can a man who is empty for the first time, attain either by perception or memory to any apprehension of replenishment, of which he has no present or past experience?

Pro. Impossible.

Soc. And yet he who desires, surely desires something?

Pro. Of course.

Soc. He does not desire that which he experiences, for he experiences thirst, and thirst is emptiness; but he desires replenishment?

Pro. True.

Soc. Then there must be something in the thirsty man which in some way apprehends replenishment?

Pro. There must.

Soc. And that cannot be the body, for the body is supposed to be emptied?

Pro. Yes.

Soc. The only remaining alternative is that the soul apprehends the replenishment by the help of memory; as is obvious, for what other way can there be?

Pro. I cannot imagine any other.

Soc. But do you see the consequence?

Pro. What is it?

Soc. That there is no such thing as desire of the body.

Pro. Why so?

Soc. Why, because the argument shows that the endeavour of every animal is to the reverse of his bodily state.

Pro. Yes.

Soc. And the impulse which leads him to the opposite of what he is experiencing proves that he has a memory of the opposite state.

Pro. True.

Soc. And the argument, having proved that memory attracts us towards the objects of desire, proves also that the impulses and the desires and the moving principle in every living being have their origin in the soul.

Pro. Most true.

Soc. The argument will not allow that our body either hungers or thirsts or has any similar experience.

Pro. Quite right.

Soc. Let me make a further observation; the argument appears to me to imply that there is a kind of life which consists in these affections.

Pro. Of what affections, and of what kind of life, are you speaking?

Soc. I am speaking of being emptied and replenished, and of all that relates to the preservation and destruction of living beings, as well as of the pain which is felt in one of these states and of the pleasure which succeeds to it.

Pro. True.

Soc. And what would you say of the intermediate state?

Pro. What do you mean by 'intermediate'?

Soc. I mean when a person is in actual suffering and yet remembers past pleasures which, if they would only return, would relieve him; but as yet he has them not. May we not say of him, that he is in an intermediate state?

There is
an inter-
mediate
life,
which
combines
a bodily
[36]
pain
with the
mental
pleasure
of hope.

Pro. Certainly.

Soc. Would you say that he was wholly pained or wholly pleased?

Pro. Nay, I should say that he has two pains; in his body there is the actual experience of pain, and in his soul longing and expectation.

Soc. What do you mean, Protarchus, by the two pains? May not a man who is empty have at one time a sure hope of being filled, and at other times be quite in despair?

Pro. Very true.

Soc. And has he not the pleasure of memory when he is hoping to be filled, and yet in that he is empty is he not at the same time in pain?

Pro. Certainly.

Soc. Then man and the other animals have at the same time both pleasure and pain?

Pro. I suppose so.

Soc. But when a man is empty and has no hope of being filled, there will be the double experience of pain. You observed this and inferred that the double experience was the single case possible.

But when
the hope
is turned
into
despair,
there is a
double
pain.

Pro. Quite true, Socrates.

Soc. Shall the enquiry into these states of feeling be made the occasion of raising a question?

Pro. What question?

Soc. Whether we ought to say that the pleasures and pains of which we are speaking are true or false? or some true and some false?

A ques-
tion.—
Can there
be false
pleasures,
as there
are false
opinions?
'No,' re-
joins Pro-
tarchus;
'opinions
may be
false, but
not plea-
sures.'

Pro. But how, Socrates, can there be false pleasures and pains?

Soc. And how, Protarchus, can there be true and false fears, or true and false expectations, or true and false opinions?

Pro. I grant that opinions may be true or false, but not pleasures.

Soc. What do you mean? I am afraid that we are raising a very serious enquiry.

Pro. There I agree.

Soc. And yet, my boy, for you are one of Philebus' boys (cp. 16 A), the point to be considered, is, whether the enquiry is relevant to the argument.

Pro. Surely.

Soc. No tedious and irrelevant discussion can be allowed; what is said should be pertinent.

Pro. Right.

Soc. I am always wondering at the question which has now been raised.

Pro. How so?

Soc. Do you deny that some pleasures are false, and others true?

Pro. To be sure I do.

Soc. Would you say that no one ever seemed to rejoice and yet did not rejoice, or seemed to feel pain and yet did not feel pain, sleeping or waking, mad or lunatic?

Pro. So we have always held, Socrates.

37
Socrates
proceeds
to discuss
the ques-
tion.

Soc. But were you right? Shall we enquire into the truth of your opinion?

Pro. I think that we should.

Soc. Let us then put into more precise terms the question which has arisen about pleasure and opinion. Is there such a thing as opinion?

Pro. Yes.

Soc. And such a thing as pleasure?

Pro. Yes.

Soc. And an opinion must be of something?

Pro. True.

Soc. And a man must be pleased by something?

Pro. Quite correct.

Soc. And whether the opinion be right or wrong, makes no difference; it will still be an opinion?

Pro. Certainly.

Soc. And he who is pleased, whether he is rightly pleased or not will always have a real feeling of pleasure?

Pro. Yes; that is also quite true.

Soc. Then, how can opinion be both true and false, and pleasure true only, although pleasure and opinion are both equally real?

Pro. Yes; that is the question.

Soc. You mean that opinion admits of truth and falsehood, and hence becomes not merely opinion, but opinion of a certain quality; and this is what you think should be examined?

Pro. Yes.

Soc. And further, even if we admit the existence of qualities in other objects, may not pleasure and pain be simple and devoid of quality?

Pro. Clearly.

Soc. But there is no difficulty in seeing that pleasure and pain as well as opinion have qualities, for they are great or small, and have various degrees of intensity; as was indeed said long ago by us.

Pro. Quite true.

Soc. And if badness attaches to any of them, Protarchus, then we should speak of a bad opinion or of a bad pleasure?

Pro. Quite true, Socrates.

Soc. And if rightness attaches to any of them, should we not speak of a right opinion or right pleasure; and in like manner of the reverse of rightness?

Pro. Certainly.

Soc. And if the thing opined be erroneous, might we not say that opinion, being erroneous, is not right or rightly opined?

Pro. Certainly.

Soc. And if we see a pleasure or pain which errs in respect of its object, shall we call that right or good, or by any honourable name?

Pro. Not if the pleasure is mistaken; how could we?

Soc. And surely pleasure often appears to accompany an opinion which is not true, but false?

Pro. Certainly it does; and in that case, Socrates, as we were saying, the opinion is false, but no one could call the actual pleasure false.

How do
these
differ
from
pleasures
based on
true
opinion?

Opinions
spring
from
memory
and per-
ception,

Soc. How eagerly, Protarchus, do you rush to the defence of pleasure!

Pro. Nay, Socrates, I only repeat what I hear.

Soc. And is there no difference, my friend, between that pleasure which is associated with right opinion and knowledge, and that which is often found in all of us associated with falsehood and ignorance?

Pro. There must be a very great difference between them.

Soc. Then, now let us proceed to contemplate this difference.

Pro. Lead, and I will follow.

Soc. Well, then, my view is—

Pro. What is it?

Soc. We agree—do we not?—that there is such a thing as false, and also such a thing as true opinion?

Pro. Yes.

Soc. And pleasure and pain, as I was just now saying, are often consequent upon these—upon true and false opinion, I mean.

Pro. Very true.

Soc. And do not opinion and the endeavour to form an opinion always spring from memory and perception?

Pro. Certainly.

Soc. Might we imagine the process to be something of this nature?

Pro. Of what nature?

Soc. An object may be often seen at a distance not very clearly, and the seer may want to determine what it is which he sees.

Pro. Very likely.

Soc. Soon he begins to interrogate himself.

Pro. In what manner?

Soc. He asks himself—'What is that which appears to be standing by the rock under the tree?' This is the question which he may be supposed to put to himself when he sees such an appearance.

Pro. True.

Soc. To which he may guess the right answer, saying as if in a whisper to himself—'It is a man.'

Pro. Very good.

Soc. Or again, he may be misled, and then he will say—'No, it is a figure made by the shepherds.'

Pro. Yes.

Soc. And if he has a companion. he repeats his thought to him in articulate sounds, and what was before an opinion, has now become a proposition.

Pro. Certainly.

Soc. But if he be walking alone when these thoughts occur to him, he may not unfrequently keep them in his mind for a considerable time.

Pro. Very true.

Soc. Well, now, I wonder whether you would agree in my explanation of this phenomenon.

Pro. What is your explanation?

Soc. I think that the soul at such times is like a book.

Pro. How so?

Soc. Memory and perception meet, and they and their attendant feelings seem to me almost to write down words in the soul, and when the inscribing feeling writes truly, then true opinion and true propositions which are the expressions of opinion, come into our souls—but when the scribe within us writes falsely, the result is false.

Pro. I quite assent and agree to your statement.

Soc. I must bespeak your favour also for another artist, who is busy at the same time in the chambers of the soul.

Pro. Who is he?

Soc. The painter, who, after the scribe has done his work, draws images in the soul of the things which he has described.

Pro. But when and how does he do this?

Soc. When a man, besides receiving from sight or some other sense certain opinions or statements, sees in his mind the images of the subjects of them;—is not this a very common mental phenomenon?

Pro. Certainly.

Soc. And the images answering to true opinions and words are true, and to false opinions and words false; are they not?

Pro. They are.

Soc. If we are right so far, there arises a further question.

Pro. What is it?

Soc. Whether we experience the feeling of which I am speaking only in relation to the present and the past, or in relation to the future also?

Pro. I should say in relation to all times alike.

Soc. Have not purely mental pleasures and pains been described already as in some cases anticipations of the bodily ones; from which we may infer that anticipatory pleasures and pains have to do with the future?

Pro. Most true.

Certainly
they do;
and then
they are
hopes.

Soc. And do all those writings and paintings which, as we were saying a little while ago, are produced in us, relate to the past and present only, and not to the future?

Pro. To the future, very much.

Soc. When you say, 'Very much,' you mean to imply that all these representations are hopes about the future, and that mankind are filled with hopes in every stage of existence?

Pro. Exactly.

Soc. Answer me another question.

Pro. What question?

Soc. A just and pious and good man is the friend of the gods; is he not?

Pro. Certainly he is.

Soc. And the unjust and utterly bad man is the reverse?

40 *Pro.* True.

Soc. And all men, as we were saying just now, are always filled with hopes?

Pro. Certainly.

Soc. And these hopes, as they are termed, are propositions which exist in the minds of each of us?

Pro. Yes.

Soc. And the fancies of hope are also pictured in us; a man may often have a vision of a heap of gold, and pleasures ensuing, and in the picture there may be a likeness of himself mightily rejoicing over his good fortune.

Pro. True.

And the
good have
true
hopes
presented
to their
minds by
the gods,
the bad
have false
pleasures
painted in
their
fancies.

Soc. And may we not say that the good, being friends of the gods, have generally true pictures presented to them, and the bad false pictures?

Pro. Certainly.

Soc. The bad, too, have pleasures painted in their fancy as well as the good; but I presume that they are false pleasures.

Pro. They are.

Soc. The bad then commonly delight in false pleasures, and the good in true pleasures?

Pro. Doubtless.

Soc. Then upon this view there are false pleasures in the souls of men which are a ludicrous imitation of the true, and there are pains of a similar character?

Pro. There are.

Soc. And did we not allow that a man who had an opinion at all had a real opinion, but often about things which had no existence either in the past, present, or future?

Pro. Quite true.

Soc. And this was the source of false opinion and opining; am I not right?

Pro. Yes.

Soc. And must we not attribute to pleasure and pain a similar real but illusory character?

Pro. How do you mean?

Soc. I mean to say that a man must be admitted to have real pleasure who is pleased with anything or anyhow; and he may be pleased about things which neither have nor have ever had any real existence, and, more often than not, are never likely to exist.

Pro. Yes, Socrates, that again is undeniable.

Soc. And may not the same be said about fear and anger and the like; are they not often false?

Pro. Quite so.

Soc. And can opinions be good or bad except in as far as they are true or false?

Pro. In no other way.

Soc. Nor can pleasures be conceived to be bad except in so far as they are false.

Pro. Nay, Socrates, that is the very opposite of truth; for no one would call pleasures and pains bad because they are false, but by reason of some other great corruption to which they are liable.

Soc. Well, of pleasures which are corrupt and caused by corruption we will hereafter speak, if we care to continue the enquiry; for the present I would rather show by another argument that there are many false pleasures existing or coming into existence in us, because this may assist our final decision.

Pro. Very true; that is to say, if there are such pleasures.

Soc. I think that there are, Protarchus; but this is an opinion which should be well assured, and not rest upon a mere assertion.

Pro. Very good.

Soc. Then now, like wrestlers, let us approach and grasp this new argument.

Pro. Proceed.

Soc. We were maintaining a little while since, that when desires, as they are termed, exist in us, then the body has separate feelings apart from the soul—do you remember?

Pro. Yes, I remember that you said so.

Soc. And the soul was supposed to desire the opposite of the bodily state, while the body was the source of any pleasure or pain which was experienced.

Pro. True.

But these false pleasures have a real existence.

Opinions are only bad if they are [41] false: Is this the case with pleasures?— Protarchus reclaims against the notion.

Recapitulation.

Soc. Then now you may infer what happens in such cases.

Pro. What am I to infer?

Soc. That in such cases pleasure and pains come simultaneously; and there is a juxtaposition of the opposite sensations which correspond to them, as has been already shown.

Pro. Clearly.

Soc. And there is another point to which we have agreed.

Pro. What is it?

Soc. That pleasure and pain both admit of more and less, and that they are of the class of infinites.

Pro. Certainly, we said so.

Soc. But how can we rightly judge of them?

Pro. How can we?

Soc. It is our intention to judge of their comparative importance and intensity, measuring pleasure against pain, and pain against pain, and pleasure against pleasure?

Pro. Yes, such is our intention, and we shall judge of them accordingly.

42

Soc. Well, take the case of sight. Does not the nearness or distance of magnitudes obscure their true proportions, and make us opine falsely; and do we not find the same illusion happening in the case of pleasures and pains?

Pro. Yes, Socrates, and in a degree far greater.

Soc. Then what we are now saying is the opposite of what we were saying before.

Pro. What was that?

Soc. Then the opinions were true and false, and infected the pleasures and pains with their own falsity.

Pro. Very true.

Pleasures
and pains
are often
false, be-
cause
they are
seen at
various
distances
and in
various
relations.

Soc. But now it is the pleasures which are said to be true and false because they are seen at various distances, and subjected to comparison; the pleasures appear to be greater and more vehement when placed side by side with the pains, and the pains when placed side by side with the pleasures.

Pro. Certainly, and for the reason which you mention.

Soc. And suppose you part off from pleasures and pains the element which makes them appear to be greater or less than they really are: you will acknowledge that this element is illusory, and you will never say that the corresponding excess or defect of pleasure or pain is real or true.

Pro. Certainly not.

Soc. Next let us see whether in another direction we may not find pleasures and pains existing and appearing in living beings, which are still more false than these.

Pro. What are they, and how shall we find them?

Soc. If I am not mistaken, I have often repeated that pains and aches and suffering and uneasiness of all sorts arise out of a corruption of nature caused by concretions, and dissolutions, and repletions, and evacuations, and also by growth and decay?

Pro. Yes, that has been often said.

Soc. And we have also agreed that the restoration of the natural state is pleasure?

Pro. Right.

Soc. But now let us suppose an interval of time at which the body experiences none of these changes.

Pro. When can that be, Socrates?

Soc. Your question, Protarchus, does not help the argument.

Pro. Why not, Socrates?

Soc. Because it does not prevent me from repeating mine.

Pro. And what was that?

Soc. Why, Protarchus, admitting that there is no such interval, I may ask what would be the necessary consequence if there were?

Pro. You mean, what would happen if the body were not changed either for good or bad?

Soc. Yes.

Pro. Why then, Socrates, I should suppose that there would be neither pleasure nor pain.

Soc. Very good; but still, if I am not mistaken, you do assert that we must always be experiencing one of them; that is what the wise tell us; for, say they, all things are ever flowing up and down.

Pro. Yes, and their words are of no mean authority.

Soc. Of course, for they are no mean authorities themselves; and I should like to avoid the brunt of their argument. Shall I tell you how I mean to escape from them? And you shall be the partner of my flight.

Pro. How?

Soc. To them we will say: 'Good; but are we, or living things in general, always conscious of what happens to us—for example, of our growth, or the like? Are we not, on the contrary, almost wholly unconscious of this and similar phenomena?' You must answer for them.

Pro. The latter alternative is the true one.

Soc. Then we were not right in saying, just now, that motions going up and down cause pleasures and pains?

Philebus

SOCRATES, PROTAR-CHUS.

These are not the only instances of false pleasures and pains. Pleasure and pain may arise from certain changes in the bodily constitution.

43

Such changes are always going on, though they are not always perceptible; only the greatest are accompanied by pleasure and pain.

Philebus

SOCRATES,
PROTAR-
CHUS.

Thus the
neutral
life re-
appears

This
neutral
life,
though
painless,
is not
pleasant.

44
Yet some
people
think that
it is.

Pro. True.

Soc. A better and more unexceptionable way of speaking will be—

Pro. What?

Soc. If we say that the great changes produce pleasures and pains, but that the moderate and lesser ones do neither.

Pro. That, Socrates, is the more correct mode of speaking.

Soc. But if this be true, the life to which I was just now referring again appears.

Pro. What life?

Soc. The life which we affirmed to be devoid either of pain or of joy.

Pro. Very true.

Soc. We may assume then that there are three lives, one pleasant, one painful, and the third which is neither; what say you?

Pro. I should say as you do that there are three of them.

Soc. But if so, the negation of pain will not be the same with pleasure.

Pro. Certainly not.

Soc. Then when you hear a person saying, that always to live without pain is the pleasantest of all things, what would you understand him to mean by that statement?

Pro. I think that by pleasure he must mean the negative of pain.

Soc. Let us take any three things; or suppose that we embellish a little and call the first gold, the second silver, and there shall be a third which is neither.

Pro. Very good.

Soc. Now, can that which is neither be either gold or silver?

Pro. Impossible.

Soc. No more can that neutral or middle life be rightly or reasonably spoken or thought of as pleasant or painful.

Pro. Certainly not.

Soc. And yet, my friend, there are, as we know, persons who say and think so.

Pro. Certainly.

Soc. And do they think that they have pleasure when they are free from pain?

Pro. They say so.

Soc. And they must think or they would not say that they have pleasure.

Pro. I suppose not.

Soc. And yet if pleasure and the negation of pain are of distinct natures, they are wrong.

Pro. But they are undoubtedly of distinct natures.

Soc. Then shall we take the view that they are three, as we were just now saying, or that they are two only—the one being a state of pain, which is an evil, and the other a cessation of pain, which is of itself a good, and is called pleasant?

Pro. But why, Socrates, do we ask the question at all? I do not see the reason.

Soc. You, Protarchus, have clearly never heard of certain enemies of our friend Philebus.

Pro. And who may they be?

Soc. Certain persons who are reputed to be masters in natural philosophy, who deny the very existence of pleasure.

Pro. Indeed!

Soc. They say that what the school of Philebus calls pleasures are all of them only avoidances of pain.

They are certain physical philosophers who affirm pleasure to be only the absence of pain.

Pro. And would you, Socrates, have us agree with them?

Soc. Why, no, I would rather use them as a sort of diviners, who divine the truth, not by rules of art, but by an instinctive repugnance and extreme detestation which a noble nature has of the power of pleasure, in which they think that there is nothing sound, and her seductive influence is declared by them to be witchcraft, and not pleasure. This is the use which you may make of them. And when you have considered the various grounds of their dislike, you shall hear from me what I deem to be true pleasures. Having thus examined the nature of pleasure from both points of view, we will bring her up for judgment.

The grounds of their dislike to pleasure may throw light on our present enquiry

Pro. Well said.

Soc. Then let us enter into an alliance with these philosophers and follow in the track of their dislike. I imagine that they would say something of this sort; they would begin at the beginning, and ask whether, if we wanted to know the nature of any quality, such as hardness, we should be more likely to discover it by looking at the hardest things, rather than at the least hard? You, Protarchus, shall answer these severe gentlemen as you answer me.

The nature of things is best seen in their greatest instances.

Pro. By all means, and I reply to them, that you should look at the greatest instances.

Soc. Then if we want to see the true nature of pleasures as a class, we should not look at the most diluted pleasures, but at the most extreme and most vehement?

45

Pro. In that every one will agree.

Soc. And the obvious instances of the greatest pleasures, as we have often said, are the pleasures of the body?

The greatest pleasures are of the

Pro. Certainly.

Soc. And are they felt by us to be or become greater, when we are sick or when we are in health? And here we must be careful in our answer, or we shall come to grief.

Pro. How will that be?

Soc. Why, because we might be tempted to answer, 'When we are in health.'

Pro. Yes, that is the natural answer.

Soc. Well, but are not those pleasures the greatest of which mankind have the greatest desires?

Pro. True.

Soc. And do not people who are in a fever, or any similar illness, feel cold or thirst or other bodily affections more intensely? Am I not right in saying that they have a deeper want and greater pleasure in the satisfaction of their want?

Pro. That is obvious as soon as it is said.

Soc. Well, then, shall we not be right in saying, that if a person would wish to see the greatest pleasures he ought to go and look, not at health, but at disease? And here you must distinguish:—do not imagine that I mean to ask whether those who are very ill have more pleasures than those who are well, but understand that I am speaking of the magnitude of pleasure; I want to know where pleasures are found to be most intense. For, as I say, we have to discover what is pleasure, and what they mean by pleasure who deny her very existence.

Pro. I think I follow you.

Soc. You will soon have a better opportunity of showing whether you do or not, Protarchus. Answer now, and tell me whether you see, I will not say more, but more intense and excessive pleasures in wantonness than in temperance? Reflect before you speak.

Pro. I understand you, and see that there is a great difference between them; the temperate are restrained by the wise man's aphorism of 'Never too much,' which is their rule, but excess of pleasure possessing the minds of fools and wantons becomes madness and makes them shout with delight.

Soc. Very good, and if this be true, then the greatest pleasures and pains will clearly be found in some vicious state of soul and body, and not in a virtuous state.

Pro. Certainly.

Soc. And ought we not to select some of these for examination, and see what makes them the greatest?

Pro. To be sure we ought.

Soc. Take the case of the pleasures which arise out of certain disorders.

Philebus

SOCRATES, PROTARCHUS.

body, not in a healthy,

but in a morbid state.

The pleasures of wantonness are more intense than those of temperance.

46

Pro. What disorders?

Soc. The pleasures of unseemly disorders, which our severe friends utterly detest.

Pro. What pleasures?

Soc. Such, for example, as the relief of itching and other ailments by scratching, which is the only remedy required. For what in Heaven's name is the feeling to be called which is thus produced in us?—Pleasure or pain?

Pro. A villainous mixture of some kind, Socrates, I should say.

Soc. I did not introduce the argument, O Protarchus, with any personal reference to Philebus, but because, without the consideration of these and similar pleasures, we shall not be able to determine the point at issue.

Pro. Then we had better proceed to analyze this family of pleasures.

Soc. You mean the pleasures which are mingled with pain?

Pro. Exactly.

Soc. There are some mixtures which are of the body, and only in the body, and others which are of the soul, and only in the soul; while there are other mixtures of pleasures with pains, common both to soul and body, which in their composite state are called sometimes pleasures and sometimes pains.

Pro. How is that?

Soc. Whenever, in the restoration or in the derangement of nature, a man experiences two opposite feelings; for example, when he is cold and is growing warm, or again, when he is hot and is becoming cool, and he wants to have the one and be rid of the other;—the sweet has a bitter, as the common saying is, and both together fasten upon him and create irritation and in time drive him to distraction.

Pro. That description is very true to nature.

Soc. And in these sorts of mixtures the pleasures and pains are sometimes equal, and sometimes one or other of them predominates?

Pro. True.

Soc. Of cases in which the pain exceeds the pleasure, an example is afforded by itching, of which we were just now speaking, and by the tingling which we feel when the boiling and fiery element is within, and the rubbing and motion[1] only relieves the surface, and does not reach the parts affected; then if you put them to the fire, and as a last resort apply cold to them, you may often produce the most intense pleasure or pain in the inner parts, which contrasts

[1] Reading with the MSS. κινήσει.

Philebus

Socrates,
Protar-
chus.

Morbid
pleasures
are such as
those of
scratch-
ing,
which are
of a
mixed
charac-
ter.

Mixed
pleasures
may be of
the body,
of the
soul, or
common
to both.

Either
element
may pre-
dominate
in the
mixture.

Instances
of mixed
pleasures:
(1) of the
body only
—the re-
lief of
itching

Philebus

47

SOCRATES,
PROTAR-
CHUS.

by
scratch-
ing;

and mingles with the pain or pleasure, as the case may be, of the outer parts; and this is due to the forcible separation of what is united, or to the union of what is separated, and to the juxtaposition of pleasure and pain.

Pro. Quite so.

Soc. Sometimes the element of pleasure prevails in a man, and the slight undercurrent of pain makes him tingle, and causes a gentle irritation; or again, the excessive infusion of pleasure creates an excitement in him,—he even leaps for joy, he assumes all sorts of attitudes, he changes all manner of colours, he gasps for breath, and is quite amazed, and utters the most irrational exclamations.

Pro. Yes, indeed.

Soc. He will say of himself, and others will say of him, that he is dying with these delights; and the more dissipated and good-for-nothing he is, the more vehemently he pursues them in every way; of all pleasures he declares them to be the greatest; and he reckons him who lives in the most constant enjoyment of them to be the happiest of mankind.

Pro. That, Socrates, is a very true description of the opinions of the majority about pleasures.

(2) com-
mon to
body and
mind—
vacuity
accom-
panied by
hope;

Soc. Yes, Protarchus, quite true of the mixed pleasures, which arise out of the communion of external and internal sensations in the body; there are also cases in which the mind contributes an opposite element to the body[1], whether of pleasure or pain, and the two unite and form one mixture. Concerning these I have already remarked, that when a man is empty he desires to be full, and has pleasure in hope and pain in vacuity. But now I must further add what I omitted before, that in all these and similar emotions in which body and mind are opposed (and they are innumerable), pleasure and pain coalesce in one.

Pro. I believe that to be quite true.

(3) of the
mind
only—

Soc. There still remains one other sort of admixture of pleasures and pains.

Pro. What is that?

Soc. The union which, as we were saying, the mind often experiences of purely mental feelings.

Pro. What do you mean?

Soc. Why, do we not speak of anger, fear, desire, sorrow, love, emulation, envy, and the like, as pains which belong to the soul only?

Pro. Yes.

---

[1] Reading περὶ δὲ τῶν ἐν αἷς ψυχὴ σώματι τἀναντία ξυμβάλλεται.

Soc. And shall we not find them also full of the most wonderful pleasures? need I remind you of the anger

> 'Which stirs even a wise man to violence,
> And is sweeter than honey and the honeycomb?'

Aṅd you remember how pleasures mingle with pains in lamentation and bereavement?

Pro. Yes, there is a natural connection between them.

Soc. And you remember also how at the sight of tragedies the spectators smile through their tears?

Pro. Certainly I do.

Soc. And are you aware that even at a comedy the soul experiences a mixed feeling of pain and pleasure?

Pro. I do not quite understand you.

Soc. I admit, Protarchus, that there is some difficulty in recognizing this mixture of feelings at a comedy.

Pro. There is, I think.

Soc. And the greater the obscurity of the case the more desirable is the examination of it, because the difficulty in detecting other cases of mixed pleasures and pains will be less.

Pro. Proceed.

Soc. I have just mentioned envy; would you not call that a pain of the soul?

Pro. Yes.

Soc. And yet the envious man finds something in the misfortunes of his neighbours at which he is pleased?

Pro. Certainly.

Soc. And ignorance, and what is termed clownishness, are surely an evil?

Pro. To be sure.

Soc. From these considerations learn to know the nature of the ridiculous.

Pro. Explain.

Soc. The ridiculous is in short the specific name which is used to describe the vicious form of a certain habit; and of vice in general it is that kind which is most at variance with the inscription at Delphi.

Pro. You mean, Socrates, 'Know thyself.'

Soc. I do; and the opposite would be, 'Know not thyself.'

Pro. Certainly.

Soc. And now, O Protarchus, try to divide this into three.

Pro. Indeed I am afraid that I cannot.

Soc. Do you mean to say that I must make the division for you?

Philebus

SOCRATES,
PROTAR-
CHUS.

a. anger;
48
b. sorrow;

c. the mixed feelings with which spectators regard tragedy and comedy;

d. envy.

From envy we proceed to the consideration of the ridiculous.

The sense of the ridiculous is excited by self-deception.

which
may be
shown
(1) about
money,

(2) about
beauty,

and (3)
about
wisdom
[49]
and
virtue.

Pro. Yes, and what is more, I beg that you will.

Soc. Are there not three ways in which ignorance of self may be shown?

Pro. What are they?

Soc. In the first place, about money; the ignorant may fancy himself richer than he is.

Pro. Yes, that is a very common error.

Soc. And still more often he will fancy that he is taller or fairer than he is, or that he has some other advantage of person which he really has not.

Pro. Of course.

Soc. And yet surely by far the greatest number err about the goods of the mind; they imagine themselves to be much better men than they are.

Pro. Yes, that is by far the commonest delusion.

Soc. And of all the virtues, is not wisdom the one which the mass of mankind are always claiming, and which most arouses in them a spirit of contention and lying conceit of wisdom?

Pro. Certainly.

Soc. And may not all this be truly called an evil condition?

Pro. Very evil.

Soc. But we must pursue the division a step further, Protarchus, if we would see in envy of the childish sort a singular mixture of pleasure and pain.

Pro. How can we make the further division which you suggest?

Those
who
deceive
them-
selves
may be
powerful
or power-
less: in
the latter
case they
are ridi-
culous.

But how
is there a
combin-
ation of
pleasure
and pain
in the
ridicu-
lous?

Soc. All who are silly enough to entertain this lying conceit of themselves may of course be divided, like the rest of mankind, into two classes—one having power and might; and the other the reverse.

Pro. Certainly.

Soc. Let this, then, be the principle of division; those of them who are weak and unable to revenge themselves, when they are laughed at, may be truly called ridiculous, but those who can defend themselves may be more truly described as strong and formidable; for ignorance in the powerful is hateful and horrible, because hurtful to others both in reality and in fiction, but powerless ignorance may be reckoned, and in truth is, ridiculous.

Pro. That is very true, but I do not as yet see where is the admixture of pleasures and pains.

Soc. Well, then, let us examine the nature of envy.

Pro. Proceed.

Soc. Is not envy an unrighteous pleasure, and also an unrighteous pain?

Pro. Most true.

Soc. There is nothing envious or wrong in rejoicing at the misfortunes of enemies?

Pro. Certainly not.

Soc. But to feel joy instead of sorrow at the sight of our friends' misfortunes—is not that wrong?

Pro. Undoubtedly.

Soc. Did we not say that ignorance was always an evil?

Pro. True.

Soc. And the three kinds of vain conceit in our friends which we enumerated—the vain conceit of beauty, of wisdom, and of wealth, are ridiculous if they are weak, and detestable when they are powerful: May we not say, as I was saying before, that our friends who are in this state of mind, when harmless to others, are simply ridiculous?

Pro. They are ridiculous.

Soc. And do we not acknowledge this ignorance of theirs to be a misfortune?

Pro. Certainly.

Soc. And do we feel pain or pleasure in laughing at it?

Pro. Clearly we feel pleasure.

Soc. And was not envy the source of this pleasure which we feel at the misfortunes of friends?

Pro. Certainly.

Soc. Then the argument shows that when we laugh at the folly of our friends, pleasure, in mingling with envy, mingles with pain, for envy has been acknowledged by us to be mental pain, and laughter is pleasant; and so we envy and laugh at the same instant.

Pro. True.

Soc. And the argument implies that there are combinations of pleasure and pain in lamentations, and in tragedy and comedy, not only on the stage, but on the greater stage of human life; and so in endless other cases.

Pro. I do not see how any one can deny what you say, Socrates, however eager he may be to assert the opposite opinion.

Soc. I mentioned anger, desire, sorrow, fear, love, emulation, envy, and similar emotions, as examples in which we should find a mixture of the two elements so often named; did I not?

Pro. Yes.

Soc. We may observe that our conclusions hitherto have had reference only to sorrow and envy and anger.

Pro. I see.

Soc. Then many other cases still remain?

Philebus

SOCRATES,
PROTAR-
CHUS.

We laugh at a friend's misfortunes through envy. Laughter is pleasant, envy is painful.

50

Combinations of pleasure and pain take place, not only on the stage, but in human life, and arise out of many other causes besides sorrow, envy, and anger.

Philebus

SOCRATES,
PROTAR-
CHUS.

But these
instances
will
suffice.

After the
mixed
pleasures
[51]
we must
consider
the un-
mixed
or true.

True
pleasures
are given
(1) by
beauty of
form,

Pro. Certainly.

Soc. And why do you suppose me to have pointed out to you the admixture which takes place in comedy? Why but to convince you that there was no difficulty in showing the mixed nature of fear and love and similar affections; and I thought that when I had given you the illustration, you would have let me off, and have acknowledged as a general truth that the body without the soul, and the soul without the body, as well as the two united, are susceptible of all sorts of admixtures of pleasures and pains; and so further discussion would have been unnecessary. And now I want to know whether I may depart; or will you keep me here until midnight? I fancy that I may obtain my release without many words; —if I promise that to-morrow I will give you an account of all these cases. But at present I would rather sail in another direction, and go to other matters which remain to be settled, before the judgment can be given which Philebus demands.

Pro. Very good, Socrates; in what remains take your own course.

Soc. Then after the mixed pleasures the unmixed should have their turn; this is the natural and necessary order.

Pro. Excellent.

Soc. These, in turn, then, I will now endeavour to indicate; for with the maintainers of the opinion that all pleasures are a cessation of pain, I do not agree, but, as I was saying, I use them as witnesses, that there are pleasures which seem only and are not, and there are others again which have great power and appear in many forms, yet are intermingled with pains, and are partly alleviations of agony and distress, both of body and mind.

Pro. Then what pleasures, Socrates, should we be right in conceiving to be true?

Soc. True pleasures are those which are given by beauty of colour and form, and most of those which arise from smells; those of sound, again, and in general those of which the want is painless and unconscious, and of which the fruition is palpable to sense and pleasant and unalloyed with pain.

Pro. Once more, Socrates, I must ask what you mean.

Soc. My meaning is certainly not obvious, and I will endeavour to be plainer. I do not mean by beauty of form such beauty as that of animals or pictures, which the many would suppose to be my meaning; but, says the argument, understand me to mean straight lines and circles, and the plane or solid figures which are formed out of them by turning-lathes and rulers and measurers of angles; for these I affirm to be not only relatively beautiful, like other things, but they are eternally and absolutely beautiful, and they have peculiar pleasures, quite unlike the pleasures of scratching. And there are colours which are of the same character, and have similar pleasures; now do you understand my meaning?

Pro. I am trying to understand, Socrates, and I hope that you will try to make your meaning clearer.

Soc. When sounds are smooth and clear, and have a single pure tone, then I mean to say that they are not relatively but absolutely beautiful, and have natural pleasures associated with them.

Pro. Yes, there are such pleasures.

Soc. The pleasures of smell are of a less ethereal sort, but they have no necessary admixture of pain; and all pleasures, however and wherever experienced, which are unattended by pains, I assign to an analogous class. Here then are two kinds of pleasures.

Pro. I understand.

Soc. To these may be added the pleasures of knowledge, if no hunger of knowledge and no pain caused by such hunger precede them.

Pro. And this is the case.

Soc. Well, but if a man who is full of knowledge loses his knowledge, are there not pains of forgetting?

Pro. Not necessarily, but there may be times of reflection, when he feels grief at the loss of his knowledge.

Soc. Yes, my friend, but at present we are enumerating only the natural perceptions, and have nothing to do with reflection.

Pro. In that case you are right in saying that the loss of knowledge is not attended with pain.

Soc. These pleasures of knowledge, then, are unmixed with pain; and they are not the pleasures of the many but of a very few.

Pro. Quite true.

Soc. And now, having fairly separated the pure pleasures and those which may be rightly termed impure, let us further add to our description of them, that the pleasures which are in excess have no measure, but that those which are not in excess have measure; the great, the excessive, whether more or less frequent, we shall be right in referring to the class of the infinite, and of the more and less, which pours through body and soul alike; and the others we shall refer to the class which has measure.

Pro. Quite right, Socrates.

Soc. Still there is something more to be considered about pleasures.

Pro. What is it?

Philebus

Socrates,
Protar-
chus.

(2) co-
lour,

(3)
sound;

(4) by
sweet
smells,

52
and (5)
by
knowl-
edge.

Excessive
pleasures
are in-
finite;
moderate
pleasures
have
measure
or limit.

The nature of purity

Soc. When you speak of purity and clearness, or of excess, abundance, greatness and sufficiency, in what relation do these terms stand to truth?

Pro. Why do you ask, Socrates?

We must
select the
pure and
not the
impure
kinds of
pleasure
and knowl-
edge for
com-
parison.

Soc. Because, Protarchus, I should wish to test pleasure and knowledge in every possible way, in order that if there be a pure and impure element in either of them, I may present the pure element for judgment, and then they will be more easily judged of by you and by me and by all of us.

Pro. Most true.

Soc. Let us investigate all the pure kinds; first selecting for consideration a single instance.

Pro. What instance shall we select?

53

Soc. Suppose that we first of all take whiteness.

Pro. Very good.

Purity is
given,
not by
quantity,
but by
quality.

Soc. How can there be purity in whiteness, and what purity? Is that purest which is greatest or most in quantity, or that which is most unadulterated and freest from any admixture of other colours?

Pro. Clearly that which is most unadulterated.

Soc. True, Protarchus; and so the purest white, and not the greatest or largest in quantity, is to be deemed truest and most beautiful?

Pro. Right.

Soc. And we shall be quite right in saying that a little pure white is whiter and fairer and truer than a great deal that is mixed.

Pro. Perfectly right.

Soc. There is no need of adducing many similar examples in illustration of the argument about pleasure; one such is sufficient to prove to us that a small pleasure or a small amount of pleasure, if pure or unalloyed with pain, is always pleasanter and truer and fairer than a great pleasure or a great amount of pleasure of another kind.

Pro. Assuredly; and the instance you have given is quite sufficient.

Wise men
say that
pleasure
is a gen-
eration.
What
does this
mean?

Soc. But what do you say of another question:—have we not heard that pleasure is always a generation, and has no true being? Do not certain ingenious philosophers teach this doctrine, and ought not we to be grateful to them?

Pro. What do they mean?

Soc. I will explain to you, my dear Protarchus, what they mean, by putting a question.

Pro. Ask, and I will answer.

Soc. I assume that there are two natures, one self-existent, and the other ever in want of something.

Pro. What manner of natures are they?

Soc. The one majestic ever, the other inferior.

Pro. You speak riddles.

Soc. You have seen loves good and fair, and also brave lovers of them.

Pro. I should think so.

Soc. Search the universe for two terms which are like these two and are present everywhere.

Pro. Yet a third time I must say[1], Be a little plainer, Socrates.

Soc. There is no difficulty, Protarchus; the argument is only in play, and insinuates that some things are for the sake of something else (relatives), and that other things are the ends to which the former class subserve (absolutes).

Pro. Your many repetitions make me slow to understand.

Soc. As the argument proceeds, my boy, I dare say that the meaning will become clearer.

Pro. Very likely.

Soc. Here are two new principles.

Pro. What are they?

Soc. One is the generation of all things, and the other is essence.

Pro. I readily accept from you both generation and essence.

Soc. Very right; and would you say that generation is for the sake of essence, or essence for the sake of generation?

Pro. You want to know whether that which is called essence is, properly speaking, for the sake of generation?

Soc. Yes.

Pro. By the gods, I wish that you would repeat your question.

Soc. I mean, O my Protarchus, to ask whether you would tell me that ship-building is for the sake of ships, or ships for the sake of ship-building? and in all similar cases I should ask the same question.

Pro. Why do you not answer yourself, Socrates?

Soc. I have no objection, but you must take your part.

Pro. Certainly.

Soc. My answer is, that all things instrumental, remedial, material, are given to us with a view to generation, and that each generation is relative to, or for the sake of, some being or essence, and that the whole of generation is relative to the whole of essence.

Pro. Assuredly.

Reading τὸ τρίτον ἔτ’ ἐρῶ (conj. Badham).

Philebus

SOCRATES, PROTARCHUS.

There are two natures, the absolute and the relative: the latter is for the sake of the former.

54

Generation is relative to essence, which is an absolute.

Absolutes
are to be
placed in
the class
of good,
relatives
in some
other
class.
Thus
pleasure,
which is a
genera-
tion and
relative,
is not a
good.
(Many
thanks to
him who
first
pointed
this out.)

It is ab-
surd to
[55]
make
pleasure
consist in
genera-
tion and
destruc-
tion;

Soc. Then pleasure, being a generation, must surely be for the sake of some essence?

Pro. True.

Soc. And that for the sake of which something else is done must be placed in the class of good, and that which is done for the sake of something else, in some other class, my good friend.

Pro. Most certainly.

Soc. Then pleasure, being a generation, will be rightly placed in some other class than that of good?

Pro. Quite right.

Soc. Then, as I said at first, we ought to be very grateful to him who first pointed out that pleasure was a generation only, and had no true being at all; for he is clearly one who laughs at the notion of pleasure being a good.

Pro. Assuredly.

Soc. And he would surely laugh also at those who make generation their highest end.

Pro. Of whom are you speaking, and what do they mean?

Soc. I am speaking of those who when they are cured of hunger or thirst or any other defect by some process of generation are delighted at the process as if it were pleasure; and they say that they would not wish to live without these and other feelings of a like kind which might be mentioned.

Pro. That is certainly what they appear to think.

Soc. And is not destruction universally admitted to be the opposite of generation?

Pro. Certainly.

Soc. Then he who chooses thus, would choose generation and destruction rather than that third sort of life, in which, as we were saying, was neither pleasure nor pain, but only the purest possible thought.

Pro. He who would make us believe pleasure to be a good is involved in great absurdities, Socrates.

Soc. Great, indeed; and there is yet another of them.

Pro. What is it?

and ab-
surd to
say (1)
that in
the body
there is
nothing
good;
(2) that
the only
good of

Soc. Is there not an absurdity in arguing that there is nothing good or noble in the body, or in anything else, but that good is in the soul only, and that the only good of the soul is pleasure; and that courage or temperance or understanding, or any other good of the soul, is not really a good?—and is there not yet a further absurdity in our being compelled to say that he who has a feeling of pain and not of pleasure is bad at the time when he is suffering pain, even though he be the best of men; and again, that he who has a feeling of pleasure, in so far as he is pleased at the time when he is pleased, in that degree excels in virtue?

Pro. Nothing, Socrates, can be more irrational than all this.

Soc. And now, having subjected pleasure to every sort of test, let us not appear to be too sparing of mind and knowledge: let us ring their metal bravely, and see if there be unsoundness in any part, until we have found out what in them is of the purest nature; and then the truest elements both of pleasure and knowledge may be brought up for judgment.

Pro. Right.

Soc. Knowledge has two parts,—the one productive, and the other educational?

Pro. True.

Soc. And in the productive or handicraft arts, is not one part more akin to knowledge, and the other less; and may not the one part be regarded as the pure, and the other as the impure?

Pro. Certainly.

Soc. Let us separate the superior or dominant elements in each of them.

Pro. What are they, and how do you separate them?

Soc. I mean to say, that if arithmetic, mensuration, and weighing be taken away from any art, that which remains will not be much.

Pro. Not much, certainly.

Soc. The rest will be only conjecture, and the better use of the senses which is given by experience and practice, in addition to a certain power of guessing, which is commonly called art, and is perfected by attention and pains.

Pro. Nothing more, assuredly.

Soc. Music, for instance, is full of this empiricism; for sounds are harmonized, not by measure, but by skilful conjecture; the music of the flute is always trying to guess the pitch of each vibrating note, and is therefore mixed up with much that is doubtful and has little which is certain.

Pro. Most true.

Soc. And the same will be found to hold good of medicine and husbandry and piloting and generalship.

Pro. Very true.

Soc. The art of the builder, on the other hand, which uses a number of measures and instruments, attains by their help to a greater degree of accuracy than the other arts.

Pro. How is that?

Soc. In ship-building and house-building, and in other branches

Philebus

SOCRATES, PROTARCHUS.

the soul is pleasure; (3) that a man is vicious when in pain and virtuous when he is pleased.

And now for knowledge: Are some kinds purer than others?

Knowledge is (1) productive and (2) educational; of the former there is a [56] pure and impure sort.

The pure elements in the productive arts are arithmetic, mensuration, and weighing; the rest is guesswork and experience.

Music,
medicine,
etc. are
less accu-
rate than
the art of
building.

Arts may
be
divided
into more
and less
exact.

Of arith-
metic and
mensu-
ration,
which
belong to
the
former
class,
there are
two
kinds,—
one pure,
the other
impure.

57

Thus we
see that as
of plea-
sure, so
of knowl-
edge,
there are
two sorts,
and one is
purer
than the
other.

of the art of carpentering, the builder has his rule, lathe, compass, line, and a most ingenious machine for straightening wood.

Pro. Very true, Socrates.

Soc. Then now let us divide the arts of which we were speaking into two kinds,—the arts which, like music, are less exact in their results, and those which, like carpentering, are more exact.

Pro. Let us make that division.

Soc. Of the latter class, the most exact of all are those which we just now spoke of as primary.

Pro. I see that you mean arithmetic, and the kindred arts of weighing and measuring.

Soc. Certainly, Protarchus; but are not these also distinguishable into two kinds?

Pro. What are the two kinds?

Soc. In the first place, arithmetic is of two kinds, one of which is popular, and the other philosophical.

Pro. How would you distinguish them?

Soc. There is a wide difference between them, Protarchus; some arithmeticians reckon unequal units; as for example, two armies, two oxen, two very large things or two very small things. The party who are opposed to them insist that every unit in ten thousand must be the same as every other unit.

Pro. Undoubtedly there is, as you say, a great difference among the votaries of the science; and there may be reasonably supposed to be two sorts of arithmetic.

Soc. And when we compare the art of mensuration which is used in building with philosophical geometry, or the art of computation which is used in trading with exact calculation, shall we say of either of the pairs that it is one or two?

Pro. On the analogy of what has preceded, I should be of opinion that they were severally two.

Soc. Right; but do you understand why I have discussed the subject?

Pro. I think so, but I should like to be told by you.

Soc. The argument has all along been seeking a parallel to pleasure, and true to that original design, has gone on to ask whether one sort of knowledge is purer than another, as one pleasure is purer than another.

Pro. Clearly; that was the intention.

Soc. And has not the argument in what has preceded, already shown that the arts have different provinces, and vary in their degrees of certainty?

Pro. Very true.

Soc. And just now did not the argument first designate a particular art by a common term, thus making us believe in the unity of that art; and then again, as if speaking of two different things, proceed to enquire whether the art as pursued by philosophers, or as pursued by non-philosophers, has more of certainty and purity?

Pro. That is the very question which the argument is asking.

Soc. And how, Protarchus, shall we answer the enquiry?

Pro. O Socrates, we have reached a point at which the difference of clearness in different kinds of knowledge is enormous.

Soc. Then the answer will be the easier.

Pro. Certainly; and let us say in reply, that those arts into which arithmetic and mensuration enter, far surpass all others; and that of these the arts or sciences which are animated by the pure philosophic impulse are infinitely superior in accuracy and truth.

Soc. Then this is your judgment; and this is the answer which, upon your authority, we will give to all masters of the art of misinterpretation?

Pro. What answer?

Soc. That there are two arts of arithmetic, and two of mensuration; and also several other arts which in like manner have this double nature, and yet only one name.

Pro. Let us boldly return this answer to the masters of whom you speak, Socrates, and hope for good luck.

Soc. We have explained what we term the most exact arts or sciences.

Pro. Very good.

Soc. And yet, Protarchus, dialectic will refuse to acknowledge us, if we do not award to her the first place.

Pro. And pray, what is dialectic?

Soc. Clearly the science which has to do with all that knowledge of which we are now speaking; for I am sure that all men who have a grain of intelligence will admit that the knowledge which has to do with being and reality, and sameness and unchangeableness, is by far the truest of all. But how would you decide this question, Protarchus?

Pro. I have often heard Gorgias maintain, Socrates, that the art of persuasion far surpassed every other; this, as he says, is by far the best of them all, for to it all things submit, not by compulsion, but of their own free will. Now, I should not like to quarrel either with you or with him.

Soc. You mean to say that you would like to desert, if you were not ashamed?

The purer sort consists of those arts into which mathematics enter; and of mathematics themselves there is a purer and an impurer kind.

Where shall we place dialectic, the truest of sciences?
[58]

Protarchus is afraid that he will offend Gorgias, if he assigns

Philebus

SOCRATES,
PROTAR-
CHUS.

the first
place to
dialectic,
and So-
crates, if
to
rhetoric.

Socrates
assures
him that
if he does
not deny
that
rhetoric
is the
most
useful of
arts and
sciences,
Gorgias
will not
quarrel
with him
[59]
for saying
that dia-
lectic is
the truest.

Dialectic
differs
from the
generality
of arts
which
have to
do with
the
change-
able and
therefore
never
attain
certainty.

Pro. As you please.

Soc. May I not have led you into a misapprehension?

Pro. How?

Soc. Dear Protarchus, I never asked which was the greatest or best or usefullest of arts or sciences, but which had clearness and accuracy, and the greatest amount of truth, however humble and little useful an art. And as for Gorgias, if you do not deny that his art has the advantage in usefulness to mankind, he will not quarrel with you for saying that the study of which I am speaking is superior in this particular of essential truth; as in the comparison of white colours, a little whiteness, if that little be only pure, was said to be superior in truth to a great mass which is impure. And now let us give our best attention and consider well, not the comparative use or reputation of the sciences, but the power or faculty, if there be such, which the soul has of loving the truth, and of doing all things for the sake of it; let us search into the pure element of mind and intelligence, and then we shall be able to say whether the science of which I have been speaking is most likely to possess the faculty, or whether there be some other which has higher claims.

Pro. Well, I have been considering, and I can hardly think that any other science or art has a firmer grasp of the truth than this.

Soc. Do you say so because you observe that the arts in general and those engaged[1] in them make use of opinion, and are resolutely engaged in the investigation of matters of opinion? Even he who supposes himself to be occupied with nature is really occupied with the things of this world, how created, how acting or acted upon. Is not this the sort of enquiry in which his life is spent?

Pro. True.

Soc. He is labouring, not after eternal being, but about things which are becoming, or which will or have become.

Pro. Very true.

Soc. And can we say that any of these things which neither are nor have been nor will be unchangeable, when judged by the strict rule of truth, ever become certain?

Pro. Impossible.

Soc. How can anything fixed be concerned with that which has no fixedness?

Pro. How indeed?

Soc. Then mind and science when employed about such changing things do not attain the highest truth?

Pro. I should imagine not.

Soc. And now let us bid farewell, a long farewell, to you or me or

[1] Reading ὅσοι.

Philebus or Gorgias, and urge on behalf of the argument a single point.

Pro. What point?

Soc. Let us say that the stable and pure and true and unalloyed has to do with the things which are eternal and unchangeable and unmixed, or if not, at any rate what is most akin to them has; and that all other things are to be placed in a second or inferior class.

Pro. Very true.

Soc. And of the names expressing cognition, ought not the fairest to be given to the fairest things?

Pro. That is natural.

Soc. And are not mind and wisdom the names which are to be honoured most?

Pro. Yes.

Soc. And these names may be said to have their truest and most exact application when the mind is engaged in the contemplation of true being?

Pro. Certainly.

Soc. And these were the names which I adduced of the rivals of pleasure?

Pro. Very true, Socrates.

Soc. In the next place, as to the mixture, here are the ingredients, pleasure and wisdom, and we may be compared to artists who have their materials ready to their hands.

Pro. Yes.

Soc. And now we must begin to mix them?

Pro. By all means.

Soc. But had we not better have a preliminary word and refresh our memories?

Pro. Of what?

Soc. Of that which I have already mentioned. Well says the proverb, that we ought to repeat twice and even thrice that which is good.

Pro. Certainly.

Soc. Well then, by Zeus, let us proceed, and I will make what I believe to be a fair summary of the argument.

Pro. Let me hear.

Soc. Philebus says that pleasure is the true end of all living beings, at which all ought to aim, and moreover that it is the chief good of all, and that the two names 'good' and 'pleasant' are correctly given to one thing and one nature; Socrates, on the other hand, begins by denying this, and further says, that in nature as in name they are two, and that wisdom partakes more than pleasure

Philebus

SOCRATES,
PROTAR-
CHUS.

Being con-
cerned
with the
eternal
and un-
change-
able, it
ranks
first.

The fair-
est
names
should be
given to
the fair-
est
things—
therefore
mind and
wisdom
are to be
assigned
to the
contem-
plation of
true
being.

Before
mixing
let us
sum up.

60

By Phile-
bus
pleasure
was af-
firmed to
be the
good:
Socrates

preferred
wisdom.

We
agreed
that the
good
must be
character-
ised by
self-suf-
fiency;

but we
found
that both
pleasure
and wis-
dom by
them-
selves are
devoid of
this
quality.

of the good. Is not and was not this what we were saying, Protarchus?

Pro. Certainly.

Soc. And is there not and was there not a further point which was conceded between us?

Pro. What was it?

Soc. That the good differs from all other things.

Pro. In what respect?

Soc. In that the being who possesses good always everywhere and in all things has the most perfect sufficiency, and is never in need of anything else.

Pro. Exactly.

Soc. And did we not endeavour to make an imaginary separation of wisdom and pleasure, assigning to each a distinct life, so that pleasure was wholly excluded from wisdom, and wisdom in like manner had no part whatever in pleasure?

Pro. We did.

Soc. And did we think that either of them alone would be sufficient?

Pro. Certainly not.

Soc. And if we erred in any point, then let any one who will, take up the enquiry again and set us right; and assuming memory and wisdom and knowledge and true opinion to belong to the same class, let him consider whether he would desire to possess or acquire,—I will not say pleasure, however abundant or intense, if he has no real perception that he is pleased, nor any consciousness of what he feels, nor any recollection, however momentary, of the feeling,—but would he desire to have anything at all, if these faculties were wanting to him? And about wisdom I ask the same question; can you conceive that any one would choose to have all wisdom absolutely devoid of pleasure, rather than with a certain degree of pleasure, or all pleasure devoid of wisdom, rather than with a certain degree of wisdom?

Pro. Certainly not, Socrates; but why repeat such questions any more?

61

Neither
therefore
ranks
first.
And be-
fore the
second
place can
be as-

Soc. Then the perfect and universally eligible and entirely good cannot possibly be either of them?

Pro. Impossible.

Soc. Then now we must ascertain the nature of the good more or less accurately, in order, as we were saying, that the second place may be duly assigned?

Pro. Right.

Soc. Have we not found a road which leads towards the good?

Pro. What road?

Soc. Supposing that a man had to be found, and you could discover in what house he lived, would not that be a great step towards the discovery of the man himself?

Pro. Certainly.

Soc. And now reason intimates to us, as at our first beginning, that we should seek the good, not in the unmixed life but in the mixed.

Pro. True.

Soc. There is greater hope of finding that which we are seeking in the life which is well mixed than in that which is not?

Pro. Far greater.

Soc. Then now let us mingle, Protarchus, at the same time offering up a prayer to Dionysus or Hephaestus, or whoever is the god who presides over the ceremony of mingling.

Pro. By all means.

Soc. Are not we the cup-bearers? and here are two fountains which are flowing at our side: one, which is pleasure, may be likened to a fountain of honey; the other, wisdom, a sober draught in which no wine mingles, is of water unpleasant but healthful; out of these we must seek to make the fairest of all possible mixtures.

Pro. Certainly.

Soc. Tell me first;—should we be most likely to succeed if we mingled every sort of pleasure with every sort of wisdom?

Pro. Perhaps we might.

Soc. But I should be afraid of the risk, and I think that I can show a safer plan.

Pro. What is it?

Soc. One pleasure was supposed by us to be truer than another, and one art to be more exact than another.

Pro. Certainly.

Soc. There was also supposed to be a difference in sciences; some of them regarding only the transient and perishing, and others the permanent and imperishable and everlasting and immutable; and when judged by the standard of truth, the latter, as we thought, were truer than the former.

Pro. Very good and right.

Soc. If, then, we were to begin by mingling the sections of each class which have the most of truth, will not the union suffice to give us the loveliest of lives, or shall we still want some elements of another kind?

Pro. I think that we ought to do what you suggest.

signed,
we must
discover
the na-
ture of
the good.

Reason
tells us
that we
should
look for
it in the
mixed
class.

Let us
then
mingle
pleasure
and wis-
dom.

Shall we
mingle
all kinds
of them,
or the
pure
only?

We can-
not ex-
clude the
impure
kinds of
knowl-
edge, for
they are
required
by the
needs of
every-
day life.

Soc. Let us suppose a man who understands justice, and has reason as well as understanding about the true nature of this and of all other things.

Pro. We will suppose such a man.

Soc. Will he have enough of knowledge if he is acquainted only with the divine circle and sphere, and knows nothing of our human spheres and circles, but uses only divine circles and measures in the building of a house?

Pro. The knowledge which is only superhuman, Socrates, is ridiculous in man.

Soc. What do you mean? Do you mean that you are to throw into the cup and mingle the impure and uncertain art which uses the false measure and the false circle?

Pro. Yes, we must, if any of us is ever to find his way home.

Soc. And am I to include music, which, as I was saying just now, is full of guesswork and imitation, and is wanting in purity?

Pro. Yes, I think that you must, if human life is to be a life at all.

Soc. Well, then, suppose that I give way, and, like a doorkeeper who is pushed and overborne by the mob, I open the door wide, and let knowledge of every sort stream in, and the pure mingle with the impure?

All the
sciences
may be
admitted,
but the
pleasures
require
more
consider-
ation.

Pro. I do not know, Socrates, that any great harm would come of having them all, if only you have the first sort.

Soc. Well, then, shall I let them all flow into what Homer poetically terms 'a meeting of the waters'?

Pro. By all means.

Soc. There—I have let him in, and now I must return to the fountain of pleasure. For we were not permitted to begin by mingling in a single stream the true portions of both according to our original intention; but the love of all knowledge constrained us to let all the sciences flow in together before the pleasures.

Pro. Quite true.

Soc. And now the time has come for us to consider about the pleasures also, whether we shall in like manner let them go all at once, or at first only the true ones.

First, let
us have
the true
ones;
secondly,
we must
have the
necessary.

Pro. It will be by far the safer course to let flow the true ones first.

Soc. Let them flow, then; and now, if there are any necessary pleasures, as there were arts and sciences necessary, must we not mingle them?

Pro. Yes; the necessary pleasures should certainly be allowed to mingle.

Soc. The knowledge of the arts has been admitted to be innocent and useful always; and if we say of pleasures in like manner that all of them are good and innocent for all of us at all times, we must let them all mingle?

Pro. What shall we say about them, and what course shall we take?

Soc. Do not ask me, Protarchus; but ask the daughters of pleasure and wisdom to answer for themselves.

Pro. How?

Soc. Tell us, O beloved—shall we call you pleasures or by some other name?—would you rather live with or without wisdom? I am of opinion that they would certainly answer as follows:

Pro. How?

Soc. They would answer, as we said before, that for any single class to be left by itself pure and isolated is not good, nor altogether possible; and that if we are to make comparisons of one class with another and choose, there is no better companion than knowledge of things in general, and likewise the perfect knowledge, if that may be, of ourselves in every respect[1].

Pro. And our answer will be:—In that ye have spoken well.

Soc. Very true. And now let us go back and interrogate wisdom and mind: Would you like to have any pleasures in the mixture? And they will reply:—'What pleasures do you mean?'

Pro. Likely enough.

Soc. And we shall take up our parable and say: Do you wish to have the greatest and most vehement pleasures for your companions in addition to the true ones? 'Why, Socrates,' they will say, 'how can we? seeing that they are the source of ten thousand hindrances to us; they trouble the souls of men, which are our habitation, with their madness; they prevent us from coming to the birth, and are commonly the ruin of the children which are born to us, causing them to be forgotten and unheeded; but the true and pure pleasures, of which you spoke, know to be of our family, and also those pleasures which accompany health and temperance, and which every Virtue, like a goddess has in her train to follow her about wherever she goes,—mingle these and not the others; there would be great want of sense in any one who desires to see a fair and perfect mixture, and to find in it what is the highest good in man and in the universe, and to divine what is the true form of good—there would be great want of sense in his allowing the pleasures, which are always in the company of folly and vice, to mingle with mind in the cup.'—Is not this a very rational and

Philebus

SOCRATES, PROTAR-CHUS.

Let us consult the pleasures and wisdom.

The pleasures say that they cannot live alone or without knowledge;

and wisdom, that she desires only true and virtuous pleasures, not all of them.

64

---

[1] Reading αὐτῶν ἡμῶν.

Truth is
an indis-
pensable
element
in the
mixture.

suitable reply, which mind has made, both on her own behalf, as well as on the behalf of memory and true opinion?

Pro. Most certainly.

Soc. And still there must be something more added, which is a necessary ingredient in every mixture.

Pro. What is that?

Soc. Unless truth enter into the composition, nothing can truly be created or subsist.

Pro. Impossible.

Soc. Quite impossible; and now you and Philebus must tell me whether anything is still wanting in the mixture, for to my way of thinking the argument is now completed, and may be compared to an incorporeal law, which is going to hold fair rule over a living body.

Pro. I agree with you, Socrates.

We are
now at
the vesti-
bule of
the good.

Soc. And may we not say with reason that we are now at the vestibule of the habitation of the good?

Pro. I think that we are.

What is
the most
precious
element
in the
mixture?

Soc. What, then, is there in the mixture which is most precious, and which is the principal cause why such a state is universally beloved by all? When we have discovered it, we will proceed to ask whether this omnipresent nature is more akin to pleasure or to mind.

Pro. Quite right; in that way we shall be better able to judge.

Soc. And there is no difficulty in seeing the cause which renders any mixture either of the highest value or of none at all.

Pro. What do you mean?

Soc. Every man knows it.

Pro. What?

Measure,
which is
the es-
sence of
beauty
and
virtue.

Soc. He knows that any want of measure and symmetry in any mixture whatever must always of necessity be fatal, both to the elements and to the mixture, which is then not a mixture, but only a confused medley which brings confusion on the possessor of it.

Pro. Most true.

Soc. And now the power of the good has retired into the region of the beautiful; for measure and symmetry are beauty and virtue all the world over.

Pro. True.

Soc. Also we said that truth was to form an element in the mixture.

65

Pro. Certainly.

Sym-
metry,

Soc. Then, if we are not able to hunt the good with one idea only, with three we may catch our prey; Beauty, Symmetry, Truth are

the three, and these taken together we may regard as the single
cause of the mixture, and the mixture as being good by reason of
the infusion of them.

Pro. Quite right.

Soc. And now, Protarchus, any man could decide well enough
whether pleasure or wisdom is more akin to the highest good, and
more honourable among gods and men.

Pro. Clearly, and yet perhaps the argument had better be pursued to the end.

Soc. We must take each of them separately in their relation to
pleasure and mind, and pronounce upon them; for we ought to see
to which of the two they are severally most akin.

Pro. You are speaking of beauty, truth, and measure?

Soc. Yes, Protarchus, take truth first, and, after passing in review
mind, truth, pleasure, pause awhile and make answer to yourself,
—as to whether pleasure or mind is more akin to truth.

Pro. There is no need to pause, for the difference between them
is palpable; pleasure is the veriest impostor in the world; and it is
said that in the pleasures of love, which appear to be the greatest,
perjury is excused by the gods; for pleasures, like children, have
not the least particle of reason in them; whereas mind is either the
same as truth, or the most like truth, and the truest.

Soc. Shall we next consider measure, in like manner, and ask
whether pleasure has more of this than wisdom, or wisdom than
pleasure?

Pro. Here is another question which may be easily answered;
for I imagine that nothing can ever be more immoderate than the
transports of pleasure, or more in conformity with measure than
mind and knowledge.

Soc. Very good; but there still remains the third test: Has mind
a greater share of beauty than pleasure, and is mind or pleasure
the fairer of the two?

Pro. No one, Socrates, either awake or dreaming, ever saw or
imagined mind or wisdom to be in aught unseemly, at any time,
past, present, or future.

Soc. Right.

Pro. But when we see some one indulging in pleasures, perhaps
in the greatest of pleasures, the ridiculous or disgraceful nature of
the action makes us ashamed; and so we put them out of sight, and
consign them to darkness, under the idea that they ought not to
meet the eye of day.

Soc. Then, Protarchus, you will proclaim everywhere, by word
of mouth to this company, and by messengers bearing the tidings

Philebus

SOCRATES,
PROTAR-
CHUS.

beauty,
and truth
are the
cause of
the mix-
ture and
of the
good in
it.

Of each
of these
three
elements
wisdom
has a
larger
share
than
pleasure.

66

The or-
der of

Philebus

SOCRATES,
PROTAR-
CHUS.

goods:—
(1) meas-
ure, the
eternal
nature;

(2) the
sym-
metrical
and per-
fect;

(3) mind
and
wisdom;

(4) sci-
ences,
arts, and
true
opinions;

(5) pure
pleasures.

far and wide, that pleasure is not the first of possessions, nor yet the second, but that in measure, and the mean, and the suitable, and the like, the eternal nature has been found.

Pro. Yes, that seems to be the result of what has been now said.

Soc. In the second class is contained the symmetrical and beautiful and perfect or sufficient, and all which are of that family.

Pro. True.

Soc. And if you reckon in the third class mind and wisdom, you will not be far wrong, if I divine aright.

Pro. I dare say.

Soc. And would you not put in the fourth class the goods which we were affirming to appertain specially to the soul—sciences and arts and true opinions as we called them? These come after the third class, and form the fourth, as they are certainly more akin to good than pleasure is.

Pro. Surely.

Soc. The fifth class are the pleasures which were defined by us as painless, being the pure pleasures of the soul herself, as we termed them, which accompany, some the sciences, and some the senses[1].

Pro. Perhaps.

Soc. And now, as Orpheus says,

'With the sixth generation cease the glory of my song.'

Here, at the sixth award, let us make an end; all that remains is to set the crown on our discourse.

Pro. True.

Soc. Then let us sum up and reassert what has been said, thus offering the third libation to the saviour Zeus.

Pro. How?

Soc. Philebus affirmed that pleasure was always and absolutely the good.

Pro. I understand; this third libation, Socrates, of which you spoke, meant a recapitulation.

Soc. Yes, but listen to the sequel; convinced of what I have just been saying, and feeling indignant at the doctrine, which is maintained, not by Philebus only, but by thousands of others, I affirmed that mind was far better and far more excellent, as an element of human life, than pleasure.

Pro. True.

Soc. But, suspecting that there were other things which were also better, I went on to say that if there was anything better than

---

[1] Reading ἐπιστήμαις τὰς δὲ κ.τ.λ.

either, then I would claim the second place for mind over pleasure, and pleasure would lose the second place as well as the first.

Pro. You did.

Soc. Nothing could be more satisfactorily shown than the unsatisfactory nature of both of them.

Pro. Very true.

Soc. The claims both of pleasure and mind to be the absolute good have been entirely disproven in this argument, because they are both wanting in self-sufficiency and also in adequacy and perfection.

Pro. Most true.

Soc. But, though they must both resign in favour of another, mind is ten thousand times nearer and more akin to the nature of the conqueror than pleasure.

Pro. Certainly.

Soc. And, according to the judgment which has now been given, pleasure will rank fifth.

Pro. True.

Soc. But not first; no, not even if all the oxen and horses and animals in the world by their pursuit of enjoyment proclaim her to be so;—although the many trusting in them, as diviners trust in birds, determine that pleasures make up the good of life, and deem the lusts of animals to be better witnesses than the inspirations of divine philosophy.

Pro. And now, Socrates, we tell you that the truth of what you have been saying is approved by the judgment of all of us.

Soc. And will you let me go?

Pro. There is a little which yet remains, and I will remind you of it, for I am sure that you will not be the first to go away from an argument.

Philebus

67
SOCRATES,
PROTAR-
CHUS.

Pleasure
is the
last and
lowest of
goods,
and not
first, even
if asserted
to be so
by all the
animals
in the
world.

GORGIAS

GORGIAS

PERSONS OF THE DIALOGUE

CALLICLES   SOCRATES   CHAEREPHON

GORGIAS   POLUS

SCENE:—*The house of Callicles*

Callicles. THE wise man, as the proverb says, is late for a fray, but not for a feast.

Socrates. And are we late for a feast?

Cal. Yes, and a delightful feast; for Gorgias has just been exhibiting to us many fine things.

Soc. It is not my fault, Callicles; our friend Chaerephon is to blame; for he would keep us loitering in the Agora.

Chaerephon. Never mind, Socrates; the misfortune of which I have been the cause I will also repair; for Gorgias is a friend of mine, and I will make him give the exhibition again either now, or, if you prefer, at some other time.

Cal. What is the matter, Chaerephon—does Socrates want to hear Gorgias?

Chaer. Yes, that was our intention in coming.

Cal. Come into my house, then; for Gorgias is staying with me, and he shall exhibit to you.

Soc. Very good, Callicles; but will he answer our questions? for I want to hear from him what is the nature of his art, and what it is which he professes and teaches; he may, as you [Chaerephon] suggest, defer the exhibition to some other time.

Cal. There is nothing like asking him, Socrates; and indeed to answer questions is a part of his exhibition, for he was saying only just now, that any one in my house might put any question to him, and that he would answer.

Soc. How fortunate! will you ask him, Chaerephon—?

Chaer. What shall I ask him?

Soc. Ask him who he is.

Chaer. What do you mean?

Soc. I mean such a question as would elicit from him, if he had

Steph.
447

SOCRATES,
CALLICLES,
CHAERE-
PHON.

119

Gorgias

SOCRATES,
GORGIAS,
CHAERE-
PHON,
POLUS.

448

Polus
offers to
take the
place of
Gorgias in
the argu-
ment.

The ques-
tion is
asked,
'What is
Gorgias?'

Answer:—
Gorgias is
one of the
best pro-
ficients in
the
noblest
art.

been a maker of shoes, the answer that he is a cobbler. Do you understand?

Chaer. I understand, and will ask him: Tell me, Gorgias, is our friend Callicles right in saying that you undertake to answer any questions which you are asked?

Gorgias. Quite right, Chaerephon: I was saying as much only just now; and I may add, that many years have elapsed since any one has asked me a new one.

Chaer. Then you must be very ready, Gorgias.

Gor. Of that, Chaerephon, you can make trial.

Polus. Yes, indeed, and if you like, Chaerephon, you may make trial of me too, for I think that Gorgias, who has been talking a long time, is tired.

Chaer. And do you, Polus, think that you can answer better than Gorgias?

Pol. What does that matter if I answer well enough for you?

Chaer. Not at all:—and you shall answer if you like.

Pol. Ask:—

Chaer. My question is this: If Gorgias had the skill of his brother Herodicus, what ought we to call him? Ought he not to have the name which is given to his brother?

Pol. Certainly.

Chaer. Then we should be right in calling him a physician?

Pol. Yes.

Chaer. And if he had the skill of Aristophon the son of Aglaophon, or of his brother Polygnotus, what ought we to call him?

Pol. Clearly, a painter.

Chaer. But now what shall we call him—what is the art in which he is skilled?

Pol. O Chaerephon, there are many arts among mankind which are experimental, and have their origin in experience, for experience makes the days of men to proceed according to art, and inexperience according to chance, and different persons in different ways are proficient in different arts, and the best persons in the best arts. And our friend Gorgias is one of the best, and the art in which he is a proficient is the noblest.

Soc. Polus has been taught how to make a capital speech, Gorgias; but he is not fulfilling the promise which he made to Chaerephon.

Gor. What do you mean, Socrates?

Soc. I mean that he has not exactly answered the question which he was asked.

Gor. Then why not ask him yourself?

Soc. But I would much rather ask you, if you are disposed to answer: for I see, from the few words which Polus has uttered, that he has attended more to the art which is called rhetoric than to dialectic.

Pol. What makes you say so, Socrates?

Soc. Because, Polus, when Chaerephon asked you what was the art which Gorgias knows, you praised it as if you were answering some one who found fault with it, but you never said what the art was.

Pol. Why, did I not say that it was the noblest of arts?

Soc. Yes, indeed, but that was no answer to the question: nobody asked what was the quality, but what was the nature, of the art, and by what name we were to describe Gorgias. And I would still beg you briefly and clearly, as you answered Chaerephon when he asked you at first, to say what this art is, and what we ought to call Gorgias: Or rather, Gorgias, let me turn to you, and ask the same question,—what are we to call you, and what is the art which you profess?

Gor. Rhetoric, Socrates, is my art.

Soc. Then I am to call you a rhetorician?

Gor. Yes, Socrates, and a good one too, if you would call me that which, in Homeric language, 'I boast myself to be.'

Soc. I should wish to do so.

Gor. Then pray do.

Soc. And are we to say that you are able to make other men rhetoricians?

Gor. Yes, that is exactly what I profess to make them, not only at Athens, but in all places.

Soc. And will you continue to ask and answer questions, Gorgias, as we are at present doing, and reserve for another occasion the longer mode of speech which Polus was attempting? Will you keep your promise, and answer shortly the questions which are asked of you?

Gor. Some answers, Socrates, are of necessity longer; but I will do my best to make them as short as possible; for a part of my profession is that I can be as short as any one.

Soc. That is what is wanted, Gorgias; exhibit the shorter method now, and the longer one at some other time.

Gor. Well, I will; and you will certainly say, that you never heard a man use fewer words.

Soc. Very good then; as you profess to be a rhetorician, and a maker of rhetoricians, let me ask you, with what is rhetoric concerned: I might ask with what is weaving concerned, and you

Marginal notes:

Gorgias

SOCRATES, GORGIAS, POLUS.

This is no answer.

449

Better:— Gorgias is a rhetorician and a teacher of rhetoric.

Gorgias

SOCRATES,
GORGIAS.

would reply (would you not?), with the making of garments?
Gor. Yes.
Soc. And music is concerned with the composition of melodies?
Gor. It is.
Soc. By Herè, Gorgias, I admire the surpassing brevity of your answers.
Gor. Yes, Socrates, I do think myself good at that.

And rhe-
toric is
concerned
with dis-
course.

Soc. I am glad to hear it; answer me in like manner about rhetoric: with what is rhetoric concerned?
Gor. With discourse.
Soc. What sort of discourse, Gorgias?—such discourse as would teach the sick under what treatment they might get well?
Gor. No.
Soc. Then rhetoric does not treat of all kinds of discourse?
Gor. Certainly not.
Soc. And yet rhetoric makes men able to speak?
Gor. Yes.
Soc. And to understand that about which they speak?
Gor. Of course.

450

Soc. But does not the art of medicine, which we were just now mentioning, also make men able to understand and speak about the sick?
Gor. Certainly.
Soc. Then medicine also treats of discourse?
Gor. Yes.
Soc. Of discourse concerning diseases?
Gor. Just so.
Soc. And does not gymnastic also treat of discourse concerning the good or evil condition of the body?
Gor. Very true.

But so are
all the
other
arts.

`   Soc.* And the same, Gorgias, is true of the other arts:—all of them treat of discourse concerning the subjects with which they severally have to do.
Gor. Clearly.
Soc. Then why, if you call rhetoric the art which treats of discourse, and all the other arts treat of discourse, do you not call them arts of rhetoric?
Gor. Because, Socrates, the knowledge of the other arts has only to do with some sort of external action, as of the hand; but there is no such action of the hand in rhetoric which works and takes effect only through the medium of discourse. And therefore I am justified in saying that rhetoric treats of discourse.
Soc. I am not sure whether I entirely understand you, but I dare

say I shall soon know better; please to answer me a question:— *Gorgias*
you would allow that there are arts?

Gor. Yes.

SOCRATES,
GORGIAS.

Soc. As to the arts generally, they are for the most part concerned with doing, and require little or no speaking; in painting, and statuary, and many other arts, the work may proceed in silence; and of such arts I suppose you would say that they do not come within the province of rhetoric.

Gor. You perfectly conceive my meaning, Socrates.

Soc. But there are other arts which work wholly through the medium of language, and require either no action or very little, as, for example, the arts of arithmetic, of calculation, of geometry, and of playing draughts; in some of these speech is pretty nearly co-extensive with action, but in most of them the verbal element is greater—they depend wholly on words for their efficacy and power: and I take your meaning to be that rhetoric is an art of this latter sort?

You mean
to say
that rhe-
toric be-
longs to
that class
of arts
which
is chiefly
concerned
with
words.

Gor. Exactly.

Soc. And yet I do not believe that you really mean to call any of these arts rhetoric; although the precise expression which you used was, that rhetoric is an art which works and takes effect only through the medium of discourse; and an adversary who wished to be captious might say, 'And so, Gorgias, you call arithmetic rhetoric.' But I do not think that you really call arithmetic rhetoric any more than geometry would be so called by you.

And yet
you
would
[451]
not call
arithmetic
rhetoric.

Gor. You are quite right, Socrates, in your apprehension of my meaning.

Soc. Well, then, let me now have the rest of my answer:—seeing that rhetoric is one of those arts which works mainly by the use of words, and there are other arts which also use words, tell me what is that quality in words with which rhetoric is concerned:—Suppose that a person asks me about some of the arts which I was mentioning just now; he might say, 'Socrates, what is arithmetic?' and I should reply to him, as you replied to me, that arithmetic is one of those arts which take effect through words. And then he would proceed to ask: 'Words about what?' and I should reply, Words about odd and even numbers, and how many there are of each. And if he asked again: 'What is the art of calculation?' I should say, That also is one of the arts which is concerned wholly with words. And if he further said, 'Concerned with what?' I should say, like the clerks in the assembly, 'as aforesaid' of arithmetic, but with a difference, the difference being that the art of calculation considers not only the quantities of odd and even numbers, but also

Illustra-
tions.

Gorgias

SOCRATES,
GORGIAS.

their numerical relations to themselves and to one another. And suppose, again, I were to say that astronomy is only words—he would ask, 'Words about what, Socrates?' and I should answer, that astronomy tells us about the motions of the stars and sun and moon, and their relative swiftness.

Gor. You would be quite right, Socrates.

Soc. And now let us have from you, Gorgias, the truth about rhe-- toric: which you would admit (would you not?) to be one of those arts which act always and fulfil all their ends through the medium of words?

Rhetoric
has to do
with
words:
about the
greatest
and best
of human
things.

Gor. True.

Soc. Words which do what? I should ask. To what class of things do the words which rhetoric uses relate?

Gor. To the greatest, Socrates, and the best of human things.

Soc. That again, Gorgias, is ambiguous; I am still in the dark: for which are the greatest and best of human things? I dare say that you have heard men singing at feasts the old drinking song, in which the singers enumerate the goods of life, first health, beauty next, thirdly, as the writer of the song says, wealth honestly obtained.

452

But
which are
they?

Gor. Yes, I know the song; but what is your drift?

Soc. I mean to say, that the producers of those things which the author of the song praises, that is to say, the physician, the trainer, the money-maker, will at once come to you, and first the physician will say: 'O Socrates, Gorgias is deceiving you, for my art is concerned with the greatest good of men and not his.' And when I ask, Who are you? he will reply, 'I am a physician.' What do you mean? I shall say. Do you mean that your art produces the greatest good? 'Certainly,' he will answer, 'for is not health the greatest good? What greater good can men have, Socrates?' And after him the trainer will come and say, 'I too, Socrates, shall be greatly surprised if Gorgias can show more good of his art than I can show of mine.' To him again I shall say, Who are you, honest friend, and what is your business? 'I am a trainer,' he will reply, 'and my business is to make men beautiful and strong in body.' When I have done with the trainer, there arrives the money-maker, and he, as I expect, will utterly despise them all. 'Consider, Socrates,' he will say, 'whether Gorgias or any one else can produce any greater good than wealth.' Well, you and I say to him, and are you a creator of wealth? 'Yes,' he replies. And who are you? 'A money-maker.' And do you consider wealth to be the greatest good of man? 'Of course,' will be his reply. And we shall rejoin: Yes; but our friend Gorgias contends that his art produces a greater good than yours. And then he will be sure to go on and ask, 'What good? Let Gorgias answer.' Now I want you, Gorgias, to imagine that this question is asked of you by them and by me; What is that which, as you say, is the greatest good of man, and of which you are the creator? Answer us.

Gor. That good, Socrates, which is truly the greatest, being that which gives to men freedom in their own persons, and to individuals the power of ruling over others in their several states.

Soc. And what would you consider this to be?

Gor. What is there greater than the word which persuades the judges in the courts, or the senators in the council, or the citizens in the assembly, or at any other political meeting?—if you have the power of uttering this word, you will have the physician your slave, and the trainer your slave, and the money-maker of whom you talk will be found to gather treasures, not for himself, but for you who are able to speak and to persuade the multitude.

Soc. Now I think, Gorgias, that you have very accurately explained what you conceive to be the art of rhetoric; and you mean to say, if I am not mistaken, that rhetoric is the artificer of persuasion, having this and no other business, and that this is her crown and end. Do you know any other effect of rhetoric over and above that of producing persuasion?

Gor. No: the definition seems to me very fair, Socrates; for persuasion is the chief end of rhetoric.

Soc. Then hear me, Gorgias, for I am quite sure that if there ever was a man who entered on the discussion of a matter from a pure love of knowing the truth, I am such a one, and I should say the same of you.

Gor. What is coming, Socrates?

Soc. I will tell you: I am very well aware that I do not know what, according to you, is the exact nature, or what are the topics of that persuasion of which you speak, and which is given by rhetoric; although I have a suspicion about both the one and the other. And I am going to ask—what is this power of persuasion which is given by rhetoric, and about what? But why, if I have a suspicion, do I ask instead of telling you? Not for your sake, but in order that the argument may proceed in such a manner as is most likely to set forth the truth. And I would have you observe, that I am right in asking this further question: If I asked, 'What sort of a painter is Zeuxis?' and you said, 'The painter of figures,' should I not be right in asking, 'What kind of figures, and where do you find them?'

Gor. Certainly.

Gorgias

SOCRATES,
GORGIAS.

Freedom
and
power,

and the
word
which
gives
them.

453

Rhetoric
is the art
of persuading-
says
Gorgias

Soc. And the reason for asking this second question would be, that there are other painters besides, who paint many other figures?

Gor. True.

Soc. But if there had been no one but Zeuxis who painted them, then you would have answered very well?

Gor. Quite so.

But so is arithmetic, so is painting.

Soc. Now I want to know about rhetoric in the same way;—is rhetoric the only art which brings persuasion, or do other arts have the same effect? I mean to say—Does he who teaches anything persuade men of that which he teaches or not?

Gor. He persuades, Socrates,—there can be no mistake about that.

Soc. Again, if we take the arts of which we were just now speaking:—do not arithmetic and the arithmeticians teach us the properties of number?

Gor. Certainly.

Soc. And therefore persuade us of them?

Gor. Yes.

Soc. Then arithmetic as well as rhetoric is an artificer of persuasion?

Gor. Clearly.

Soc. And if any one asks us what sort of persuasion, and about what,—we shall answer, persuasion which teaches the quantity of odd and even; and we shall be able to show that all the other arts of which we were just now speaking are artificers of persuasion, and of what sort, and about what.

454

Gor. Very true.

Soc. Then rhetoric is not the only artificer of persuasion?

Gor. True.

Soc. Seeing, then, that not only rhetoric works by persuasion, but that other arts do the same, as in the case of the painter, a question has arisen which is a very fair one: Of what persuasion is rhetoric the artificer, and about what?—is not that a fair way of putting the question?

Of what persuasion is rhetoric the artificer?

Gor. I think so.

Soc. Then, if you approve the question, Gorgias, what is the answer?

Of persuasion in the courts and assemblies about the just and unjust.

Gor. I answer, Socrates, that rhetoric is the art of persuasion in courts of law and other assemblies, as I was just now saying, and about the just and unjust.

Soc. And that, Gorgias, was what I was suspecting to be your notion; yet I would not have you wonder if by-and-by I am found repeating a seemingly plain question; for I ask not in order to confute you, but as I was saying that the argument may proceed consecutively, and that we may not get the habit of anticipating and suspecting the meaning of one another's words; I would have you develop your own views in your own way, whatever may be your hypothesis.

Gor. I think that you are quite right, Socrates.

Soc. Then let me raise another question; there is such a thing as 'having learned'?

Gor. Yes.

Soc. And there is also 'having believed'?

Gor. Yes.

Soc. And is the 'having learned' the same as 'having believed,' and are learning and belief the same things?

Gor. In my judgment, Socrates, they are not the same.

Soc. And your judgment is right, as you may ascertain in this way:—If a person were to say to you, 'Is there, Gorgias, a false belief as well as a true?'—you would reply, if I am not mistaken, that there is.

Gor. Yes.

Soc. Well, but is there a false knowledge as well as a true?

Gor. No.

Soc. No, indeed; and this again proves that knowledge and belief differ.

Gor. Very true.

Soc. And yet those who have learned as well as those who have believed are persuaded?

Gor. Just so.

Soc. Shall we then assume two sorts of persuasion,—one which is the source of belief without knowledge, as the other is of knowledge?

Gor. By all means.

Soc. And which sort of persuasion does rhetoric create in courts of law and other assemblies about the just and unjust, the sort of persuasion which gives belief without knowledge, or that which gives knowledge?

Gor. Clearly, Socrates, that which only gives belief.

Soc. Then rhetoric, as would appear, is the artificer of a persuasion which creates belief about the just and unjust, but gives no instruction about them?

Gor. True.

Soc. And the rhetorician does not instruct the courts of law or other assemblies about things just and unjust, but he creates belief about them; for no one can be supposed to instruct such a vast multitude about such high matters in a short time?

Gorgias

SOCRATES,
GORGIAS.

Neither is
the rheto-
rician
taken into
counsel
when
anything
has to be
done.

Gor. Certainly not.

Soc. Come, then, and let us see what we really mean about rhetoric; for I do not know what my own meaning is as yet. When the assembly meets to elect a physician or a shipwright or any other craftsman, will the rhetorician be taken into counsel? Surely not. For at every election he ought to be chosen who is most skilled; and, again, when walls have to be built or harbours or docks to be constructed, not the rhetorician but the master workman will advise; or when generals have to be chosen and an order of battle arranged, or a proposition taken, then the military will advise and not the rhetoricians: what do you say, Gorgias? Since you profess to be a rhetorician and a maker of rhetoricians, I cannot do better than learn the nature of your art from you. And here let me assure you that I have your interest in view as well as my own. For likely enough some one or other of the young men present might desire to become your pupil, and in fact I see some, and a good many too, who have this wish, but they would be too modest to question you. And therefore when you are interrogated by me, I would have you imagine that you are interrogated by them. 'What is the use of coming to you, Gorgias?' they will say—'about what will you teach us to advise the state?—about the just and unjust only, or about those other things also which Socrates has just mentioned?' How will you answer them?

But, says
Gorgias,
he will
persuade
people to
do it.

Gor. I like your way of leading us on, Socrates, and I will endeavour to reveal to you the whole nature of rhetoric. You must have heard, I think, that the docks and the walls of the Athenians and the plan of the harbour were devised in accordance with the counsels, partly of Themistocles, and partly of Pericles, and not at the suggestion of the builders.

Soc. Such is the tradition, Gorgias, about Themistocles; and I myself heard the speech of Pericles when he advised us about the middle wall.

456

Gor. And you will observe, Socrates, that when a decision has to be given in such matters the rhetoricians are the advisers; they are the men who win their point.

Soc. I had that in my admiring mind, Gorgias, when I asked what is the nature of rhetoric, which always appears to me, when I look at the matter in this way, to be a marvel of greatness.

Gor. A marvel, indeed, Socrates, if you only knew how rhetoric comprehends and holds under her sway all the inferior arts. Let me offer you a striking example of this. On several occasions I have been with my brother Herodicus or some other physician to see one of his patients, who would not allow the physician to give him medicine, or apply a knife or hot iron to him; and I have persuaded him to do for me what he would not do for the physician just by the use of rhetoric. And I say that if a rhetorician and a physician were to go to any city, and had there to argue in the Ecclesia or any other assembly as to which of them should be elected state-physician, the physician would have no chance; but he who could speak would be chosen if he wished; and in a contest with a man of any other profession the rhetorician more than any one would have the power of getting himself chosen, for he can speak more persuasively to the multitude than any of them, and on any subject. Such is the nature and power of the art of rhetoric! And yet, Socrates, rhetoric should be used like any other competitive art, not against everybody,—the rhetorician ought not to abuse his strength any more than a pugilist or pancratiast or other master of fence;—because he has powers which are more than a match either for friend or enemy, he ought not therefore to strike, stab, or slay his friends. Suppose a man to have been trained in the palestra and to be a skilful boxer,—he in the fulness of his strength goes and strikes his father or mother or one of his familiars or friends; but that is no reason why the trainers or fencing-masters should be held in detestation or banished from the city;—surely not. For they taught their art for a good purpose, to be used against enemies and evil-doers, in self-defence not in aggression, and others have perverted their instructions, and turned to a bad use their own strength and skill. But not on this account are the teachers bad, neither is the art in fault, or bad in itself; I should rather say that those who make a bad use of the art are to blame. And the same argument holds good of rhetoric; for the rhetorician can speak against all men and upon any subject,—in short, he can persuade the multitude better than any other man of anything which he pleases, but he should not therefore seek to defraud the physician or any other artist of his reputation merely because he has the power; he ought to use rhetoric fairly, as he would also use his athletic powers. And if after having become a rhetorician he makes a bad use of his strength and skill, his instructor surely ought not on that account to be held in detestation or banished. For he was intended by his teacher to make a good use of his instructions, but he abuses them. And therefore he is the person who ought to be held in detestation, banished, and put to death, and not his instructor.

Soc. You, Gorgias, like myself, have had great experience of disputations, and you must have observed, I think, that they do not always terminate in mutual edification, or in the definition by either party of the subjects which they are discussing; but dis-

Gorgias

SOCRATES, GORGIAS.

The rhetorician more than a match for a man of any other profession.

His pupils may make a bad use [457] of his instructions, but he is not to be blamed for this.

If Gorgias, like Socrates, is one of

Gorgias

SOCRATES,
GORGIAS,
CHAERE-
PHON,
CAL-
LICLES.

those who
rejoice
in being
refuted,
he would
like to
cross-
examine
him; if
not, not.

458

agreements are apt to arise—somebody says that another has not spoken truly or clearly; and then they get into a passion and begin to quarrel, both parties conceiving that their opponents are arguing from personal feeling only and jealousy of themselves, not from any interest in the question at issue. And sometimes they will go on abusing one another until the company at last are quite vexed at themselves for ever listening to such fellows. Why do I say this? Why, because I cannot help feeling that you are now saying what is not quite consistent or accordant with what you were saying at first about rhetoric. And I am afraid to point this out to you, lest you should think that I have some animosity against you, and that I speak, not for the sake of discovering the truth, but from jealousy of you. Now if you are one of my sort, I should like to cross-examine you, but if not I will let you alone. And what is my sort? you will ask. I am one of those who are very willing to be refuted if I say anything which is not true, and very willing to refute any one else who says what is not true, and quite as ready to be refuted as to refute; for I hold that this is the greater gain of the two, just as the gain is greater of being cured of a very great evil than of curing another. For I imagine that there is no evil which a man can endure so great as an erroneous opinion about the matters of which we are speaking; and if you claim to be one of my sort, let us have the discussion out, but if you would rather have done, no matter;—let us make an end of it.

Gor. I should say, Socrates, that I am quite the man whom you indicate; but, perhaps, we ought to consider the audience, for, before you came, I had already given a long exhibition, and if we proceed the argument may run on to a great length. And therefore I think that we should consider whether we may not be detaining some part of the company when they are wanting to do something else.

Delight of
the audi-
ence at
the pros-
pect of an
argu-
ment.

Chaer. You hear the audience cheering, Gorgias and Socrates, which shows their desire to listen to you; and for myself, Heaven forbid that I should have any business on hand which would take me away from a discussion so interesting and so ably maintained.

Cal. By the gods, Chaerephon, although I have been present at many discussions, I doubt whether I was ever so much delighted before, and therefore if you go on discoursing all day I shall be the better pleased.

Soc. I may truly say, Callicles, that I am willing, if Gorgias is.

Gor. After all this, Socrates, I should be disgraced if I refused, especially as I have promised to answer all comers; in accordance with the wishes of the company, then, do you begin, and ask of me any question which you like.

Soc. Let me tell you then, Gorgias, what surprises me in your words; though I dare say that you may be right, and I may have misunderstood your meaning. You say that you can make any man, who will learn of you, a rhetorician?

Gor. Yes.

Soc. Do you mean that you will teach him to gain the ears of the multitude on any subject, and this not by instruction but by persuasion?

Gor. Quite so.

Soc. You were saying, in fact, that the rhetorician will have greater powers of persuasion than the physician even in a matter of health?

Gor. Yes, with the multitude,—that is.

Soc. You mean to say, with the ignorant; for with those who know he cannot be supposed to have greater powers of persuasion.

The rhe-
torician
has great-
er powers
of per-
cuasion
with the
mob than
e. g. the
physician.

Gor. Very true.

Soc. But if he is to have more power of persuasion than the physician, he will have greater power than he who knows?

Gor. Certainly.

Soc. Although he is not a physician:—is he?

Gor. No.

Soc. And he who is not a physician must, obviously, be ignorant of what the physician knows.

The more
ignorant
therefore
will have
more
power
than he
who
knows.

Gor. Clearly.

Soc. Then, when the rhetorician is more persuasive than the physician, the ignorant is more persuasive with the ignorant than he who has knowledge?—is not that the inference?

Gor. In the case supposed:—Yes.

Soc. And the same holds of the relation of rhetoric to all the other arts; the rhetorician need not know the truth about things; he has only to discover some way of persuading the ignorant that he has more knowledge than those who know?

Gor. Yes, Socrates, and is not this a great comfort?—not to have learned the other arts, but the art of rhetoric only, and yet to be in no way inferior to the professors of them?

Soc. Whether the rhetorician is or is not inferior on this account is a question which we will hereafter examine if the enquiry is likely to be of any service to us; but I would rather begin by asking, whether he is or is not as ignorant of the just and unjust, base and honourable, good and evil, as he is of medicine and the other

And is the
rhetori-
cian as
ignorant
of good
and evil,
just and
unjust, as
[460]
about
special
arts; or
will
Gorgias
teach him
these
things
first?

He must
be taught.

He who
has
learned
what is
just, is
admitted
to be just
and to act
justly.
But if so,
the rheto-
rician,
having
learned
what is
just, must
act justly,
and can
never

arts; I mean to say, does he really know anything of what is good and evil, base or honourable, just or unjust in them; or has he only a way with the ignorant of persuading them that he not knowing is to be esteemed to know more about these things than some one else who knows? Or must the pupil know these things and come to you knowing them before he can acquire the art of rhetoric? If he is ignorant, you who are the teacher of rhetoric will not teach him —it is not your business; but you will make him seem to the multitude to know them, when he does not know them; and seem to be a good man, when he is not. Or will you be unable to teach him rhetoric at all, unless he knows the truth of these things first? What is to be said about all this? By heavens, Gorgias, I wish that you would reveal to me the power of rhetoric, as you were saying that you would.

Gor. Well, Socrates, I suppose that if the pupil does chance not to know them, he will have to learn of me these things as well.

Soc. Say no more, for there you are right; and so he whom you make a rhetorician must either know the nature of the just and unjust already, or he must be taught by you.

Gor. Certainly.

Soc. Well, and is not he who has learned carpentering a carpenter?

Gor. Yes.

Soc. And he who has learned music a musician?

Gor. Yes.

Soc. And he who has learned medicine is a physician, in like manner? He who has learned anything whatever is that which his knowledge makes him.

Gor. Certainly.

Soc. And in the same way, he who has learned what is just is just?

Gor. To be sure.

Soc. And he who is just may be supposed to do what is just?

Gor. Yes.

Soc. And must not[1] the just man always desire to do what is just?

Gor. That is clearly the inference.

Soc. Surely, then, the just man will never consent to do injustice?

Gor. Certainly not.

Soc. And according to the argument the rhetorician must be a just man?

Gor. Yes.

---

[1] Omitting the words τὸν ῥητορικὸν δίκαιον εἶναι and δὲ in next clause.

Soc. And will therefore never be willing to do injustice?

Gor. Clearly not.

Soc. But do you remember saying just now that the trainer is not to be accused or banished if the pugilist makes a wrong use of his pugilistic art; and in like manner, if the rhetorician makes a bad and unjust use of rhetoric, that is not to be laid to the charge of his teacher, who is not to be banished, but the wrong-doer himself who made a bad use of his rhetoric—he is to be banished—was not that said?

Gor. Yes, it was.

Soc. But now we are affirming that the aforesaid rhetorician will never have done injustice at all?

Gor. True.

Soc. And at the very outset, Gorgias, it was said that rhetoric treated of discourse, not [like arithmetic] about odd and even, but about just and unjust? Was not this said?

Gor. Yes.

Soc. I was thinking at the time, when I heard you saying so, that rhetoric, which is always discoursing about justice, could not possibly be an unjust thing. But when you added, shortly afterwards, that the rhetorician might make a bad use of rhetoric I noted with surprise the inconsistency into which you had fallen; and I said, that if you thought, as I did, that there was a gain in being refuted, there would be an advantage in going on with the question, but if not, I would leave off. And in the course of our investigations, as you will see yourself, the rhetorician has been acknowledged to be incapable of making an unjust use of rhetoric, or of willingness to do injustice. By the dog, Gorgias, there will be a great deal of discussion, before we get at the truth of all this.

Polus. And do even you, Socrates, seriously believe what you are now saying about rhetoric? What! because Gorgias was ashamed to deny that the rhetorician knew the just and the honourable and the good, and admitted that to any one who came to him ignorant of them he could teach them, and then out of this admission there arose a contradiction—the thing which you so dearly love, and to which not he, but you, brought the argument by your captious questions—[do you seriously believe that there is any truth in all this?] For will any one ever acknowledge that he does not know, or cannot teach, the nature of justice? The truth is, that there is great want of manners in bringing the argument to such a pass.

The para-
doxes of
Socrates
arouse the
ire of
Polus.

Soc. Illustrious Polus, the reason why we provide ourselves with friends and children is, that when we get old and stumble, a

Socrates
is willing
enough to
receive his
correc-
tion, if
he will
only be
brief.

'Am I to
be de-
prived of
speech in
a free
state?'

462
'Am I to
be com-
pelled to
listen?'

younger generation may be at hand to set us on our legs again in our words and in our actions: and now, if I and Gorgias are stumbling, here are you who should raise us up; and I for my part engage to retract any error into which you may think that I have fallen—upon one condition:

Pol. What condition?

Soc. That you contract, Polus, the prolixity of speech in which you indulged at first.

Pol. What! do you mean that I may not use as many words as I please?

Soc. Only to think, my friend, that having come on a visit to Athens, which is the most free-spoken state in Hellas, you when you got there, and you alone, should be deprived of the power of speech—that would be hard indeed. But then consider my case: —shall not I be very hardly used, if, when you are making a long oration, and refusing to answer what you are asked, I am compelled to stay and listen to you, and may not go away? I say rather, if you have a real interest in the argument, or, to repeat my former expression, have any desire to set it on its legs, take back any statement which you please; and in your turn ask and answer, like myself and Gorgias—refute and be refuted: for I suppose that you would claim to know what Gorgias knows— would you not?

Pol. Yes.

Soc. And you, like him, invite any one to ask you about anything which he pleases, and you will know how to answer him?

Pol. To be sure.

Soc. And now, which will you do, ask or answer?

Pol. I will ask; and do you answer me, Socrates, the same question which Gorgias, as you suppose, is unable to answer: What is rhetoric?

Soc. Do you mean what sort of an art?

Pol. Yes.

Socrates
in his
answer
contrives
to give
Polus a
lesson.

Soc. To say the truth, Polus, it is not an art·at all, in my opinion.

Pol. Then what, in your opinion, is rhetoric?

Soc. A thing which, as I was lately reading in a book of yours, you say that you have made an art.

Pol. What thing?

Soc. I should say a sort of experience.

Pol. Does rhetoric seem to you to be an experience?

Soc. That is my view, but you may be of another mind.

Pol. An experience in what?

Soc. An experience in producing a sort of delight and gratification.

Pol. And if able to gratify others, must not rhetoric be a fine thing?

Soc. What are you saying, Polus? Why do you ask me whether rhetoric is a fine thing or not, when I have not as yet told you what rhetoric is?

Pol. Did I not hear you say that rhetoric was a sort of experience?

Soc. Will you, who are so desirous to gratify others, afford a slight gratification to me?

Pol. I will.

Soc. Will you ask me, what sort of an art is cookery?

Pol. What sort of an art is cookery?

Soc. Not an art at all, Polus.

Pol. What then?

Soc. I should say an experience.

Pol. In what? I wish that you would explain to me.

Soc. An experience in producing a sort of delight and gratification, Polus.

Pol. Then are cookery and rhetoric the same?

Soc. No, they are only different parts of the same profession.

Pol. Of what profession?

Soc. I am afraid that the truth may seem discourteous; and I hesitate to answer, lest Gorgias should imagine that I am making fun of his own profession. For whether or no this is that art of rhetoric which Gorgias practises I really cannot tell:—from what he was just now saying, nothing appeared of what he thought of his art, but the rhetoric which I mean is a part of a not very creditable whole.

Gor. A part of what, Socrates? Say what you mean, and never mind me.

Soc. In my opinion then, Gorgias, the whole of which rhetoric is a part is not an art at all, but the habit of a bold and ready wit, which knows how to manage mankind: this habit I sum up under the word 'flattery;' and it appears to me to have many other parts, one of which is cookery, which may seem to be an art, but, as I maintain, is only an experience or routine and not an art:— another part is rhetoric, and the art of attiring and sophistry are two others: thus there are four branches, and four different things answering to them. And Polus may ask, if he likes, for he has not as yet been informed, what part of flattery is rhetoric: he did not see that I had not yet answered him when he proceeded to ask a further question: Whether I do not think rhetoric a fine thing? But I shall not tell him whether rhetoric is a fine thing or not,

He puts
rhetoric
and cook-
ery in the
same
class;

463

and that
class is
flattery.

Rhetoric
is the
shadow of
a part of
politics.

'But what
in the
world
does this
mean?'

464

Returning
to first
principles,
Socrates
assumes
the exist-
ence of
souls and
bodies
which
may or
may not
be in a
good con-
dition,
real or
apparent.

To the
soul cor-
responds
the art of
politics
which has
two parts,
legislation
and jus-
tice, and
to the

until I have first answered, 'What is rhetoric?' For that would not be right, Polus; but I shall be happy to answer, if you will ask me, What part of flattery is rhetoric?

Pol. I will ask, and do you answer? What part of flattery is rhetoric?

Soc. Will you understand my answer? Rhetoric, according to my view, is the ghost or counterfeit of a part of politics.

Pol. And noble or ignoble?

Soc. Ignoble, I should say, if I am compelled to answer, for I call what is bad ignoble:—though I doubt whether you understand what I was saying before.

Gor. Indeed, Socrates, I cannot say that I understand myself.

Soc. I do not wonder, Gorgias; for I have not as yet explained myself, and our friend Polus, colt by name and colt by nature, is apt to run away[1].

Gor. Never mind him, but explain to me what you mean by saying that rhetoric is the counterfeit of a part of politics.

Soc. I will try, then, to explain my notion of rhetoric, and if I am mistaken, my friend Polus shall refute me. We may assume the existence of bodies and of souls?

Gor. Of course.

Soc. You would further admit that there is a good condition of either of them?

Gor. Yes.

Soc. Which condition may not be really good, but good only in appearance? I mean to say, that there are many persons who appear to be in good health, and whom only a physician or trainer will discern at first sight not to be in good health.

Gor. True.

Soc. And this applies not only to the body, but also to the soul: in either there may be that which gives the appearance of health and not the reality?

Gor. Yes, certainly.

Soc. And now I will endeavour to explain to you more clearly what I mean: The soul and body being two, have two arts corresponding to them: there is the art of politics attending on the soul; and another art attending on the body, of which I know no single name, but which may be described as having two divisions, one of them gymnastic, and the other medicine. And in politics there is a legislative part, which answers to gymnastic, as justice does to medicine; and the two parts run into one another, justice having to do with the same subject as legislation, and med-

[1] There is an untranslatable play on the name 'Polus,' which means 'a colt.'

icine with the same subject as gymnastic, but with a difference. Now, seeing that there are these four arts, two attending on the body and two on the soul for their highest good; flattery knowing, or rather guessing their natures, has distributed herself into four shams or simulations of them; she puts on the likeness of some one or other of them, and pretends to be that which she simulates, and having no regard for men's highest interests, is ever making pleasure the bait of the unwary, and deceiving them into the belief that she is of the highest value to them. Cookery simulates the disguise of medicine, and pretends to know what food is the best for the body; and if the physician and the cook had to enter into a competition in which children were the judges, or men who had no more sense than children, as to which of them best understands the goodness or badness of food, the physician would be starved to death. A flattery I deem this to be and of an ignoble sort, Polus, for to you I am now addressing myself, because it aims at pleasure without any thought of the best. An art I do not call it, but only an experience, because it is unable to explain or to give a reason of the nature of its own applications. And I do not call any irrational thing an art; but if you dispute my words, I am prepared to argue in defence of them.

Cookery, then, I maintain to be a flattery which takes the form of medicine; and tiring, in like manner, is a flattery which takes the form of gymnastic, and is knavish, false, ignoble, illiberal, working deceitfully by the help of lines, and colours, and enamels, and garments, and making men affect a spurious beauty to the neglect of the true beauty which is given by gymnastic.

I would rather not be tedious, and therefore I will only say, after the manner of the geometricians, (for I think that by this time you will be able to follow,)

as tiring : gymnastic : : cookery : medicine;

or rather,

as tiring : gymnastic : : sophistry : legislation;

and

as cookery : medicine : : rhetoric : justice.

And this, I say, is the natural difference between the rhetorician and the sophist, but by reason of their near connection, they are apt to be jumbled up together; neither do they know what to make of themselves, nor do other men know what to make of them. For if the body presided over itself, and were not under the guidance of the soul, and the soul did not discern and discriminate between cookery and medicine, but the body was made the judge of them, and the rule of judgment was the bodily delight which was given

Gorgias
SOCRATES
body corresponds another nameless art of training which has two parts, medicine and gymnastic; and these four have four shams corre-
[465]
sponding to them.

The shams are cooking, dressing up, sophistry, rhetoric

Socrates
excuses
himself
for the
length at
which he
has
spoken.
466

by them, then the word of Anaxagoras, that word with which you, friend Polus, are so well acquainted, would prevail far and wide: 'Chaos' would come again, and cookery, health, and medicine would mingle in an indiscriminate mass. And now I have told you my notion of rhetoric, which is, in relation to the soul, what cookery is to the body. I may have been inconsistent in making a long speech, when I would not allow you to discourse at length. But I think that I may be excused, because you did not understand me, and could make no use of my answer when I spoke shortly, and therefore I had to enter into an explanation. And if I show an equal inability to make use of yours, I hope that you will speak at equal length; but if I am able to understand you, let me have the benefit of your brevity, as is only fair: And now you may do what you please with my answer.

Pol. What do you mean? do you think that rhetoric is flattery?

Soc. Nay, I said a part of flattery; if at your age, Polus, you cannot remember, what will you do by-and-by, when you get older?

Pol. And are the good rhetoricians meanly regarded in states, under the idea that they are flatterers?

Soc. Is that a question or the beginning of a speech?

Pol. I am asking a question.

Soc. Then my answer is, that they are not regarded at all.

Polus
cannot be
made to
under-
stand that
rhetori-
cians have
no real
power in
a state,
because
they do
not do
what they
ultimately
will, but
only
what they
think
best.

Pol. How not regarded? Have they not very great power in states?

Soc. Not if you mean to say that power is a good to the possessor.

Pol. And that is what I do mean to say.

Soc. Then, if so, I think that they have the least power of all the citizens.

Pol. What! are they not like tyrants? They kill and despoil and exile any one whom they please.

Soc. By the dog, Polus, I cannot make out at each deliverance of yours, whether you are giving an opinion of your own, or asking a question of me.

Pol. I am asking a question of you.

Soc. Yes, my friend, but you ask two questions at once.

Pol. How two questions?

Soc. Why, did you not say just now that the rhetoricians are like tyrants, and that they kill and despoil or exile any one whom they please?

Pol. I did.

Soc. Well then, I say to you that here are two questions in one, and I will answer both of them. And I tell you, Polus, that rhetoricians and tyrants have the least possible power in states, as I was just now saying; for they do literally nothing which they will, but only what they think best.

Pol. And is not that a great power?

Soc. Polus has already said the reverse.

Soc. No, by the great—what do you call him?—not you, for you say that power is a good to him who has the power.

Pol. I do.

Soc. And would you maintain that if a fool does what he thinks best, this is a good, and would you call this great power?

Pol. I should not.

Soc. Then you must prove that the rhetorician is not a fool, and that rhetoric is an art and not a flattery—and so you will have refuted me; but if you leave me unrefuted, why, the rhetoricians who do what they think best in states, and the tyrants, will have nothing upon which to congratulate themselves, if as you say, power be indeed a good, admitting at the same time that what is done without sense is an evil.

Pol. Yes; I admit that.

Soc. How then can the rhetoricians or the tyrants have great power in states, unless Polus can refute Socrates, and prove to him that they do as they will?

Pol. This fellow —

Soc. I say that they do not do as they will;—now refute me.

Pol. Why, have you not already said that they do as they think best?

Soc. And I say so still.

Pol. Then surely they do as they will?

Soc. I deny it.

Pol. But they do what they think best?

Soc. Aye.

Pol. That, Socrates, is monstrous and absurd.

Soc. Good words, good Polus, as I may say in your own peculiar style; but if you have any questions to ask of me, either prove that I am in error or give the answer yourself.

Pol. Very well, I am willing to answer that I may know what you mean.

Soc. Do men appear to you to will that which they do, or to will that further end for the sake of which they do a thing? when they take medicine, for example, at the bidding of a physician, do they will the drinking of the medicine which is painful, or the health for the sake of which they drink?

Pol. Clearly, the health.

Soc. And when men go on a voyage or engage in business, they

Gorgias

SOCRATES,
POLUS,

For a fool
[467]
and a flat-
terer can-
not know
what is
good.

do not will that which they are doing at the time; for who would desire to take the risk of a voyage or the trouble of business?— But they will, to have the wealth for the sake of which they go on a voyage.

Pol. Certainly.

A man
cannot
will un-
less he
knows the
ultimate
good for
the sake
of which
he acts.

Soc. And is not this universally true? If a man does something for the sake of something else, he wills not that which he does, but that for the sake of which he does it.

Pol. Yes.

Soc. And are not all things either good or evil, or intermediate and indifferent?

Pol. To be sure, Socrates.

Soc. Wisdom and health and wealth and the like you would call goods, and their opposites evils?

Pol. I should.

468

Soc. And the things which are neither good nor evil, and which partake sometimes of the nature of good and at other times of evil, or of neither, are such as sitting, walking, running, sailing; or, again, wood, stones, and the like:—these are the things which you call neither good nor evil?

Pol. Exactly so.

Soc. Are these indifferent things done for the sake of the good, or the good for the sake of the indifferent?

Pol. Clearly, the indifferent for the sake of the good.

Soc. When we walk we walk for the sake of the good, and under the idea that it is better to walk, and when we stand we stand equally for the sake of the good?

Pol. Yes.

Soc. And when we kill a man we kill him or exile him or despoil him of his goods, because, as we think, it will conduce to our good?

Pol. Certainly.

Soc. Men who do any of these things do them for the sake of the good?

Pol. Yes.

Soc. And did we not admit that in doing something for the sake of something else, we do not will those things which we do, but that other thing for the sake of which we do them?

Pol. Most true.

Soc. Then we do not will simply to kill a man or to exile him or to despoil him of his goods, but we will to do that which conduces to our good, and if the act is not conducive to our good we do not will it; for we will, as you say, that which is our good, but that which is neither good nor evil, or simply evil, we do not will. Why are you silent, Polus? Am I not right?

Pol. You are right.

Soc. Hence we may infer, that if any one, whether he be a tyrant or a rhetorician, kills another or exiles another or deprives him of his property, under the idea that the act is for his own interests when really not for his own interests, he may be said to do what seems best to him?

Pol. Yes.

Soc. But does he do what he wills if he does what is evil? Why do you not answer?

Pol. Well, I suppose not.

Soc. Then if great power is a good as you allow, will such a one have great power in a state?

Pol. He will not.

Soc. Then I was right in saying that a man may do what seems good to him in a state, and not have great power, and not do what he wills?

Pol. As though you, Socrates, would not like to have the power of doing what seemed good to you in the state, rather than not; you would not be jealous when you saw any one killing or despoiling or imprisoning whom he pleased, Oh, no!

Soc. Justly or unjustly, do you mean?

Pol. In either case is he not equally to be envied?

Soc. Forbear, Polus!

Pol. Why 'forbear'?

Soc. Because you ought not to envy wretches who are not to be envied, but only to pity them.

Pol. And are those of whom I spoke wretches?

Soc. Yes, certainly they are.

Pol. And so you think that he who slays any one whom he pleases, and justly slays him, is pitiable and wretched?

Soc. No, I do not say that of him: but neither do I think that he is to be envied.

Pol. Were you not saying just now that he is wretched?

Soc. Yes, my friend, if he killed another unjustly, in which case he is also to be pitied; and he is not to be envied if he killed him justly.

Pol. At any rate you will allow that he who is unjustly put to death is wretched, and to be pitied?

Soc. Not so much, Polus, as he who kills him, and not so much as he who is justly killed.

No man
does what
he wills
who does
what is
evil.

469

He who
makes a
bad use of
power is
not to be
envied,
but pitied.

Pol. How can that be, Socrates?

Soc. That may very well be, inasmuch as doing injustice is the greatest of evils.

Pol. But is it the greatest? Is not suffering injustice a greater evil?

Soc. Certainly not.

Pol. Then would you rather suffer than do injustice?

Soc. I should not like either, but if I must choose between them, I would rather suffer than do.

Pol. Then you would not wish to be a tyrant?

Soc. Not if you mean by tyranny what I mean.

Pol. I mean, as I said before, the power of doing whatever seems good to you in a state, killing, banishing, doing in all things as you like.

A tyrant
has no
real
power
any more
than a
man who
runs out
into the
Agora
carrying
a dagger.

Soc. Well then, illustrious friend, when I have said my say, do you reply to me. Suppose that I go into a crowded Agora, and take a dagger under my arm. Polus, I say to you, I have just acquired rare power, and become a tyrant; for if I think that any of these men whom you see ought to be put to death, the man whom I have a mind to kill is as good as dead; and if I am disposed to break his head or tear his garment, he will have his head broken or his garment torn in an instant. Such is my great power in this city. And if you do not believe me, and I show you the dagger, you would probably reply: Socrates, in that sort of way any one may have great power—he may burn any house which he pleases, and the docks and triremes of the Athenians, and all their other vessels, whether public or private—but can you believe that this mere doing as you think best is great power?

Pol. Certainly not such doing as this.

Soc. But can you tell me why you disapprove of such a power?

Pol. I can.

Soc. Why then?

Pol. Why, because he who did as you say would be certain to be punished.

Soc. And punishment is an evil?

Pol. Certainly.

Soc. And you would admit once more, my good sir, that great power is a benefit to a man if his actions turn out to his advantage, and that this is the meaning of great power; and if not, then his power is an evil and is no power. But let us look at the matter in another way:—do we not acknowledge that the things of which we were speaking, the infliction of death, and exile, and the deprivation of property are sometimes a good and sometimes not a good?

Pol. Certainly.

Soc. About that you and I may be supposed to agree?

Pol. Yes.

Soc. Tell me, then, when do you say that they are good and when that they are evil—what principle do you lay down?

Pol. I would rather, Socrates, that you should answer as well as ask that question.

Soc. Well, Polus, since you would rather have the answer from me, I say that they are good when they are just, and evil when they are unjust.

Even
what we
common-
ly call the
evils of
life may
be goods
in dis-
guise.

Pol. You are hard of refutation, Socrates, but might not a child refute that statement?

Soc. Then I shall be very grateful to the child, and equally grateful to you if you will refute me and deliver me from my fool-ishness. And I hope that refute me you will, and not weary of doing good to a friend.

Pol. Yes, Socrates, and I need not go far or appeal to antiquity; events which happened only a few days ago are enough to refute you, and to prove that many men who do wrong are happy.

Soc. What events?

Pol. You see, I presume, that Archelaus the son of Perdiccas is now the ruler of Macedonia?

Soc. At any rate I hear that he is.

Pol. And do you think that he is happy or miserable?

Soc. I cannot say, Polus, for I have never had any acquaintance with him.

Pol. And cannot you tell at once, and without having an acquaintance with him, whether a man is happy?

Soc. Most certainly not.

Pol. Then clearly, Socrates, you would say that you did not even know whether the great king was a happy man?

Soc. And I should speak the truth; for I do not know how he stands in the matter of education and justice.

Pol. What! and does all happiness consist in this?

Soc. Yes, indeed, Polus, that is my doctrine; the men and women who are gentle and good are also happy, as I maintain, and the unjust and evil are miserable.

Pol. Then, according to your doctrine, the said Archelaus is miserable?

Soc. Yes, my friend, if he is wicked.

Pol. That he is wicked I cannot deny; for he had no title at all to the throne which he now occupies, he being only the son of a woman who was the slave of Alcetas the brother of Perdiccas; he

Gorgias

SOCRATES,
POLUS.

of the un-
just by
the story
of Arche-
laus, who
has lately
by many
crimes
gained the
throne of
Mace-
donia.

himself therefore in strict right was the slave of Alcetas; and if he had meant to do rightly he would have remained his slave, and then, according to your doctrine, he would have been happy. But now he is unspeakably miserable, for he has been guilty of the greatest crimes: in the first place he invited his uncle and master, Alcetas, to come to him, under the pretence that he would restore to him the throne which Perdiccas has usurped, and after entertaining him and his son Alexander, who was his own cousin, and nearly of an age with him, and making them drunk, he threw them into a waggon and carried them off by night, and slew them, and got both of them out of the way; and when he had done all this wickedness he never discovered that he was the most miserable of all men, and was very far from repenting: shall I tell you how he showed his remorse? he had a younger brother, a child of seven years old, who was the legitimate son of Perdiccas, and to him of right the kingdom belonged; Archelaus, however, had no mind to bring him up as he ought and restore the kingdom to him; that was not his notion of happiness; but not long afterwards he threw him into a well and drowned him, and declared to his mother Cleopatra that he had fallen in while running after a goose, and had been killed. And now as he is the greatest criminal of all the Macedonians, he may be supposed to be the most miserable and not the happiest of them, and I dare say that there are many Athenians, and you would be at the head of them, who would rather be any other Macedonian than Archelaus!

Socrates
sees no
force in
such
argu-
ments.

Soc. I praised you at first, Polus, for being a rhetorician rather than a reasoner. And this, as I suppose, is the sort of argument with which you fancy that a child might refute me, and by which I stand refuted when I say that the unjust man is not happy. But, my good friend, where is the refutation? I cannot admit a word which you have been saying.

Pol. That is because you will not; for you surely must think as I do.

The mul-
titude of
witnesses
are
nothing
to him.
[472]
He must
convince
his oppo-
nent and
himself
by argu-
ment.

Soc. Not so, my simple friend, but because you will refute me after the manner which rhetoricians practise in courts of law. For there the one party think that they refute the other when they bring forward a number of witnesses of good repute in proof of their allegations, and their adversary has only a single one or none at all. But this kind of proof is of no value where truth is the aim; a man may often be sworn down by a multitude of false witnesses who have a great air of respectability. And in this argument nearly every one, Athenian and stranger alike, would be on your side, if you should bring witnesses in disproof of my statement;

—you may, if you will, summon Nicias the son of Niceratus, and let his brothers, who gave the row of tripods which stand in the precincts of Dionysus, come with him; or you may summon Aristocrates, the son of Scellius, who is the giver of that famous offering which is at Delphi; summon, if you will, the whole house of Pericles, or any other great Athenian family whom you choose;—they will all agree with you: I only am left alone and cannot agree, for you do not convince me; although you produce many false witnesses against me, in the hope of depriving me of my inheritance, which is the truth. But I consider that nothing worth speaking of will have been effected by me unless I make you the one witness of my words; nor by you, unless you make me the one witness of yours; no matter about the rest of the world. For there are two ways of refutation, one which is yours and that of the world in general; but mine is of another sort—let us compare them, and see in what they differ. For, indeed, we are at issue about matters which to know is honourable and not to know disgraceful; to know or not to know happiness and misery—that is the chief of them. And what knowledge can be nobler? or what ignorance more disgraceful than this? And therefore I will begin by asking you whether you do not think that a man who is unjust and doing injustice can be happy, seeing that you think Archelaus unjust, and yet happy? May I assume this to be your opinion?

Pol. Certainly.

Soc. But I say that this is an impossibility—here is one point about which we are at issue:—very good. And do you mean to say also that if he meets with retribution and punishment he will still be happy?

Pol. Certainly not; in that case he will be most miserable.

Soc. On the other hand, if the unjust be not punished, then, according to you, he will be happy?

Pol. Yes.

Soc. But in my opinion, Polus, the unjust or doer of unjust actions is miserable in any case,—more miserable, however, if he be not punished and does not meet with retribution, and less miserable if he be punished and meets with retribution at the hands of gods and men.

Pol. You are maintaining a strange doctrine, Socrates.

Soc. I shall try to make you agree with me, O my friend, for as a friend I regard you. Then these are the points at issue between us—are they not? I was saying that to do is worse than to suffer injustice?

Pol. Exactly so.

According to Polus the unjust man may be happy if he is unpunished: Socrates maintains that he is more happy, or less unhappy, if [473] he meets with retribution.

Gorgias

SOCRATES,
POLUS.

Soc. And you said the opposite?

Pol. Yes.

Soc. I said also that the wicked are miserable, and you refuted me?

Pol. By Zeus, I did.

Soc. In your own opinion, Polus.

Pol. Yes, and I rather suspect that I was in the right.

Soc. You further said that the wrong-doer is happy if he be unpunished?

Pol. Certainly.

Soc. And I affirm that he is most miserable, and that those who are punished are less miserable—are you going to refute this proposition also?

Pol. A proposition which is harder of refutation than the other, Socrates.

Soc. Say rather, Polus, impossible; for who can refute the truth?

What nonsense! Do you mean that the man who expires among tortures is happier than the successful tyrant?

Pol. What do you mean? If a man is detected in an unjust attempt to make himself a tyrant, and when detected is racked, mutilated, has his eyes burned out, and after having had all sorts of great injuries inflicted on him, and having seen his wife and children suffer the like, is at last impaled or tarred and burned alive, will he be happier than if he escape and become a tyrant, and continue all through life doing what he likes and holding the reins of government, the envy and admiration both of citizens and strangers? Is that the paradox which, as you say, cannot be refuted?

Soc. There again, noble Polus, you are raising hobgoblins instead of refuting me; just now you were calling witnesses against me. But please to refresh my memory a little; did you say—'in an unjust attempt to make himself a tyrant'?

Pol. Yes, I did.

Neither is to be called happy if both are wicked.

Soc. Then I say that neither of them will be happier than the other,—neither he who unjustly acquires a tyranny, nor he who suffers in the attempt, for of two miserables one cannot be the happier, but that he who escapes and becomes a tyrant is the more miserable of the two. Do you laugh, Polus? Well, this is a new kind of refutation,—when any one says anything, instead of refuting him to laugh at him.

Why refute what nobody believes? Ask the company.

Pol. But do you not think, Socrates, that you have been sufficiently refuted, when you say that which no human being will allow? Ask the company.

Soc. O Polus, I am not a public man, and only last year, when my tribe were serving as Prytanes, and it became my duty as their president to take the votes, there was a laugh at me, because I was unable to take them. And as I failed then, you must not ask me to count the suffrages of the company now; but if, as I was saying, you have no better argument than numbers, let me have a turn, and do you make trial of the sort of proof which, as I think, is required; for I shall produce one witness only of the truth of my words, and he is the person with whom I am arguing; his suffrage I know how to take; but with the many I have nothing to do, and do not even address myself to them. May I ask then whether you will answer in turn and have your words put to the proof? For I certainly think that I and you and every man do really believe, that to do is a greater evil than to suffer injustice: and not to be punished than to be punished.

Pol. And I should say neither I, nor any man: would you yourself, for example, suffer rather than do injustice?

Soc. Yes, and you, too; I or any man would.

Pol. Quite the reverse; neither you, nor I, nor any man.

Soc. But will you answer?

Pol. To be sure, I will; for I am curious to hear what you can have to say.

Soc. Tell me, then, and you will know, and let us suppose that I am beginning at the beginning: which of the two, Polus, in your opinion, is the worst?—to do injustice or to suffer?

Pol. I should say that suffering was worst.

Soc. And which is the greater disgrace?—Answer.

Pol. To do.

Soc. And the greater disgrace is the greater evil?

Pol. Certainly not.

Soc. I understand you to say, if I am not mistaken, that the honourable is not the same as the good, or the disgraceful as the evil?

Pol. Certainly not.

Soc. Let me ask a question of you: When you speak of beautiful things, such as bodies, colours, figures, sounds, institutions, do you not call them beautiful in reference to some standard: bodies, for example, are beautiful in proportion as they are useful, or as the sight of them gives pleasure to the spectators; can you give any other account of personal beauty?

Pol. I cannot.

Soc. And you would say of figures or colours generally that they were beautiful, either by reason of the pleasure which they give, or of their use, or of both?

Pol. Yes, I should.

Soc. And you would call sounds and music beautiful for the same reason?

Pol. I should.

Soc. Laws and institutions also have no beauty in them except in so far as they are useful or pleasant or both?

Pol. I think not.

Soc. And may not the same be said of the beauty of knowledge?

Pol. To be sure, Socrates; and I very much approve of your measuring beauty by the standard of pleasure and utility.

All things may be measured by the standard of pleasure and utility or of pain and evil.

Soc. And deformity or disgrace may be equally measured by the opposite standard of pain and evil?

Pol. Certainly.

Soc. Then when of two beautiful things one exceeds in beauty, the measure of the excess is to be taken in one or both of these; that is to say, in pleasure or utility or both?

Pol. Very true.

Soc. And of two deformed things, that which exceeds in deformity or disgrace, exceeds either in pain or evil—must it not be so?

Pol. Yes.

Soc. But then again, what was the observation which you just now made, about doing and suffering wrong? Did you not say, that suffering wrong was more evil, and doing wrong more disgraceful?

Pol. I did.

If to do is, as Polus admits, more disgraceful than to endure wrong, it must also be more evil.

Soc. Then, if doing wrong is more disgraceful than suffering, the more disgraceful must be more painful and must exceed in pain or in evil or both: does not that also follow?

Pol. Of course.

Soc. First, then, let us consider whether the doing of injustice exceeds the suffering in the consequent pain: Do the injurers suffer more than the injured?

Pol. No, Socrates; certainly not.

Soc. Then they do not exceed in pain?

Pol. No.

Soc. But if not in pain, then not in both?

Pol. Certainly not.

Soc. Then they can only exceed in the other?

Pol. Yes.

Soc. That is to say, in evil?

Pol. True.

Soc. Then doing injustice will have an excess of evil, and will therefore be a greater evil than suffering injustice?

Pol. Clearly.

Soc. But have not you and the world already agreed that to do injustice is more disgraceful than to suffer?

Pol. Yes.

Soc. And that is now discovered to be more evil?

Pol. True.

Soc. And would you prefer a greater evil or a greater dishonour to a less one? Answer, Polus, and fear not; for you will come to no harm if you nobly resign yourself into the healing hand of the argument as to a physician without shrinking, and either say 'Yes' or 'No' to me.

Pol. I should say 'No.'

Soc. Would any other man prefer a greater to a less evil?

Pol. No, not according to this way of putting the case, Socrates.

Soc. Then I said truly, Polus, that neither you, nor I, nor any man, would rather, do than suffer injustice; for to do injustice is the greater evil of the two.

Pol. That is the conclusion.

Soc. You see, Polus, when you compare the two kinds of refutations, how unlike they are. All men, with the exception of myself, are of your way of thinking; but your single assent and witness are enough for me,—I have no need of any other, I take your suffrage, and am regardless of the rest. Enough of this, and now let us proceed to the next question; which is, Whether the greatest of evils to a guilty man is to suffer punishment, as you supposed, or whether to escape punishment is not a greater evil, as I supposed. Consider:—You would say that to suffer punishment is another name for being justly corrected when you do wrong?

The next
question:
Is it bet-
ter for the
guilty to
suffer or
not to
suffer
punish-
ment?

Pol. I should.

Soc. And would you not allow that all just things are honourable in so far as they are just? Please to reflect, and tell me your opinion.

Pol. Yes, Socrates, I think that they are.

Soc. Consider again:—Where there is an agent, must there not also be a patient?

Pol. I should say so.

Soc. And will not the patient suffer that which the agent does, and will not the suffering have the quality of the action? I mean, for example, that if a man strikes, there must be something which is stricken?

Pol. Yes.

Soc. And if the striker strikes violently or quickly, that which is struck will be struck violently or quickly?

Pol. True.

Soc. And the suffering to him who is stricken is of the same nature as the act of him who strikes?

Pol. Yes.

Soc. And if a man burns. there is something which is burned?

Gorgias

Socrates,
Polus.

Pol. Certainly.

Soc. And if he burns in excess or so as to cause pain, the thing burned will be burned in the same way?

Pol. Truly.

Soc. And if he cuts, the same argument holds—there will be something cut?

Pol. Yes.

Soc. And if the cutting be great or deep or such as will cause pain, the cut will be of the same nature?

Pol. That is evident.

Soc. Then you would agree generally to the universal proposition which I was just now asserting: that the affection of the patient answers to the act of the agent?

Pol. I agree.

Soc. Then, as this is admitted, let me ask whether being punished is suffering or acting?

Pol. Suffering, Socrates; there can be no doubt of that.

Soc. And suffering implies an agent?

Pol. Certainly, Socrates; and he is the punisher.

Soc. And he who punishes rightly, punishes justly?

Pol. Yes.

Soc. And therefore he acts justly?

Pol. Justly.

Soc. Then he who is punished and suffers retribution, suffers justly?

Pol. That is evident.

Soc. And that which is just has been admitted to be honourable?

Pol. Certainly.

Soc. Then the punisher does what is honourable, and the punished suffers what is honourable?

Pol. True.

Soc. And if what is honourable, then what is good, for the honourable is either pleasant or useful?

Pol. Certainly.

Soc. Then he who is punished suffers what is good?

Pol. That is true.

Soc. Then he is benefited?

Pol. Yes.

Soc. Do I understand you to mean what I mean by the term 'benefited? I mean, that if he be justly punished his soul is improved.

Pol. Surely.

Soc. Then he who is punished is delivered from the evil of his soul?

Since the affection of the patient answers to the act of the agent, it follows that he who is punished justly suffers justly, and therefore honourably,

477

Pol. Yes.

Soc. And is he not then delivered from the greatest evil? Look at the matter in this way:—In respect of a man's estate, do you see any greater evil than poverty?

Pol. There is no greater evil.

Soc. Again, in a man's bodily frame, you would say that the evil is weakness and disease and deformity?

Pol. I should.

Soc. And do you not imagine that the soul likewise has some evil of her own?

Pol. Of course.

Soc. And this you would call injustice and ignorance and cowardice, and the like?

Pol. Certainly.

Soc. So then, in mind, body, and estate, which are three, you have pointed out three corresponding evils—injustice, disease, poverty?

Pol. True.

Soc. And which of the evils is the most disgraceful?—Is not the most disgraceful of them injustice, and in general the evil of the soul?

Pol. By far the most.

Soc. And if the most disgraceful, then also the worst?

Pol. What do you mean, Socrates?

Soc. I mean to say, that what is most disgraceful has been already admitted to be most painful or hurtful, or both.

Pol. Certainly.

Soc. And now injustice and all evil in the soul has been admitted by us to be most disgraceful?

Pol. It has been admitted.

Soc. And most disgraceful either because most painful and causing excessive pain, or most hurtful, or both?

Pol. Certainly.

Soc. And therefore to be unjust and intemperate, and cowardly and ignorant, is more painful than to be poor and sick?

Pol. Nay, Socrates; the painfulness does not appear to me to follow from your premises.

Soc. Then, if, as you would argue, not more painful, the evil of the soul is of all evils the most disgraceful; and the excess of disgrace must be caused by some preternatural greatness, or extraordinary hurtfulness of the evil.

Pol. Clearly.

Soc. And that which exceeds most in hurtfulness will be the greatest of evils?

Gorgias

SOCRATES,
POLUS.

soul is
more
painful
than that
of the
body.

478

Pol. Yes.

Soc. Then injustice and intemperance, and in general the depravity of the soul, are the greatest of evils!

Pol. That is evident.

Soc. Now, what art is there which delivers us from poverty? Does not the art of making money?

Pol. Yes.

Soc. And what art frees us from disease? Does not the art of medicine?

Pol. Very true.

Soc. And what from vice and injustice? If you are not able to answer at once, ask yourself whither we go with the sick, and to whom we take them.

Pol. To the physicians, Socrates.

Soc. And to whom do we go with the unjust and intemperate?

Pol. To the judges, you mean.

Soc.—Who are to punish them?

Pol. Yes.

Soc. And do not those who rightly punish others, punish them in accordance with a certain rule of justice?

Pol. Clearly.

Soc. Then the art of money-making frees a man from poverty; medicine from disease; and justice from intemperance and injustice?

Pol. That is evident.

Soc. Which, then, is the best of these three?

Pol. Will you enumerate them?

Soc. Money-making, medicine, and justice.

Pol. Justice, Socrates, far excels the two others.

Soc. And justice, if the best, gives the greatest pleasure or advantage or both?

Pol. Yes.

Soc. But is the being healed a pleasant thing, and are those who are being healed pleased?

Pol. I think not.

Soc. A useful thing, then?

Pol. Yes.

Punish-
ment is
the deliv-
erance
from evil,
and he
who is
punished,

Soc. Yes, because the patient is delivered from a great evil; and this is the advantage of enduring the pain—that you get well?

Pol. Certainly.

Soc. And would he be the happier man in his bodily condition, who is healed, or who never was out of health?

Pol. Clearly he who was never out of health.

Soc. Yes; for happiness surely does not consist in being delivered from evils, but in never having had them.

Pol. True.

Soc. And suppose the case of two persons who have some evil in their bodies, and that one of them is healed and delivered from evil, and another is not healed, but retains the evil—which of them is the most miserable?

Pol. Clearly he who is not healed.

Soc. And was not punishment said by us to be a deliverance from the greatest of evils, which is vice?

Pol. True.

Soc. And justice punishes us, and makes us more just, and is the medicine of our vice?

Pol. True

Soc. He, then, has the first place in the scale of happiness who has never had vice in his soul; for this has been shown to be the greatest of evils.

Pol. Clearly.

Soc. And he has the second place, who is delivered from vice?

Pol. True.

Soc. That is to say, he who receives admonition and rebuke and punishment?

Pol. Yes.

Soc. Then he lives worst, who, having been unjust, has no deliverance from injustice?

Pol. Certainly.

Soc. That is, he lives worst who commits the greatest crimes, and who, being the most unjust of men, succeeds in escaping rebuke or correction or punishment; and this, as you say, has been accomplished by Archelaus and other tyrants and rhetoricians and potentates [1]?

Pol. True.

Soc. May not their way of proceeding, my friend, be compared to the conduct of a person who is afflicted with the worst of diseases and yet contrives not to pay the penalty to the physician for his sins against his constitution, and will not be cured, because, like a child, he is afraid of the pain of being burned or cut:—Is not that a parallel case?

Pol. Yes, truly.

Soc. He would seem as if he did not know the nature of health and bodily vigour; and if we are right, Polus, in our previous conclusions, they are in a like case who strive to evade justice, which

[1] Cp. Rep. ix. 579, 580.

Gorgias

SOCRATES, POLUS.

like him who is healed, is happier than he who is not punished or not healed.

Happiest of all is he who is just; happy in the second degree he who is delivered from injustice by punishment, most deluded [479] and most unhappy of all he who lives on, enjoying the fruit of his crimes.

they see to be painful, but are blind to the advantage which ensues from it, not knowing how far more miserable a companion a diseased soul is than a diseased body; a soul, I say, which is corrupt and unrighteous and unholy. And hence they do all that they can to avoid punishment and to avoid being released from the greatest of evils; they provide themselves with money and friends, and cultivate to the utmost their powers of persuasion. But if we, Polus, are right, do you see what follows, or shall we draw out the consequences in form?

Pol. If you please.

Soc. Is it not a fact that injustice, and the doing of injustice, is the greatest of evils?

Pol. That is quite clear.

Soc. And further, that to suffer punishment is the way to be released from this evil?

Pol. True.

Soc. And not to suffer, is to perpetuate the evil?

Pol. Yes.

Soc. To do wrong, then, is second only in the scale of evils; but to do wrong and not to be punished, is first and greatest of all?

Pol. That is true.

Soc. Well, and was not this the point in dispute, my friend? You deemed Archelaus happy, because he was a very great criminal and unpunished: I, on the other hand, maintained that he or any other who like him has done wrong and has not been punished, is, and ought to be, the most miserable of all men; and that the doer of injustice is more miserable than the sufferer; and he who escapes punishment, more miserable than he who suffers.—Was not that what I said?

Pol. Yes.

Soc. And it has been proved to be true?

Pol. Certainly.

Soc. Well, Polus, but if this is true, where is the great use of rhetoric? If we admit what has been just now said, every man ought in every way to guard himself against doing wrong, for he will thereby suffer great evil?

Pol. True.

Injustice,
if not removed,
will become the
cancer of
the soul.

Soc. And if he, or any one about whom he cares, does wrong, he ought of his own accord to go where he will be immediately punished; he will run to the judge, as he would to the physician, in order that the disease of injustice may not be rendered chronic and become the incurable cancer of the soul; must we not allow this consequence, Polus, if our former admissions are to stand:—is any other inference consistent with them?

Pol. To that, Socrates, there can be but one answer.

Soc. Then rhetoric is of no use to us, Polus, in helping a man to excuse his own injustice, or that of his parents or friends, or children or country; but may be of use to any one who holds that instead of excusing he ought to accuse—himself above all, and in the next degree his family or any of his friends who may be doing wrong; he should bring to light the iniquity and not conceal it, that so the wrong-doer may suffer and be made whole; and he should even force himself and others not to shrink, but with closed eyes like brave men to let the physician operate with knife or searing iron, not regarding the pain, in the hope of attaining the good and the honourable; let him who has done things worthy of stripes, allow himself to be scourged, if of bonds, to be bound, if of a fine, to be fined, if of exile, to be exiled, if of death, to die, himself being the first to accuse himself and his own relations, and using rhetoric to this end, that his and their unjust actions may be made manifest, and that they themselves may be delivered from injustice, which is the greatest evil. Then, Polus, rhetoric would indeed be useful. Do you say 'Yes' or 'No' to that?

Pol. To me, Socrates, what you are saying appears very strange, though probably in agreement with your premises.

Soc. Is not this the conclusion, if the premises are not disproven?

Pol. Yes; it certainly is.

Soc. And from the opposite point of view, if indeed it be our duty to harm another, whether an enemy or not—I except the case of self-defence —then I have to be upon my guard—but if my enemy injures a third person, then in every sort of way, by word as well as deed, I should try to prevent his being punished, or appearing before the judge; and if he appears, I should contrive that he should escape, and not suffer punishment: if he has stolen a sum of money, let him keep what he has stolen and spend it on him and his, regardless of religion and justice; and if he have done things worthy of death, let him not die, but rather be immortal in his wickedness; or, if this is not possible, let him at any rate be allowed to live as long as he can. For such purposes, Polus, rhetoric may be useful, but is of small if of any use to him who is not intending to commit injustice; at least, there was no such use discovered by us in the previous discussion.

Cal. Tell me, Chaerephon, is Socrates in earnest, or is he joking?

Chaer. I should say, Callicles, that he is in most profound earnest; but you may as well ask him.

Gorgias

Socrates,
Cal-
licles,
Chaere-
phon,
Polus.

The only use of rhetoric is that it enables a man to expose his own injustice and to petition for speedy punishment.

A slighter and secondary [481] use of rhetoric in self-defence against an enemy, or in preventing the punishment of an enemy.

Callicles
asks in
amaze-
ment
whether
Socrates
really
means
what he
says.
I am only
repeating
the words
of phil-
osophy,
whose
lover I
am. For
as you
love the
Athenian
people,
and their
namesake
[482]
Demus, so
I have
two loves,
philoso-
phy and
Alcibi-
ades.

The son
of Clei-
nias is
incon-
stant, but
philoso-
phy is
ever the
same: she
it is
whom
you have
to refute:
I am only
her
mouth-
piece.

Cal. By the gods, and I will. Tell me, Socrates, are you in earnest, or only in jest? For if you are in earnest, and what you say is true, is not the whole of human life turned upside down; and are we not doing, as would appear, in everything the opposite of what we ought to be doing?

Soc. O Callicles, if there were not some community of feelings among mankind, however varying in different persons—I mean to say, if every man's feelings were peculiar to himself and were not shared by the rest of his species—I do not see how we could ever communicate our impressions to one another. I make this remark because I perceive that you and I have a common feeling. For we are lovers both, and both of us have two loves apiece:—I am the lover of Alcibiades, the son of Cleinias, and of philosophy; and you of the Athenian Demus, and of Demus the son of Pyrilampes. Now, I observe that you, with all your cleverness, do not venture to contradict your favourite in any word or opinion of his; but as he changes you change, backwards and forwards. When the Athenian Demus denies anything that you are saying in the assembly, you go over to his opinion; and you do the same with Demus, the fair young son of Pyrilampes. For you have not the power to resist the words and ideas of your loves; and if a person were to express surprise at the strangeness of what you say from time to time when under their influence, you would probably reply to him, if you were honest, that you cannot help saying what your loves say unless they are prevented; and that you can only be silent when they are. Now you must understand that my words are an echo too, and therefore you need not wonder at me; but if you want to silence me, silence philosophy, who is my love, for she is always telling me what I am now telling you, my friend; neither is she capricious like my other love, for the son of Cleinias says one thing to-day and another thing to-morrow, but philosophy is always true. She is the teacher at whose words you are now wondering, and you have heard her yourself. Her you must refute, and either show, as I was saying, that to do injustice and to escape punishment is not the worst of all evils; or, if you leave her word unrefuted, by the dog the god of Egypt, I declare, O Callicles, that Callicles will never be at one with himself, but that his whole life will be a discord. And yet, my friend, I would rather that my lyre should be inharmonious, and that there should be no music in the chorus which I provided; aye, or that the whole world should be at odds with me, and oppose me, rather than that I myself should be at odds with myself, and contradict myself.

Cal. O Socrates, you are a regular declaimer, and seem to be running riot in the argument. And now you are declaiming in this way because Polus has fallen into the same error himself of which he accused Gorgias:—for he said that when Gorgias was asked by you, whether, if some one came to him who wanted to learn rhetoric, and did not know justice, he would teach him justice, Gorgias in his modesty replied that he would, because he thought that mankind in general would be displeased if he answered 'No;' and then in consequence of this admission, Gorgias was compelled to contradict himself, that being just the sort of thing in which you delight. Whereupon Polus laughed at you deservedly, as I think; but now he has himself fallen into the same trap. I cannot say very much for his wit when he conceded to you that to do is more dishonourable than to suffer injustice, for this was the admission which led to his being entangled by you; and because he was too modest to say what he thought, he had his mouth stopped. For the truth is, Socrates, that you, who pretend to be engaged in the pursuit of truth, are appealing now to the popular and vulgar notions of right, which are not natural, but only conventional. Convention and nature are generally at variance with one another: and hence, if a person is too modest to say what he thinks, he is compelled to contradict himself; and you, in your ingenuity perceiving the advantage to be thereby gained, slyly ask of him who is arguing conventionally a question which is to be determined by the rule of nature; and if he is talking of the rule of nature, you slip away to custom: as, for instance, you did in this very discussion about doing and suffering injustice. When Polus was speaking of the conventionally dishonourable, you assailed him from the point of view of nature; for by the rule of nature, to suffer injustice is the greater disgrace because the greater evil; but conventionally, to do evil is the more disgraceful. For the suffering of injustice is not the part of a man, but of a slave, who indeed had better die than live; since when he is wronged and trampled upon, he is unable to help himself, or any other about whom he cares. The reason, as I conceive, is that the makers of laws are the majority who are weak; and they make laws and distribute praises and censures with a view to themselves and to their own interests; and they terrify the stronger sort of men, and those who are able to get the better of them, in order that they may not get the better of them; and they say, that dishonesty is shameful and unjust; meaning, by the word injustice, the desire of a man to have more than his neighbours; for knowing their own inferiority, I suspect that they are too glad of equality. And therefore the endeavour to have more than the many, is conventionally said to be shameful and unjust, and is called injustice [1], whereas

Polus was vanquished because he refused to take a bold line.

Callicles would return to [483] the rule of nature in the lower sense of the term.

Convention was only introduced by the weak majority in order to protect themselves against the few strong.

[1] Cp. Rep. ii. 359

Gorgias

CAL-
LICLES.

nature herself intimates that it is just for the better to have more than the worse, the more powerful than the weaker; and in many ways she shows, among men as well as among animals, and indeed among whole cities and races, that justice consists in the superior ruling over and having more than the inferior. For on what principle of justice did Xerxes invade Hellas, or his father the Scythians? (not to speak of numberless other examples). Nay, but these are the men who act according to nature; yes, by Heaven, and according to the law of nature: not, perhaps, according to that artificial law, which we invent and impose upon our fellows, of whom we take the best and strongest from their youth upwards, and tame

484

A man of courage would easily break down the guards of convention.

them like young lions,—charming them with the sound of the voice, and saying to them, that with equality they must be content, and that the equal is the honourable and the just. But if there were a man who had sufficient force, he would shake off and break through, and escape from all this; he would trample under foot all our formulas and spells and charms, and all our laws which are against nature: the slave would rise in rebellion and be lord over us, and the light of natural justice would shine forth. And this I take to be the sentiment of Pindar, when he says in his poem, that

'Law is the king of all, of mortals as well as of immortals;'

this, as he says,

Pindar.

'Makes might to be right, doing violence with highest hand; as I infer from the deeds of Heracles, for without buying them—' [1]

A little philosophy not a bad thing in youth.

—I do not remember the exact words, but the meaning is, that without buying them, and without their being given to him, he carried off the oxen of Geryon, according to the law of natural right, and that the oxen and other possessions of the weaker and inferior properly belong to the stronger and superior. And this is true, as you may ascertain, if you will leave philosophy and go on to higher things: for philosophy, Socrates, if pursued in moderation and at the proper age, is an elegant accomplishment, but too much philosophy is the ruin of human life. Even if a man has good parts, still, if he carries philosophy into later life, he is necessarily ignorant of all those things which a gentleman and a person of honour ought to know; he is inexperienced in the laws of the State, and in the language which ought to be used in the dealings of man with man, whether private or public, and utterly ignorant of the pleasures and desires of mankind and of human character in general. And people of this sort, when they betake themselves to

[1] Fragm. Incert. 151 (Böckh).

politics or business, are as ridiculous as I imagine the politicians to be, when they make their appearance in the arena of philosophy. For, as Euripides says,

Gorgias

CAL-
LICLES.

'Every man shines in that and pursues that, and devotes the greatest portion of the day to that in which he most excels [1],'

Euripides.

but anything in which he is inferior, he avoids and depreciates, and praises the opposite from partiality to himself, and because he thinks that he will thus praise himself. The true principle is to unite them. Philosophy, as a part of education, is an excellent thing, and there is no disgrace to a man while he is young in pursuing such a study; but when he is more advanced in years, the thing becomes ridiculous, and I feel towards philosophers as I do towards those who lisp and imitate children. For I love to see a little child, who is not of an age to speak plainly, lisping at his play; there is an appearance of grace and freedom in his utterance, which is natural to his childish years. But when I hear some small creature carefully articulating its words, I am offended; the sound is disagreeable, and has to my ears the twang of slavery. So when I hear a man lisping, or see him playing like a chlid, his behaviour appears to me ridiculous and unmanly and worthy of stripes. And I have the same feeling about students of philosophy; when I see a youth thus engaged, —the study appears to me to be in character, and becoming a man of liberal education, and him who neglects philosophy I regard as an inferior man, who will never aspire to anything great or noble. But if I see him continuing the study in later life, and not leaving off, I should like to beat him, Socrates; for, as I was saying, such a one, even though he have good natural parts, becomes effeminate. He flies from the busy centre and the market-place, in which, as the poet says, men become distinguished; he creeps into a corner for the rest of his life, and talks in a whisper with three or four admiring youths, but never speaks out like a freeman in a satisfactory manner. Now I, Socrates, am very well inclined towards you, and my feeling may be compared with that of Zethus towards Amphion, in the play of Euripides, whom I was mentioning just now: for I am disposed to say to you much what Zethus said to his brother, that you, Socrates, are careless about the things of which you ought to be careful; and that you

485

But the study should not be continued into later life.

'Who have a soul so noble, are remarkable for a puerile exterior;
Neither in a court of justice could you state a case, or give any reason or proof,
Or offer valiant counsel on another's behalf.'

486

[1] Antiope, fragm. 20 (Dindorf).

And you must not be offended, my dear Socrates, for I am speaking out of good-will towards you, if I ask whether you are not ashamed of being thus defenceless; which I affirm to be the condition not of you only but of all those who will carry the study of philosophy too far. For suppose that some one were to take you, or any one of your sort, off to prison, declaring that you had done wrong when you had done no wrong, you must allow that you would not know what to do:—there you would stand giddy and gaping, and not having a word to say; and when you went up before the Court, even if the accuser were a poor creature and not good for much, you would die if he were disposed to claim the penalty of death. And yet, Socrates, what is the value of

'An art which converts a man of sense into a fool,'

who is helpless, and has no power to save either himself or others, when he is in the greatest danger and is going to be despoiled by his enemies of all his goods, and has to live, simply deprived of his rights of citizenship?—he being a man who, if I may use the expression, may be boxed on the ears with impunity. Then, my good friend, take my advice, and refute no more:

'Learn the philosophy of business, and acquire the reputation of wisdom. But leave to others these niceties,'

whether they are to be described as follies or absurdities:

'For they will only Give you poverty for the inmate of your dwelling.'

Cease, then, emulating these paltry splitters of words, and emulate only the man of substance and honour, who is well to do.

Callicles
the de-
sired
touch-
stone of
Socrates.

Soc. If my soul, Callicles, were made of gold, should I not rejoice to discover one of those stones with which they test gold, and the very best possible one to which I might bring my soul; and if the stone and I agreed in approving of her training, then I should know that I was in a satisfactory state, and that no other test was needed by me.

Cal. What is your meaning, Socrates?

Soc. I will tell you; I think that I have found in you the desired touchstone.

Cal. Why?

Soc. Because I am sure that if you agree with me in any of the opinions which my soul forms, I have at last found the truth indeed. For I consider that if a man is to make a complete trial of the good or evil of the soul, he ought to have three qualities— knowledge, good-will, outspokenness, which are all possessed by you. Many whom I meet are unable to make trial of me, because they are not wise as you are; others are wise, but they will not tell me the truth, because they have not the same interest in me which you have; and these two strangers, Gorgias and Polus, are undoubtedly wise men and my very good friends, but they are not outspoken enough, and they are too modest. Why, their modesty is so great that they are driven to contradict themselves, first one and then the other of them, in the face of a large company, on matters of the highest moment. But you have all the qualities in which these others are deficient, having received an excellent education; to this many Athenians can testify. And you are my friend. Shall I tell you why I think so? I know that you, Callicles, and Tisander of Aphidnae, and Andron the son of Androtion, and Nauoicydes of the deme of Cholarges, studied together: there were four of you, and I once heard you advising with one another as to the extent to which the pursuit of philosophy should be carried, and, as I know, you came to the conclusion that the study should not be pushed too much into detail. You were cautioning one another not to be overwise; you were afraid that too much wisdom might unconsciously to yourselves be the ruin of you. And now when I hear you giving the same advice to me which you then gave to your most intimate friends, I have a sufficient evidence of your real good-will to me. And of the frankness of your nature and freedom from modesty I am assured by yourself, and the assurance is confirmed by your last speech. Well then, the inference in the present case clearly is, that if you agree with me in an argument about any point, that point will have been sufficiently tested by us, and will not require to be submitted to any further test. For you could not have agreed with me, either from lack of knowledge or from superfluity of modesty, nor yet from a desire to deceive me, for you are my friend, as you tell me yourself. And therefore when you and I are agreed, the result will be the attainment of perfect truth. Now there is no nobler enquiry, Callicles, than that which you censure me for making,—What ought the character of a man to be, and what his pursuits, and how far is he to go, both in maturer years and in youth? For be assured that if I err in my own conduct I do not err intentionally, but from ignorance. Do not then desist from advising me, now that you have begun, until I have learned clearly what this is which I am to practise, and how I may acquire it. And if you find me assenting to your words, and hereafter not doing that to which I assented, call me 'dolt,' and deem me unworthy of receiving further instruction. Once more, then, tell me what you and Pindar mean by natural justice: Do

Gorgias

SOCRATES.

Other men have not the knowledge or frankness or goodwill which is required; and they are too modest. His sincerity is shown by his consistency.

488

Gorgias

SOCRATES,
CAL-
LICLES.

you not mean that the superior should take the property of the inferior by force; that the better should rule the worse, the noble have more than the mean? Am I not right in my recollection?

Cal. Yes; that is what I was saying, and so I still aver.

But still
he would
ask, What
Callicles
means
by the
superior?

Soc. And do you mean by the better the same as the superior? for I could not make out what you were saying at the time—whether you meant by the superior the stronger, and that the weaker must obey the stronger, as you seemed to imply when you said that great cities attack small ones in accordance with natural right, because they are superior and stronger, as though the superior and stronger and better were the same; or whether the better may be also the inferior and weaker, and the superior the worse, or whether better is to be defined in the same way as superior: this is the point which I want to have cleared up. Are the superior and better and stronger the same or different?

Cal. I say unequivocally that they are the same.

He means
the better
and
stronger,
and there-
fore the
many
who
make the
laws,
which are
noble be-
cause they
are made
by the
better.

[489]
And the
many are
also of
opinion
that to do
is more
disgrace-
ful than
to suffer
injustice.

Soc. Then the many are by nature superior to the one, against whom, as you were saying, they make the laws?

Cal. Certainly.

Soc. Then the laws of the many are the laws of the superior?

Cal. Very true.

Soc. Then they are the laws of the better; for the superior class are far better, as you were saying?

Cal. Yes.

Soc. And since they are superior, the laws which are made by them are by nature good?

Cal. Yes.

Soc. And are not the many of opinion, as you were lately saying, that justice is equality, and that to do is more disgraceful than to suffer injustice?—is that so or not? Answer, Callicles, and let no modesty be found to come in the way[1]; do the many think, or do they not think thus?—I must beg of you to answer, in order that if you agree with me I may fortify myself by the assent of so competent an authority.

Cal. Yes; the opinion of the many is what you say.

Soc. Then not only custom but nature also affirms that to do is more disgraceful than to suffer injustice, and that justice is equality; so that you seem to have been wrong in your former assertion, when accusing me you said that nature and custom are opposed, and that I, knowing this, was dishonestly playing between them, appealing to custom when the argument is about nature, and to nature when the argument is about custom?

[1] Cp. what is said of Gorgias by Callicles at p. 482.

Cal. This man will never cease talking nonsense. At your age, Socrates, are you not ashamed to be catching at words and chuckling over some verbal slip? do you not see—have I not told you already, that by superior I mean better: do you imagine me to say, that if a rabble of slaves and nondescripts, who are of no use except perhaps for their physical strength, get together, their ipsissima verba are laws?

Soc. Ho! my philosopher, is that your line?

Cal. Certainly.

Soc. I was thinking, Callicles, that something of the kind must have been in your mind, and that is why I repeated the question, —What is the superior? I wanted to know clearly what you meant; for you surely do not think that two men are better than one, or that your slaves are better than you because they are stronger? Then please to begin again, and tell me who the better are, if they are not the stronger; and I will ask you, great Sir, to be a little milder in your instructions, or I shall have to run away from you.

Cal. You are ironical.

Soc. No, by the hero Zethus, Callicles, by whose aid you were just now saying (486 A) many ironical things against me, I am not:—tell me, then, whom you mean by the better?

Cal. I mean the more excellent.

Soc. Do you not see that you are yourself using words which have no meaning and that you are explaining nothing?—will you tell me whether you mean by the better and superior the wiser, or if not, whom?

Cal. Most assuredly, I do mean the wiser.

Soc. Then according to you, one wise man may often be superior to ten thousand fools, and he ought to rule them, and they ought to be his subjects, and he ought to have more than they should. This is what I believe that you mean (and you must not suppose that I am word-catching), if you allow that the one is superior to the ten thousand?

Cal. Yes; that is what I mean, and that is what I conceive to be natural justice—that the better and wiser should rule and have more than the inferior.

Soc. Stop there, and let me ask you what you would say in this case: Let us suppose that we are all together as we are now; there are several of us, and we have a large common store of meats and drinks, and there are all sorts of persons in our company having various degrees of strength and weakness, and one of us, being physician, is wiser in the matter of food than all the rest, and he is probably stronger than some and not so strong as others of us—

Gorgias

SOCRATES,
CAL-
LICLES.

'Of course
I don't
mean the
mob.'

Then
once
more,—
Who are
the bet-
ter?

490
The wis-
er: the
one wise
among
ten thou-
sand
fools,—he
ought to
rule.

But this is
contrary
to the
analogy
of the
other
arts.

will he not, being wiser, be also better than we are, and our superior in this matter of food?

Cal. Certainly.

Soc. Either, then, he will have a larger share of the meats and drinks, because he is better, or he will have the distribution of all of them by reason of his authority, but he will not expend or make use of a larger share of them on his own person, or if he does, he will be punished;—his share will exceed that of some, and be less than that of others, and if he be the weakest of all, he being the best of all will have the smallest share of all, Callicles:—am I not right, my friend?

Callicles
is disgust-
ed at the
common-
place par-
allels of
Socrates.

Cal. You talk about meats and drinks and physicians and other nonsense; I am not speaking of them.

Soc. Well, but do you admit that the wiser is the better? Answer 'Yes' or 'No.'

Cal. Yes.

Soc. And ought not the better to have a larger share?

Cal. Not of meats and drinks.

Soc. I understand: then, perhaps, of coats—the skilfullest weaver ought to have the largest coat, and the greatest number of them, and go about clothed in the best and finest of them?

Cal. Fudge about coats!

Soc. Then the skilfullest and best in making shoes ought to have the advantage in shoes; the shoemaker, clearly, should walk about in the largest shoes, and have the greatest number of them?

Cal. Fudge about shoes! What nonsense are you talking?

Soc. Or, if this is not your meaning, perhaps you would say that the wise and good and true husbandman should actually have a larger share of seeds, and have as much seed as possible for his own land?

Cal. How you go on, always talking in the same way, Socrates!

Soc. Yes, Callicles, and also about the same things.

Cal. Yes, by the Gods, you are literally always talking of cobblers and fullers and cooks and doctors, as if this had to do with our argument.

Soc. But why will you not tell me in what a man must be superior and wiser in order to claim a larger share; will you neither accept a suggestion, nor offer one?

Cal. I have already told you. In the first place, I mean by superiors not cobblers or cooks, but wise politicians who understand the administration of a state, and who are not only wise, but also valiant and able to carry out their designs, and not the men to faint from want of soul.

Soc. See now, most excellent Callicles, how different my charge against you is from that which you bring against me, for you reproach me with always saying the same; but I reproach you with never saying the same about the same things, for at one time you were defining the better and the superior to be the stronger, then again as the wiser, and now you bring forward a new notion; the superior and the better are now declared by you to be the more courageous: I wish, my good friend, that you would tell me, once for all, whom you affirm to be the better and superior, and in what they are better?

Cal. I have already told you that I mean those who are wise and courageous in the administration of a state—they ought to be the rulers of their states, and justice consists in their having more than their subjects.

Soc. But whether rulers or subjects will they or will they not have more than themselves, my friend?

Cal. What do you mean?

Soc. I mean that every man is his own ruler; but perhaps you think that there is no necessity for him to rule himself; he is only required to rule others?

Cal. What do you mean by his 'ruling over himself'?

Soc. A simple thing enough; just what is commonly said, that a man should be temperate and master of himself, and ruler of his own pleasures and passions.

Cal. What innocence! you mean those fools,—the temperate?

Soc. Certainly:—any one may know that to be my meaning.

Cal. Quite so, Socrates; and they are really fools, for how can a man be happy who is the servant of anything? On the contrary, I plainly assert, that he who would truly live ought to allow his desires to wax to the uttermost, and not to chastise them; but when they have grown to their greatest he should have courage and intelligence to minister to them and to satisfy all his longings. And this I affirm to be natural justice and nobility. To this however the many cannot attain; and they blame the strong man because they are ashamed of their own weakness, which they desire to conceal, and hence they say that intemperance is base. As I have remarked already, they enslave the nobler natures, and being unable to satisfy their pleasures, they praise temperance and justice out of their own cowardice. For if a man had been originally the son of a king, or had a nature capable of acquiring an empire or a tyranny or sovereignty, what could be more truly base or evil than temperance—to a man like him, I say, who might freely be enjoying every good, and has no one to stand in his way, and yet has ad-

Gorgias

SOCRATES, CALLICLES.

Socrates is accused of always saying the same things: he accuses Callicles of never saying the same about the same.

Callicles reasserts his doctrine that the esteem in which [492] virtue and justice are held is due only to men's fear for themselves. No man who has the power to enjoy himself practices self-control.

Gorgias

SOCRATES,
CAL-
LICLES.

·mitted custom and reason and the opinion of other men to be lords over him?—must not he be in a miserable plight whom the reputation of justice and temperance hinders from giving more to his friends than to his enemies, even though he be a ruler in his city? Nay, Socrates, for you profess to be a votary of the truth, and the truth is this:—that luxury and intemperance and licence, if they be provided with means, are virtue and happiness—all the rest is a mere bauble, agreements contrary to nature, foolish talk of men, nothing worth[1].

Soc. There is a noble freedom, Callicles, in your way of approaching the argument; for what you say is what the rest of the world think, but do not like to say. And I must beg of you to persevere, that the true rule of human life may become manifest. Tell me, then:—you say, do you not, that in the rightly-developed man the passions ought not to be controlled, but that we should let them grow to the utmost and somehow or other satisfy them, and that this is virtue?

Cal. Yes; I do.

Soc. Then those who want nothing are not truly said to be happy?

To live
without
pleasure
or passion
is to be
dead.

Cal. No indeed, for then stones and dead men would be the happiest of all.

Soc. But surely life according to your view is an awful thing; and indeed I think that Euripides may have been right in saying,

'Who knows if life be not death and death life;'

493
No; the
true
death, as
Pythago-
rean phil-
osophy
tells us, is
to pour
water out
of a vessel
full of
holes into
a colander
full of
holes.

and that we are very likely dead; I have heard a philosopher say that at this moment we are actually dead, and that the body (σῶμα) is our tomb (σῆμα [2]), and that the part of the soul which is the seat of the desires is liable to be tossed about by words and blown up and down; and some ingenious person, probably a Sicilian or an Italian, playing with the word, invented a tale in which he called the soul—because of its believing and make-believe nature—a vessel [3], and the ignorant he called the uninitiated or leaky, and the place in the souls of the uninitiated in which desires are seated, being the intemperate and incontinent part, he compared to a vessel full of holes, because it can never be satisfied. He is not of your way of thinking, Callicles, for he declares. that of all the souls in Hades, meaning the invisible world (ἀειδὲς), these uninitiated or leaky persons are the most miserable, and that

---

[1] Cp. Rep. i. 348.
[2] Cp. Phaedr. 250 C.
[3] An untranslateable pun,—διὰ τὸ πιθανόν τε καὶ πιστικὸν ὠνόμασε πίθον.

they pour water into a vessel which is full of holes out of a colander which is similarly perforated. The colander, as my informer assures me, is the soul, and the soul which he compares to a colander is the soul of the ignorant, which is likewise full of holes, and therefore incontinent, owing to a bad memory and want of faith. These notions are strange enough, but they show the principle which, if I can, I would fain prove to you; that you should change your mind, and, instead of the intemperate and insatiate life, choose that which is orderly and sufficient and has a due provision for daily needs. Do I make any impression on you, and are you coming over to the opinion that the orderly are happier than the intemperate? Or do I fail to persuade you, and, however many tales I rehearse to you, do you continue of the same opinion still?

Cal. The latter, Socrates, is more like the truth.

Soc. Well, I will tell you another image, which comes out of the same school:—Let me request you to consider how far you would accept this as an account of the two lives of the temperate and intemperate in a figure:—There are two men, both of whom have a number of casks; the one man has his casks sound and full, one of wine, another of honey, and a third of milk, besides others filled with other liquids, and the streams which fill them are few and scanty, and he can only obtain them with a great deal of toil and difficulty; but when his casks are once filled he has no need to feed them any more, and has no further trouble with them or care about them. The other, in like manner, can procure streams, though not without difficulty; but his vessels are leaky and unsound, and night and day he is compelled to be filling them, and if he pauses for a moment, he is in an agony of pain. Such are their respective lives:—And now would you say that the life of the intemperate is happier than that of the temperate? Do I not convince you that the opposite is the truth?

Cal. You do not convince me, Socrates, for the one who has filled himself has no longer any pleasure left; and this, as I was just now saying, is the life of a stone: he has neither joy nor sorrow after he is once filled; but the pleasure depends on the superabundance of the influx.

Soc. But the more you pour in, the greater the waste; and the holes must be large for the liquid to escape.

Cal. Certainly.

Soc. The life which you are now depicting is not that of a dead man, or of a stone, but of a cormorant; you mean that he is to be hungering and eating?

Cal. Yes.

The temperate man is the sound, the intemperate the leaky vessel.

494

The life of desire and pleasure is not to be compared to a full vessel, but to an ever-running stream.

Soc. And he is to be thirsting and drinking?

Cal. Yes, that is what I mean; he is to have all his desires about him, and to be able to live happily in the gratification of them.

Soc. Capital, excellent; go on as you have begun, and have no shame; I, too, must disencumber myself of shame: and first, will you tell me whether you include itching and scratching, provided you have enough of them and pass your life in scratching, in your notion of happiness?

Cal. What a strange being you are, Socrates! a regular mob-orator.

Soc. That was the reason, Callicles, why I scared Polus and Gorgias, until they were too modest to say what they thought; but you will not be too modest and will not be scared, for you are a brave man. And now, answer my question.

Cal. I answer, that even the scratcher would live pleasantly.

Soc. And if pleasantly, then also happily?

Cal. To be sure.

Soc. But what if the itching is not confined to the head? Shall I pursue the question? And here, Callicles, I would have you consider how you would reply if consequences are pressed upon you, especially if in the last resort you are asked, whether the life of a catamite is not terrible, foul, miserable? Or would you venture to say, that they too are happy, if they only get enough of what they want?

Callicles
professes
a virtu-
ous indig-
nation at
the very
mention
of the
conse-
quences
of his
[495]
own doc-
trine.

Cal. Are you not ashamed, Socrates, of introducing such topics into the argument?

Soc. Well, my fine friend, but am I the introducer of these topics, or he who says without any qualification that all who feel pleasure in whatever manner are happy, and who admits of no distinction between good and bad pleasures? And I would still ask, whether you say that pleasure and good are the same, or whether there is some pleasure which is not a good?

Cal. Well, then, for the sake of consistency, I will say that they are the same.

Soc. You are breaking the original agreement, Callicles, and will no longer be a satisfactory companion in the search after truth, if you say what is contrary to your real opinion.

Cal. Why, that is what you are doing too, Socrates.

Soc. Then we are both doing wrong. Still, my dear friend, I would ask you to consider whether pleasure, from whatever source derived, is the good; for, if this be true, then the disagreeable consequences which have been darkly intimated must follow, and many others.

Cal. That, Socrates, is only your opinion.

Soc. And do you, Callicles, seriously maintain what you are saying?

Cal. Indeed I do.

Soc. Then, as you are in earnest, shall we proceed with the argument?

Cal. By all means[1].

Soc. Well, if you are willing to proceed, determine this question for me:—There is something, I presume, which you would call knowledge?

Cal. There is.

Soc. And were you not saying just now, that some courage implied knowledge?

Cal. I was.

Soc. And you were speaking of courage and knowledge as two things different from one another?

Cal. Certainly I was.

Soc. And would you say that pleasure and knowledge are the same, or not the same?

Cal. Not the same, O man of wisdom.

Soc. And would you say that courage differed from pleasure?

Cal. Certainly.

Soc. Well, then, let us remember that Callicles, the Acharnian, says that pleasure and good are the same; but that knowledge and courage are not the same, either with one another, or with the good.

Cal. And what does our friend Socrates, of Foxton, say—does he assent to this, or not?

Soc. He does not assent; neither will Callicles, when he sees himself truly. You will admit, I suppose, that good and evil fortune are opposed to each other?

Cal. Yes.

Soc. And if they are opposed to each other, then, like health and disease, they exclude one another; a man cannot have them both, or be without them both, at the same time?

Cal. What do you mean?

Soc. Take the case of any bodily affection:—a man may have the complaint in his eyes which is called ophthalmia?

Cal. To be sure.

Soc. But he surely cannot have the same eyes well and sound at the same time?

Cal. Certainly not.

____
[1] Or, 'I am in profound earnest.'

Callicles, having admitted that pleasure and good are the same, is led to make the further admission that pleasure and knowledge and courage are different.

496

Soc. And when he has got rid of his ophthalmia, has he got rid of the health of his eyes too? Is the final result, that he gets rid of them both together?

Cal. Certainly not.

Soc. That would surely be marvellous and absurd?

Cal. Very.

A man
may have
good and
evil by
turns, but
not at the
same
time.

Soc. I suppose that he is affected by them, and gets rid of them in turns?

Cal. Yes.

Soc. And he may have strength and weakness in the same way, by fits?

Cal. Yes.

Soc. Or swiftness and slowness?

Cal. Certainly.

Soc. And does he have and not have good and happiness, and their opposites, evil and misery, in a similar alternation[1]?

Cal. Certainly he has.

Soc. If then there be anything which a man has and has not at the same time, clearly that cannot be good and evil—do we agree? Please not to answer without consideration.

Cal. I entirely agree.

Soc. Go back now to our former admissions.—Did you say that to hunger, I mean the mere state of hunger, was pleasant or painful?

Cal. I said painful, but that to eat when you are hungry is pleasant.

Soc. I know; but still the actual hunger is painful: am I not right?

Cal. Yes.

Soc. And thirst, too, is painful?

Cal. Yes, very.

Soc. Need I adduce any more instances, or would you agree that all wants or desires are painful?

Cal. I agree, and therefore you need not adduce any more instances.

Soc. Very good. And you would admit that to drink, when you are thirsty, is pleasant?

Cal. Yes.

Soc. And in the sentence which you have just uttered, the word 'thirsty' implies pain?

Cal. Yes.

[1] Cp. Rep. iv. 436.

Soc. And the word 'drinking' is expressive of pleasure, and of the satisfaction of the want?

Cal. Yes.

Soc. There is pleasure in drinking?

Cal. Certainly.

Soc. When you are thirsty?

Cal. Yes.

Soc. And in pain?

Cal. Yes.

Soc. Do you see the inference:—that pleasure and pain are simultaneous, when you say that being thirsty, you drink? For are they not simultaneous, and do they not affect at the same time the same part, whether of the soul or the body?—which of them is affected cannot be supposed to be of any consequence: Is not this true?

Cal. It is.

Soc. You said also, that no man could have good and evil fortune at the same time?

Cal. Yes, I did.

Soc. But you admitted, that when in pain a man might also have pleasure?

Cal. Clearly.

Soc. Then pleasure is not the same as good fortune, or pain the same as evil fortune, and therefore the good is not the same as the pleasant?

Cal. I wish I knew, Socrates, what your quibbling means.

Soc. You know, Callicles, but you affect not to know.

Cal. Well, get on, and don't keep fooling: then you will know what a wiseacre you are in your admonition of me.

Soc. Does not a man cease from his thirst and from his pleasure in drinking at the same time?

Cal. I do not understand what you are saying.

Gor. Nay, Callicles, answer, if only for our sakes;—we should like to hear the argument out.

Cal. Yes, Gorgias, but I must complain of the habitual trifling of Socrates; he is always arguing about little and unworthy questions.

Gor. What matter? Your reputation, Callicles, is not at stake. Let Socrates argue in his own fashion.

Cal. Well, then, Socrates, you shall ask these little peddling questions, since Gorgias wishes to have them.

Soc. I envy you, Callicles, for having been initiated into the great mysteries before you were initiated into the lesser. I thought that this was not allowable. But to return to our argument:—Does

But he
may have
pleasure
and pain
at the
same
time.

497

Therefore
pleasure
and pain
are not
the same
as good
and evil.

not a man cease from thirsting and from the pleasure of drinking at the same moment?

Cal. True.

Soc. And if he is hungry, or has any other desire, does he not cease from the desire and the pleasure at the same moment?

Cal. Very true.

Soc. Then he ceases from pain and pleasure at the same moment?

Cal. Yes.

Soc. But he does not cease from good and evil at the same moment, as you have admitted: do you still adhere to what you said?

Cal. Yes, I do; but what is the inference?

Soc. Why, my friend, the inference is that the good is not the same as the pleasant, or the evil the same as the painful; there is a cessation of pleasure and pain at the same moment; but not of good and evil, for they are different. How then can pleasure be the same as good, or pain as evil? And I would have you look at the matter in another light, which could hardly, I think, have been considered by you when you identified them: Are not the good good because they have good present with them, as the beautiful are those who have beauty present with them?

Cal. Yes.

Soc. And do you call the fools and cowards good men? For you were saying just now that the courageous and the wise are the good —would you not say so?

Cal. Certainly.

Soc. And did you never see a foolish child rejoicing?

Cal. Yes, I have.

Soc. And a foolish man too?

Cal. Yes, certainly; but what is your drift?

Soc. Nothing particular, if you will only answer.

Cal. Yes, I have.

Soc. And did you ever see a sensible man rejoicing or sorrowing?

Cal. Yes.

Soc. Which rejoice and sorrow most—the wise or the foolish?

Cal. They are much upon a par, I think, in that respect.

Soc. Enough: And did you ever see a coward in battle?

Cal. To be sure.

Soc. And which rejoiced most at the departure of the enemy, the coward or the brave?

Cal. I should say 'most' of both; or at any rate, they rejoiced about equally.

Soc. No matter; then the cowards, and not only the brave, rejoice?

Another
point of
view.

498

Cal. Greatly.

Soc. And the foolish; so it would seem?

Cal. Yes.

Soc. And are only the cowards pained at the approach of their enemies, or are the brave also pained?

Cal. Both are pained.

Soc. And are they equally pained?

Cal. I should imagine that the cowards are more pained.

Soc. And are they not better pleased at the enemy's departure?

Cal. I dare say.

Soc. Then are the foolish and the wise and the cowards and the brave all pleased and pained, as you were saying, in nearly equal degree; but are the cowards more pleased and pained than the brave?

Cal. Yes.

Soc. But surely the wise and brave are the good, and the foolish and the cowardly are the bad?

Cal. Yes.

Soc. Then the good and the bad are pleased and pained in a nearly equal degree?

Cal. Yes.

Good is in proportion to pleasure, and the bad are often as much or more pleased than the good.

Soc. Then are the good and bad good and bad in a nearly equal degree, or have the bad the advantage both in good and evil? [i. e. in having more pleasure and more pain.]

Cal. I really do not know what you mean.

Soc. Why, do you not remember saying that the good were good because good was present with them, and the evil because evil; and that pleasures were goods and pains evils?

Cal. Yes, I remember.

Soc. And are not these pleasures or goods present to those who re-joice—if they do rejoice?

Cal. Certainly.

Soc. Then those who rejoice are good when goods are present with them?

Cal. Yes.

Soc. And those who are in pain have evil or sorrow present with them?

Cal. Yes.

Soc. And would you still say that the evil are evil by reason of the presence of evil?

Cal. I should.

Soc. Then those who rejoice are good, and those who are in pain evil?

Cal. Yes.

Soc. The degrees of good and evil vary with the degrees of pleasure and of pain?

Cal. Yes.

Soc. Have the wise man and the fool, the brave and the coward, joy and pain in nearly equal degrees? or would you say that the coward has more?

Cal. I should say that he has.

Soc. Help me then to draw out the conclusion which follows from 499 our admissions; for it is good to repeat and review what is good twice and thrice over, as they say. Both the wise man and the brave man we allow to be good?

Cal. Yes.

Soc. And the foolish man and the coward to be evil?

Cal. Certainly.

Soc. And he who has joy is good?

Cal. Yes.

Soc. And he who is in pain is evil?

Cal. Certainly.

Soc. The good and evil both have joy and pain, but, perhaps, the evil has more of them?

Cal. Yes.

Therefore the bad man is as good as the good, or perhaps even better. *Soc.* Then must we not infer, that the bad man is as good and bad as the good, or, perhaps, even better?—is not this a further inference which follows equally with the preceding from the assertion that the good and the pleasant are the same:—can this be denied, Callicles?

Cal. I have been listening and making admissions to you, Socrates; and I remark that if a person grants you anything in play, you, like a child, want to keep hold and will not give it back. But do you really suppose that I or any other human being denies that some pleasures are good and others bad?

Soc. Alas, Callicles, how unfair you are! you certainly treat me as if I were a child, sometimes saying one thing, and then another, as if you were meaning to deceive me. And yet I thought at first that you were my friend, and would not have deceived me if you Socrates begins again with some obvious truisms. could have helped. But I see that I was mistaken; and now I suppose that I must make the best of a bad business, as they said of old, and take what I can get out of you.—Well, then, as I understand you to say, I may assume that some pleasures are good and others evil?

Cal. Yes.

Soc. The beneficial are good, and the hurtful are evil?

Cal. To be sure.

Soc. And the beneficial are those which do some good, and the hurtful are those which do some evil?

Cal. Yes.

Soc. Take, for example, the bodily pleasures of eating and drinking, which we were just now mentioning—you mean to say that those which promote health, or any other bodily excellence, are good, and their opposites evil?

Cal. Certainly.

Soc. And in the same way there are good pains and there are evil pains?

Cal. To be sure.

Soc. And ought we not to choose and use the good pleasures and pains?

Cal. Certainly.

Soc. But not the evil?

Cal. Clearly.

Soc. Because, if you remember, Polus and I have agreed that all our actions are to be done for the sake of the good;—and will you agree with us in saying, that the good is the end of all our actions, and that all our actions are to be done for the sake of the good, and not the good for the sake of them?—will you add a third vote to our two?

Cal. I will.

Soc. Then pleasure, like everything else, is to be sought for the sake of that which is good, and not that which is good for the sake of pleasure?

Cal. To be sure.

Soc. But can every man choose what pleasures are good and what are evil, or must he have art or knowledge of them in detail?

Cal. He must have art.

Soc. Let me now remind you of what I was saying to Gorgias and Polus; I was saying, as you will not have forgotten, that there were some processes which aim only at pleasure, and know nothing of a better and worse, and there are other processes which know good and evil. And I considered that cookery, which I do not call an art, but only an experience, was of the former class, which is concerned with pleasure, and that the art of medicine was of the class which is concerned with the good. And now, by the god of friendship, I must beg you, Callicles, not to jest, or to imagine that I am jesting with you; do not answer at random and contrary to your real opinion; —for you will observe that we are arguing about the way of human life; and to a man who has any sense at all, what question can be

500

more serious than this?—whether he should follow after that way of life to which you exhort me, and act what you call the manly part of speaking in the assembly, and cultivating rhetoric, and engaging in public affairs, according to the principles now in vogue; or whether he should pursue the life of philosophy;—and in what the latter way differs from the former. But perhaps we had better first try to distinguish them, as I did before, and when we have come to an agreement that they are distinct, we may proceed to consider in what they differ from one another, and which of them we should choose. Perhaps, however, you do not even now understand what I mean?

Cal. No, I do not.

Soc. Then I will explain myself more clearly: seeing that you and I have agreed that there is such a thing as good, and that there is such a thing as pleasure, and that pleasure is not the same as good, and that the pursuit and process of acquisition of the one, that is pleasure, is different from the pursuit and process of acquisition of the other, which is good—I wish that you would tell me whether you agree with me thus far or not—do you agree?

Cal. I do.

Socrates
[501]
repeats
his dis-
tinction
between
true arts
and flat-
teries or
shams,

Soc. Then I will proceed, and ask whether you also agree with me, and whether you think that I spoke the truth when I further said to Gorgias and Polus that cookery in my opinion is only an experience, and not an art at all; and that whereas medicine is an art, and attends to the nature and constitution of the patient, and has principles of action and reason in each case, cookery in attending upon pleasure never regards either the nature or reason of that pleasure to which she devotes herself, but goes straight to her end, nor ever considers or calculates anything, but works by experience and routine, and just preserves the recollection of what she has usually done when producing pleasure. And first, I would have you consider whether I have proved what I was saying, and then whether there are not other similar processes which have to do with the soul—some of them processes of art, making a provision for the soul's highest interest—others despising the interest, and, as in the previous case, considering only the pleasure of the soul, and how this may be acquired, but not considering what pleasures are good or bad, and having no other aim but to afford gratification, whether good or bad. In my opinion, Callicles, there are such processes, and this is the sort of thing which I term flattery, whether concerned with the body or the soul, or whenever employed with a view to pleasure and without any consideration of good and evil. And now

I wish that you would tell me whether you agree with us in this notion, or whether you differ.

Cal. I do not differ; on the contrary, I agree; for in that way I shall soonest bring the argument to an end, and shall oblige my friend Gorgias.

Soc. And is this notion true of one soul, or of two or more?

Cal. Equally true of two or more.

Soc. Then a man may delight a whole assembly, and yet have no regard for their true interests?

Cal. Yes.

Soc. Can you tell me the pursuits which delight mankind—or rather, if you would prefer, let me ask, and do you answer, which of them belong to the pleasurable class, and which of them not? In the first place, what say you of flute-playing? Does not that appear to be an art which seeks only pleasure, Callicles, and thinks of nothing else?

Cal. I assent.

Soc. And is not the same true of all similar arts, as, for example, the art of playing the lyre at festivals?

Cal. Yes.

Soc. And what do you say of the choral art and of dithyrambic poetry?—are not they of the same nature? Do you imagine that Cinesias the son of Meles cares about what will tend to the moral improvement of his hearers, or about what will give pleasure to the multitude?

Cal. There can be no mistake about Cinesias, Socrates.

Soc. And what do you say of his father, Meles the harp-player? Did he perform with any view to the good of his hearers? Could he be said to regard even their pleasure? For his singing was an infliction to his audience. And of harp playing and dithyrambic poetry in general, what would you say? Have they not been invented wholly for the sake of pleasure?

Cal. That is my notion of them.

Soc. And as for the Muse of Tragedy, that solemn and august personage—what are her aspirations? Is all her aim and desire only to give pleasure to the spectators, or does she fight against them and refuse to speak of their pleasant vices, and willingly proclaim in word and song truths welcome and unwelcome?—which in your judgment is her character?

Cal. There can be no doubt, Socrates, that Tragedy has her face turned towards pleasure and the gratification of the audience.

Soc. And is not that the sort of thing, Callicles, which we were just now describing as flattery?

Gorgias

SOCRATES,
CAL-
LICLES.

to which
Callicles
pretends
to give
assent.

There are
arts
which
delight
mankind
but which
never
consider
the soul's
higher
interest.

502

Gorgias

SOCRATES,
CAL-
LICLES.

Cal. Quite true.

Soc. Well now, suppose that we strip all poetry of song and rhythm and metre, there will remain speech [1]?

Cal. To be sure.

Soc. And this speech is addressed to a crowd of people?

Cal. Yes.

Soc. Then poetry is a sort of rhetoric?

Cal. True.

Soc. And do not the poets in the theatres seem to you to be rhetoricians?

Cal. Yes.

Poetry is of the nature of flattery.

Soc. Then now we have discovered a sort of rhetoric which is addressed to a crowd of men, women, and children, freemen and slaves. And this is not much to our taste, for we have described it as having the nature of flattery.

Cal. Quite true.

Oratory, too, as practised regards the interest of the speaker rather than the good of the people.

Soc. Very good. And what do you say of that other rhetoric which addresses the Athenian assembly and the assemblies of freemen in other states? Do the rhetoricians appear to you always to aim at what is best, and do they seek to improve the citizens by their speeches, or are they too, like the rest of mankind, bent upon giving them pleasure, forgetting the public good in the thought of their own interest, playing with the people as with children, and trying to amuse them, but never considering whether they are better or worse for this?

503

Cal. I must distinguish. There are some who have a real care of the public in what they say, while others are such as you describe.

There might be a higher style of oratory; and Callicles thinks that such really existed in the great days of old, the days of Miltiades and Themistocles and Pericles.

Soc. I am contented with the admission that rhetoric is of two sorts; one, which is mere flattery and disgraceful declamation; the other, which is noble and aims at the training and improvement of the souls of the citizens, and strives to say what is best, whether welcome or unwelcome, to the audience; but have you ever known such a rhetoric; or if you have, and can point out any rhetorician who is of this stamp, who is he?

Cal. But, indeed, I am afraid that I cannot tell you of any such among the orators who are at present living.

Soc. Well, then, can you mention any one of a former generation, who may be said to have improved the Athenians, who found them worse and made them better, from the day that he began to make speeches? for, indeed, I do not know of such a man.

Cal. What! did you never hear that Themistocles was a good

---

[1] Cp. Rep. iii. 392 foll.

man, and Cimon and Miltiades and Pericles, who is just lately dead, and whom you heard yourself?

Soc. Yes, Callicles, they were good men, if, as you said at first, true virtue consists only in the satisfaction of our own desires and those of others; but if not, and if, as we were afterwards compelled to acknowledge, the satisfaction of some desires makes us better, and of others, worse, and we ought to gratify the one and not the other, and there is an art in distinguishing them,—can you tell me of any of these statesmen who did distinguish them?

Yet even these famous men had no ideal or standard.

Cal. No, indeed, I cannot.

Soc. Yet, surely, Callicles, if you look you will find such a one. Suppose that we just calmly consider whether any of these was such as I have described. Will not the good man, who says whatever he says with a view to the best, speak with a reference to some standard and not at random, just as all other artists, whether the painter, the builder, the shipwright, or any other look all of them to their own work, and do not select and apply at random what they apply, but strive to give a definite form to it? The artist disposes all things in order, and compels the one part to harmonize and accord with the other part, until he has constructed a regular and systematic whole; and this is true of all artists, and in the same way the trainers and physicians, of whom we spoke before, give order and regularity to the body: do you deny this?

Some standard needed other than a man's interest

Cal. No; I am ready to admit it.

Soc. Then the house in which order and regularity prevail is good; that in which there is disorder, evil?

Order is good, disorder evil, in a ship, in a human body, in a human soul.

Cal. Yes.

Soc. And the same is true of a ship?

Cal. Yes.

Soc. And the same may be said of the human body?

Cal. Yes.

Soc. And what would you say of the soul? Will the good soul be that in which disorder is prevalent, or that in which there is harmony and order?

Cal. The latter follows from our previous admissions.

Soc. What is the name which is given to the effect of harmony and order in the body?

Cal. I suppose that you mean health and strength?

Soc. Yes, I do; and what is the name which you would give to the effect of harmony and order in the soul? Try and discover a name for this as well as for the other.

Cal. Why not give the name yourself, Socrates?

Soc. Well, if you had rather that I should, I will; and you shall say whether you agree with me, and if not, you shall refute and answer me. 'Healthy,' as I conceive, is the name which is given to the regular order of the body, whence comes health and every other bodily excellence: is that true or not?

Cal. True.

From
order and
law
spring
temper-
ance and
justice.

Soc. And 'lawful' and 'law' are the names which are given to the regular order and action of the soul, and these make men lawful and orderly:—and so we have temperance and justice: have we not?

Cal. Granted.

The true
rhetori-
cian will
seek to
implant
these
virtues, to
implant
justice
and take
away
injustice.

Soc. And will not the true rhetorician who is honest and understands his art have his eye fixed upon these, in all the words which he addresses to the souls of men, and in all his actions, both in what he gives and in what he takes away? Will not his aim be to implant justice in the souls of his citizens and take away injustice, to implant temperance and take away intemperance, to implant every virtue and take away every vice? Do you not agree?

Cal. I agree.

505

Soc. For what use is there, Callicles, in giving to the body of a sick man who is in a bad state of health a quantity of the most delightful food or drink or any other pleasant thing, which may be really as bad for him as if you gave him nothing, or even worse if rightly estimated. Is not that true?

Cal. I will not say No to it.

The body
of the
sick and
the soul
of the
wicked
must be
chastised
and im-
proved.

Soc. For in my opinion there is no profit in a man's life if his body is in an evil plight—in that case his life also is evil: am I not right?

Cal. Yes.

Soc. When a man is in health the physicians will generally allow him to eat when he is hungry and drink when he is thirsty, and to satisfy his desires as he likes, but when he is sick they hardly suffer him to satisfy his desires at all: even you will admit that?

Cal. Yes.

Soc. And does not the same argument hold of the soul, my good sir? While she is in a bad state and is senseless and intemperate and unjust and unholy, her desires ought to be controlled, and she ought to be prevented from doing anything which does not tend to her own improvement.

Cal. Yes.

Soc. Such treatment will be better for the soul herself?

Cal. To be sure.

Soc. And to restrain her from her appetites is to chastise her?

Cal. Yes.

Soc. Then restraint or chastisement is better for the soul than intemperance or the absence of control, which you were just now preferring?

Cal. I do not understand you, Socrates, and I wish that you would ask some one who does.

Soc. Here is a gentleman who cannot endure to be improved or to subject himself to that very chastisement of which the argument speaks!

Cal. I do not heed a word of what you are saying, and have only answered hitherto out of civility to Gorgias.

Soc. What are we to do, then? Shall we break off in the middle?

Cal. You shall judge for yourself.

Soc. Well, but people say that 'a tale should have a head and not break off in the middle,' and I should not like to have the argument going about without a head[1]; please then to go on a little longer, and put the head on.

Cal. How tyrannical you are, Socrates! I wish that you and your argument would rest, or that you would get some one else to argue with you.

Soc. But who else is willing?—I want to finish the argument.

Cal. Cannot you finish without my help, either talking straight on, or questioning and answering yourself?

Soc. Must I then say with Epicharmus, 'Two men spoke before, but now one shall be enough'? I suppose that there is absolutely no help. And if I am to carry on the enquiry by myself, I will first of all remark that not only I but all of us should have an ambition to know what is true and what is false in this matter, for the discovery of the truth is a common good. And now I will proceed to argue according to my own notion. But if any of you think that I arrive at conclusions which are untrue you must interpose and refute me, for I do not speak from any knowledge of what I am saying; I am an enquirer like yourselves, and therefore, if my opponent says anything which is of force, I shall be the first to agree with him. I am speaking on the supposition that the argument ought to be completed; but if you think otherwise let us leave off and go our ways.

Gor. I think, Socrates, that we should not go our ways until you have completed the argument; and this appears to me to be the wish of the rest of the company; I myself should very much like to hear what more you have to say.

Soc. I too, Gorgias, should have liked to continue the argument with Callicles, and then I might have given him an 'Amphion' in

[1] Cp. Laws vi. 752 A.

Gorgias

SOCRATES, GORGIAS, CALLICLES.

Callicles does not wish to be improved.

506

return for his 'Zethus'[1]; but since you, Callicles, are unwilling to continue, I hope that you will listen, and interrupt me if I seem to you to be in error. And if you refute me, I shall not be angry with you as you are with me, but I shall inscribe you as the greatest of benefactors on the tablets of my soul.

Cal. My good fellow, never mind me, but get on.

The pleasant not the same as the good, and is to be sought only for the sake of the good; and we are good when good is present in us, and good is the effect of order and truth and art.

Soc. Listen to me, then, while I recapitulate the argument:—Is the pleasant the same as the good? Not the same. Callicles and I are agreed about that. And is the pleasant to be pursued for the sake of the good? or the good for the sake of the pleasant? The pleasant is to be pursued for the sake of the good. And that is pleasant at the presence of which we are pleased, and that is good at the presence of which we are good? To be sure. And we are good, and all good things whatever are good when some virtue is present in us or them? That, Callicles, is my conviction. But the virtue of each thing, whether body or soul, instrument or creature, when given to them in the best way comes to them not by chance but as the result of the order and truth and art which are imparted to them: Am I not right? I maintain that I am. And is not the virtue of each thing dependent on order or arrangement? Yes, I say. And that which makes a thing good is the proper order inhering in each thing? Such is my view. And is not the soul which has an order of her own better than that which has no order? Certainly. And the soul which has order is orderly? Of course. And

507

that which is orderly is temperate? Assuredly. And the temperate soul is good? No other answer can I give, Callicles dear; have you any?

Cal. Go on, my good fellow.

Soc. Then I shall proceed to add, that if the temperate soul is the good soul, the soul which is in the opposite condition, that is, the foolish and intemperate, is the bad soul. Very true.

The temperate soul is the good soul, just in relation to men, and holy in relation to gods, and is therefore happy; and the intemper-

And will not the temperate man do what is proper, both in relation to the gods and to men;—for he would not be temperate if he did not? Certainly he will do what is proper. In his relation to other men he will do what is just; and in his relation to the gods he will do what is holy; and he who does what is just and holy must be just and holy? Very true. And must he not be courageous? for the duty of a temperate man is not to follow or to avoid what he ought not, but what he ought, whether things or men or pleasures or pains, and patiently to endure when he ought; and therefore, Callicles, the temperate man, being, as we have described, also just and courageous and holy, cannot be other than a perfectly

[1] p. 485.

good man, nor can the good man do otherwise than well and perfectly whatever he does; and he who does well must of necessity be happy and blessed, and the evil man who does evil, miserable: now this latter is he whom you were applauding—the intemperate who is the opposite of the temperate. Such is my position, and these things I affirm to be true. And if they are true, then I further affirm that he who desires to be happy must pursue and practise temperance and run away from intemperance as fast as his legs will carry him: he had better order his life so as not to need punishment; but if either he or any of his friends, whether private individual or city, are in need of punishment, then justice must be done and he must suffer punishment, if he would be happy. This appears to me to be the aim which a man ought to have, and towards which he ought to direct all the energies both of himself and of the state, acting so that he may have temperance and justice present with him and be happy, not suffering his lusts to be unrestrained, and in the never-ending desire to satisfy them leading a robber's life. Such a one is the friend neither of God nor man, for he is incapable of communion, and he who is incapable of communion is also incapable of friendship. And philosophers tell us, Callicles, that communion and friendship and orderliness and temperance and justice bind together heaven and earth and gods and men, and that this universe is therefore called Cosmos or order, not disorder or misrule, my friend. But although you are a philosopher you seem to me never to have observed that geometrical equality is mighty, both among gods and men; you think that you ought to cultivate inequality or excess, and do not care about geometry.—Well, then, either the principle that the happy are made happy by the possession of justice and temperance, and the miserable miserable by the possession of vice, must be refuted, or, if it is granted, what will be the consequences? All the consequences which I drew before, Callicles, and about which you asked me whether I was in earnest when I said that a man ought to accuse himself and his son and his friend if he did anything wrong, and that to this end he should use his rhetoric—all those consequences are true. And that which you thought that Polus was led to admit out of modesty is true, viz. that, to do injustice, if more disgraceful than to suffer, is in that degree worse; and the other position, which, according to Polus, Gorgias admitted out of modesty, that he who would truly be a rhetorician ought to be just and have a knowledge of justice, has also turned out to be true.

And now, these things being as we have said, let us proceed in the next place to consider whether you are right in throwing in

508

my teeth that I am unable to help myself or any of my friends or kinsmen, or to save them in the extremity of danger, and that I am in the power of another like an outlaw to whom any one may do what he likes,—he may box my ears, which was a brave saying of yours; or take away my goods or banish me, or even do his worst and kill me; a condition which, as you say, is the height of disgrace. My answer to you is one which has been already often repeated, but may as well be repeated once more. I tell you, Callicles, that to be boxed on the ears wrongfully is not the worst evil which can befall a man, nor to have my purse or my body cut open, but that to smite and slay me and mine wrongfully is far more disgraceful and more evil; aye, and to despoil and enslave and pillage, or in any way at all to wrong me and mine, is far more disgraceful and evil to the doer of the wrong than to me who am the

509 sufferer. These truths, which have been already set forth as I state them in the previous discussion, would seem now to have been fixed and riveted by us, if I may use an expression which is certainly bold, in words which are like bonds of iron and adamant; and unless you or some other still more enterprising hero shall break them, there is no possibility of denying what I say. For my position has always been, that I myself am ignorant how these things are, but that I have never met any one who could say other-

The
greatest
evil to do
injustice,
but there
is a great-
er still,
not to be
punished
for doing
injustice.

wise, any more than you can, and not appear ridiculous. This is my position still, and if what I am saying is true, and injustice is the greatest of evils to the doer of injustice, and yet there is if possible a greater than this greatest of evils[1], in an unjust man not suffering retribution, what is that defence of which the want will make a man truly ridiculous? Must not the defence be one which will avert the greatest of human evils? And will not the worst of all defences be that with which a man is unable to defend himself or his family or his friends?—and next will come that which is unable to avert the next greatest evil; thirdly that which is unable to avert the third greatest evil; and so of other evils. As is the greatness of evil so is the honour of being able to avert them in their several degrees, and the disgrace of not being able to avert them. Am I not right, Callicles?

Cal. Yes, quite right.

Soc. Seeing then that there are these two evils, the doing injustice and the suffering injustice—and we affirm that to do injustice is a greater, and to suffer injustice a lesser evil—by what devices can a man succeed in obtaining the two advantages, the one of not doing and the other of not suffering injustice? must he have the

[1] Cp. Republic, 9. 578 ff.

power, or only the will to obtain them? I mean to ask whether a man will escape injustice if he has only the will to escape, or must he have provided himself with the power?

Cal. He must have provided himself with the power; that is clear.

Soc. And what do you say of doing injustice? Is the will only sufficient, and will that prevent him from doing injustice, or must he have provided himself with power and art; and if he have not studied and practised, will he be unjust still? Surely you might say, Callicles, whether you think that Polus and I were right in admitting the conclusion that no one does wrong voluntarily, but that all do wrong against their will?

Cal. Granted, Socrates, if you will only have done.

Soc. Then, as would appear, power and art have to be provided in order that we may do no injustice?

Cal. Certainly.

Soc. And what art will protect us from suffering injustice, if not wholly, yet as far as possible? I want to know whether you agree with me; for I think that such an art is the art of one who is either a ruler or even tyrant himself, or the equal and companion of the ruling power.

Cal. Well said, Socrates; and please to observe how ready I am to praise you when you talk sense.

Soc. Think and tell me whether you would approve of another view of mine: To me every man appears to be most the friend of him who is most like to him—like to like, as ancient sages say: Would you not agree to this?

Cal. I should.

Soc. But when the tyrant is rude and uneducated, he may be expected to fear any one who is his superior in virtue, and will never be able to be perfectly friendly with him.

Cal. That is true.

Soc. Neither will he be the friend of any one who is greatly his inferior, for the tyrant will despise him, and will never seriously regard him as a friend.

Cal. That again is true.

Soc. Then the only friend worth mentioning, whom the tyrant can have, will be one who is of the same character, and has the same likes and dislikes, and is at the same time willing to be subject and subservient to him; he is the man who will have power in the state, and no one will injure him with impunity:—is not that so?

Cal. Yes.

Gorgias

SOCRATES, CAL-
LICLES.

510

The tyrant naturally hates both his superiors and inferiors: he likes only those who resemble him in character.

And the
way to be
a great
man and
not to
suffer in-
jury is to
become
like him.
And there
can be no
[511]
greater
evil to
him than
this.

Soc. And if a young man begins to ask how he may become great and formidable, this would seem to be the way—he will accustom himself, from his youth upward, to feel sorrow and joy on the same occasions as his master, and will contrive to be as like him as possible?

Cal. Yes.

Soc. And in this way he will have accomplished, as you and your friends would say, the end of becoming a great man and not suffering injury?

Cal. Very true.

Soc. But will he also escape from doing injury? Must not the very opposite be true, if he is to be like the tyrant in his injustice, and to have influence with him? Will he not rather contrive to do as much wrong as possible, and not be punished?

Cal. True.

Soc. And by the imitation of his master and by the power which he thus acquires will not his soul become bad and corrupted, and will not this be the greatest evil to him?

Cal. You always contrive somehow or other, Socrates, to invert everything: do you not know that he who imitates the tyrant will, if he has a mind, kill him who does not imitate him and take away his goods?

But how
provok-
ing that
the bad
man
should
slay the
good!

Nay, but
we should
not al-
ways
study the
arts
whi·h
save us
from
death;—
the art
of swim-
ming, the
art of the
pilot, &c.

The pilot
demands
a very
moderate

Soc. Excellent Callicles, I am not deaf, and I have heard that a great many times from you and from Polus and from nearly every man in the city, but I wish that you would hear me too. I dare say that he will kill him if he has a mind—the bad man will kill the good and true.

Cal. And is not that just the provoking thing?

Soc. Nay, not to a man of sense, as the argument shows: do you think that all our cares should be directed to prolonging life to the uttermost, and to the study of those arts which secure us from danger always; like that art of rhetoric which saves men in courts of law, and which you advise me to cultivate?

Cal. Yes, truly, and very good advice too.

Soc. Well, my friend, but what do you think of swimming; is that an art of any great pretensions?

Cal. No, indeed.

Soc. And yet surely swimming saves a man from death, and there are occasions on which he must know how to swim. And if you despise the swimmers, I will tell you of another and greater art, the art of the pilot, who not only saves the souls of men, but also their bodies and properties from the extremity of danger, just like rhetoric. Yet his art is modest and unpresuming: it has no airs or pretences of doing anything extraordinary, and, in return for the same salvation which is given by the pleader, demands only two obols, if he brings us from Aegina to Athens, or for the longer voyage from Pontus or Egypt, at the utmost two drachmae, when he has saved, as I was just now saying, the passenger and his wife and children and goods, and safely disembarked them at the Piraeus,— this is the payment which he asks in return for so great a boon; and he who is the master of the art, and has done all this, gets out and walks about on the sea-shore by his ship in an unassuming way. For he is able to reflect and is aware that he cannot tell which of his fellow-passengers he has benefited, and which of them he has injured in not allowing them to be drowned. He knows that they are just the same when he has disembarked them as when they embarked, and not a whit better either in their bodies or in their souls; and he considers that if a man who is afflicted by great and incurable bodily diseases is only to be pitied for having escaped, and is in no way benefited by him in having been saved from drowning, much less he who has great and incurable diseases, not of the body, but of the soul, which is the more valuable part of him; neither is life worth having nor of any profit to the bad man, whether he be delivered from the sea, or the law-courts, or any other devourer;—and so he reflects that such a one had better not live, for he cannot live well[1].

And this is the reason why the pilot, although he is our saviour, is not usually conceited, any more than the engineer, who is not at all behind either the general, or the pilot, or any one else, in his saving power, for he sometimes saves whole cities. Is there any comparison between him and the pleader? And if he were to talk, Callicles, in your grandiose style, he would bury you under a mountain of words, declaring and insisting that we ought all of us to be engine-makers, and that no other profession is worth thinking about; he would have plenty to say. Nevertheless you despise him and his art, and sneeringly call him an engine-maker, and you will not allow your daughters to marry his son, or marry your son to his daughters. And yet, on your principle, what justice or reason is there in your refusal? What right have you to despise the engine-maker, and the others whom I was just now mentioning? I know that you will say, 'I am better, and better born.' But if the better is not what I say, and virtue consists only in a man saving himself and his, whatever may be his character, then your censure of the engine-maker, and of the physician, and of the other arts of salvation, is ridiculous. O my friend! I want you to see that the noble

[1] Cp. Rep. iii. 407 E.

Gorgias

SOCRATES.

payment as the fare of a passenger from Athens to Aegina, because he is not certain whether salvation from [512] death be a good or an evil.

The engineer, too:— how much better than the pleader!

He too is another of your saviours; but you despise him, whereas you ought to esteem him highly.

513

I want
you to
consider
whether
you can
possibly
become
great
among
the
people
unless
you be-
come
like them.

and the good may possibly be something different from saving and
being saved:—May not he who is truly a man cease to care about
living a certain time?—he knows, as women say, that no man can
escape fate, and therefore he is not fond of life; he leaves all that
with God, and considers in what way he can best spend his appointed term;—whether by assimilating himself to the constitution
under which he lives, as you at this moment have to consider how
you may become as like as possible to the Athenian people, if you
mean to be in their good graces, and to have power in the state;
whereas I want you to think and see whether this is for the interest
of either of us;—I would not have us risk that which is dearest
on the acquisition of this power, like the Thessalian enchantresses,
who, as they say, bring down the moon from heaven at the risk of
their own perdition. But if you suppose that any man will show
you the art of becoming great in the city, and yet not conforming
yourself to the ways of the city, whether for better or worse, then
I can only say that you are mistaken, Callicles; for he who would
deserve to be the true natural friend of the Athenian Demus, aye,
or of Pyrilampes' darling who is called after them, must be by
nature like them, and not an imitator only. He, then, who will
make you most like them, will make you as you desire, a statesman and orator: for every man is pleased when he is spoken to
in his own language and spirit, and dislikes any other. But perhaps you, sweet Callicles, may be of another mind. What do you
say?

Cal. Somehow or other your words, Socrates, always appear to
me to be good words; and yet, like the rest of the world, I am not
quite convinced by them[1].

Callicles
inclines
for an
instant to
the Gos-
pel of
Socrates,
but the
love of
the world
and of
popular-
ity over-
comes
him.

Two pro-
cesses of

Soc. The reason is, Callicles, that the love of Demus which abides
in your soul is an adversary to me; but I dare say that if we recur
to these same matters, and consider them more thoroughly, you
may be convinced for all that. Please, then, to remember that
there are two processes of training all things, including body and
soul; in the one, as we said, we treat them with a view to pleasure,
and in the other with a view to the highest good, and then we do
not indulge but resist them: was not that the distinction which we
drew?

Cal. Very true.

Soc. And the one which had pleasure in view was just a vulgar
flattery:—was not that another of our conclusions?

Cal. Be it so, if you will have it.

[1] Cp. Symp. 216: 1 Alcib. 135.

Soc. And the other had in view the greatest improvement of that which was ministered to, whether body or soul?

Cal. Quite true.

Soc. And must we not have the same end in view in the treatment of our city and citizens? Must we not try and make them as good as possible? For we have already discovered that there is no use in imparting to them any other good, unless the mind of those who are to have the good, whether money, or office, or any other sort of power, be gentle and good. Shall we say that?

Cal. Yes, certainly, if you like.

Soc. Well, then, if you and I, Callicles, were intending [1] to set about some public business, and were advising one another to undertake buildings, such as walls, docks or temples of the largest size, ought we not to examine ourselves, first, as to whether we know or do not know the art of building, and who taught us?—would not that be necessary, Callicles?

Cal. True.

Soc. In the second place, we should have to consider whether we had ever constructed any private house, either of our own or for our friends, and whether this building of ours was a success or not; and if upon consideration we found that we had had good and eminent masters, and had been successful in constructing many fine buildings, not only with their assistance, but without them, by our own unaided skill—in that case prudence would not dissuade us from proceeding to the construction of public works. But if we had no master to show, and only a number of worthless buildings or none at all, then, surely, it would be ridiculous in us to attempt public works, or to advise one another to undertake them. Is not this true?

Cal. Certainly.

Soc. And does not the same hold in all other cases? If you and I were physicians, and were advising one another that we were competent to practise as state-physicians, should I not ask about you, and would you not ask about me, Well, but how about Socrates himself, has he good health? and was any one else ever known to be cured by him, whether slave or freeman? And I should make the same enquiries about you. And if we arrived at the conclusion that no one, whether citizen or stranger, man or woman, had ever been any the better for the medical skill of either of us, then, by Heaven, Callicles, what an absurdity to think that we or any human being should be so silly as to set up as state-physicians and advise others like ourselves to do the same, without having

[1] Reading with the majority of MSS. πράξοντες.

Gorgias

SOCRATES, LICLES. CAL-

training one having [514] a view to pleasure, the other to good.

And we must train our citizens with a view to their good; and, as in other arts, we must show that we can be trusted to improve them.

Gorgias

SOCRATES,
CAL-
LICLES.

515

And now,
Callicles,
what are
you who
are a
public
character
doing for
the im-
prove-
ment of
the citi-
zens?

first practised in private, whether successfully or not, and acquired experience of the art! Is not this, as they say, to begin with
the big jar when you are learning the potter's art; which is a foolish thing?

Cal. True.

Soc. And now, my friend, as you are already beginning to be a
public character, and are admonishing and reproaching me for not
being one, suppose that we ask a few questions of one another. Tell
me, then, Callicles, how about making any of the citizens better?
Was there ever a man who was once vicious, or unjust, or intemperate, or foolish, and became by the help of Callicles good and
noble? Was there ever such a man, whether citizen or stranger,
slave or freeman? Tell me, Callicles, if a person were to ask these
questions of you, what would you answer? Whom would you say
that you had improved by your conversation? There may have
been good deeds of this sort which were done by you as a private
person, before you came forward in public. Why will you not
answer?

Cal. You are contentious, Socrates.

Callicles
makes no
answer.

Soc. Nay, I ask you, not from a love of contention, but because
I really want to know in what way you think that affairs should
be administered among us—whether, when you come to the administration of them, you have any other aim but the improvement
of the citizens? Have we not already admitted many times over
that such is the duty of a public man? Nay, we have surely said
so; for if you will not answer for yourself I must answer for you.

Or how
did
Pericles
and the
great of
old bene-
fit the
citizens?

But if this is what the good man ought to effect for the benefit of
his own state, allow me to recall to you the names of those whom
you were just now mentioning, Pericles, and Cimon, and Miltiades,
and Themistocles, and ask whether you still think that they were
good citizens.

Cal. I do.

Soc. But if they were good, then clearly each of them must have
made the citizens better instead of worse?

Cal. Yes.

Soc. And, therefore, when Pericles first began to speak in the
assembly, the Athenians were not so good as when he spoke last?

Cal. Very likely.

Soc. Nay, my friend, 'likely' is not the word; for if he was a
good citizen, the inference is certain.

Cal. And what difference does that make?

Soc. None; only I should like further to know whether the
Athenians are supposed to have been made better by Pericles, or,

on the contrary, to have been corrupted by him; for I hear that he was the first who gave the people pay, and made them idle and cowardly, and encouraged them in the love of talk and of money.

Cal. You heard that, Socrates, from the laconising set who bruise their ears.

Soc. But what I am going to tell you now is not mere hearsay, but well known both to you and me: that at first, Pericles was glorious and his character unimpeached by any verdict of the Athenians—this was during the time when they were not so good —yet afterwards, when they had been made good and gentle by him, at the very end of his life they convicted him of theft, and almost put him to death, clearly under the notion that he was a malefactor.

Cal. Well, but how does that prove Pericles' badness?

Soc. Why, surely you would say that he was a bad manager of asses or horses or oxen, who had received them originally neither kicking nor butting nor biting him, and implanted in them all these savage tricks? Would he not be a bad manager of any animals who received them gentle, and made them fiercer than they were when he received them? What do you say?

Cal. I will do you the favour of saying 'yes.'

Soc. And will you also do me the favour of saying whether man is an animal?

Cal. Certainly he is.

Soc. And was not Pericles a shepherd of men?

Cal. Yes.

Soc. And if he was a good political shepherd, ought not the animals who were his subjects, as we were just now acknowledging, to have become more just, and not more unjust?

Cal. Quite true.

Soc. And are not just men gentle, as Homer says?—or are you of another mind?

Cal. I agree.

Soc. And yet he really did make them more savage than he received them, and their savageness was shown towards himself; which he must have been very far from desiring.

Cal. Do you want me to agree with you?

Soc. Yes, if I seem to you to speak the truth.

Cal. Granted then.

Soc. And if they were more savage, must they not have been more unjust and inferior?

Cal. Granted again.

Soc. Then upon this view, Pericles was not a good statesman?

Gorgias
SOCRATES, CAL-
LICLES.

Pericles corrupted them by giving them pay.
[516]
He made them worse instead of better, for they all but put him to death.

Cimon
was os-
tracised;

Themis-
tocles
was
exiled;
Miltiades
was near-
ly thrown
from the
rock.

517
The older
statesmen
no better
than the
existing
ones.

The older
statesmen
not able
really to
elevate
the state
to a high-
er level,
but more
capable
of grati-
fying its
desires.

Cal. That is, upon your view.

Soc. Nay, the view is yours, after what you have admitted. Take the case of Cimon again. Did not the very persons whom he was serving ostracize him, in order that they might not hear his voice for ten years? and they did just the same to Themistocles, adding the penalty of exile; and they voted that Miltiades, the hero of Marathon, should be thrown into the pit of death, and he was only saved by the Prytanis. And yet, if they had been really good men, as you say, these things would never have happened to them. For the good charioteers are not those who at first keep their place, and then, when they have broken-in their horses, and themselves become better charioteers, are thrown out—that is not the way either in charioteering or in any profession.—What do you think?

Cal. I should think not.

Soc. Well, but if so, the truth is as I have said already, that in the Athenian State no one has ever shown himself to be a good statesman—you admitted that this was true of our present statesmen, but not true of former ones, and you preferred them to the others; yet they have turned out to be no better than our present ones; and therefore, if they were rhetoricians, they did not use the true art of rhetoric or of flattery, or they would not have fallen out of favour.

Cal. But surely, Socrates, no living man ever came near any one of them in his performances.

Soc. O, my dear friend, I say nothing against them regarded as the serving-men of the State; and I do think that they were certainly more serviceable than those who are living now, and better able to gratify the wishes of the State; but as to transforming those desires and not allowing them to have their way, and using the powers which they had, whether of persuasion or of force, in the improvement of their fellow-citizens, which is the prime object of the truly good citizen, I do not see that in these respects they were a whit superior to our present statesmen, although I do admit that they were more clever at providing ships and walls and docks, and all that. You and I have a ridiculous way, for during the whole time that we are arguing, we are always going round and round to the same point, and constantly misunderstanding one another. If I am not mistaken, you have admitted and acknowledged more than once, that there are two kinds of operations which have to do with the body, and two which have to do with the soul: one of the two is ministerial, and if our bodies are hungry provides food for them, and if they are thirsty gives them drink, or if they are cold supplies them with garments, blankets, shoes, and all that they crave. I use the same images as before intentionally, in order that you may understand me the better. The purveyor of the articles may provide them either wholesale or retail, or he may be the maker of any of them,—the baker, or the cook, or the weaver, or the shoemaker, or the currier; and in so doing, being such as he is, he is naturally supposed by himself and every one to minister to the body. For none of them know that there is another art—an art of gymnastic and medicine which is the true minister of the body, and ought to be the mistress of all the rest, and to use their results according to the knowledge which she has and they have not, of the real good or bad effects of meats and drinks on the body. All other arts which have to do with the body are servile and menial and illiberal; and gymnastic and medicine are, as they ought to be, their mistresses. Now, when I say that all this is equally true of the soul, you seem at first to know and understand and assent to my words, and then a little while afterwards you come repeating, Has not the State had good and noble citizens? and when I ask you who they are, you reply, seemingly quite in earnest, as if I had asked, Who are or have been good trainers?—and you had replied, Thearion, the baker, Mithoecus, who wrote the Sicilian cookery-book, Sarambus, the vintner: these are ministers of the body, first-rate in their art; for the first makes admirable loaves, the second excellent dishes, and the third capital wine;—to me these appear to be the exact parallel of the statesmen whom you mention. Now you would not be altogether pleased if I said to you, My friend, you know nothing of gymnastics; those of whom you are speaking to me are only the ministers and purveyors of luxury, who have no good or noble notions of their art, and may very likely be filling and fattening men's bodies and gaining their approval, although the result is that they lose their original flesh in the long run, and become thinner than they were before; and yet they, in their simplicity, will not attribute their diseases and loss of flesh to their entertainers; but when in after years the unhealthy surfeit brings the attendant penalty of disease, he who happens to be near them at the time, and offers them advice, is accused and blamed by them, and if they could they would do him some harm; while they proceed to eulogize the men who have been the real authors of the mischief. And that, Callicles, is just what you are now doing. You praise the men who feasted the citizens and satisfied their desires, and people say that they have made the city great, not seeing that the swollen and ulcerated condition of the State is to be attributed to these elder statesmen; for they have filled the city full of harbours and docks and walls and revenues and all that, and have left no room for justice and temperance. And when the crisis of the disorder comes, the people will blame the ad-

518

You might as well say that the cook or the baker is a good trainer as that they were great statesmen.

519

Gorgias

SOCRATES,
CAL-
LICLES.

The
statesman
like the
Sophist;
neither
has any
right to
accuse
their fol-
lowers of
wronging
them;
they
should
have
taught
them
better.

visers of the hour, and applaud Themistocles and Cimon and Pericles, who are the real authors of their calamities; and if you are not careful they may assail you and my friend Alcibiades, when they are losing not only their new acquisitions, but also their original possessions; not that you are the authors of these misfortunes of theirs, although you may perhaps be accessories to them. A great piece of work is always being made, as I see and am told, now as of old, about our statesmen. When the State treats any of them as malefactors, I observe that there is a great uproar and indignation at the supposed wrong which is done to them; 'after all their many services to the State, that they should unjustly perish,'—so the tale runs. But the cry is all a lie; for no statesman ever could be unjustly put to death by the city of which he is the head. The case of the professed statesman is, I believe, very much like that of the professed sophist; for the sophists, although they are wise men, are nevertheless guilty of a strange piece of folly; professing to be teachers of virtue, they will often accuse their disciples of wronging them, and defrauding them of their pay, and showing no gratitude for their services. Yet what can be more absurd than that men who have become just and good, and whose injustice has been taken away from them, and who have had justice implanted in them by their teachers, should act unjustly by reason of the injustice which is not in them? Can anything be more irrational, my friends, than this? You, Callicles, compel me to be a mob-orator, because you will not answer.

Cal. And you are the man who cannot speak unless there is some one to answer?

Soc. I suppose that I can; just now, at any rate, the speeches which I am making are long enough because you refuse to answer me. But I adjure you by the god of friendship, my good sir, do tell me whether there does not appear to you to be a great inconsistency in saying that you have made a man good, and then blaming him for being bad?

Cal. Yes, it appears so to me.

520   *Soc.* Do you never hear our professors of education speaking in this inconsistent manner?

Cal. Yes, but why talk of men who are good for nothing?

Soc. I would rather say, why talk of men who profess to be rulers, and declare that they are devoted to the improvement of the city, and nevertheless upon occasion declaim against the utter vileness of the city:—do you think that there is any difference between one and the other? My good friend, the sophist and the rhetorician, as I was saying to Polus, are the same, or nearly the same; but you ignorantly fancy that rhetoric is a perfect thing, and sophistry a thing to be despised; whereas the truth is, that sophistry is as much superior to rhetoric as legislation is to the practice of law, or gymnastic to medicine. The orators and sophists, as I am inclined to think, are the only class who cannot complain of the mischief ensuing to themselves from that which they teach others, without in the same breath accusing themselves of having done no good to those whom they profess to benefit. Is not this a fact?

Cal. Certainly it is.

Soc. If they were right in saying that they make men better, then they are the only class who can afford to leave their remuneration to those who have been benefited by them. Whereas if a man has been benefited in any other way, if, for example, he has been taught to run by a trainer, he might possibly defraud him of his pay, if the trainer left the matter to him, and made no agreement with him that he should receive money as soon as he had given him the utmost speed; for not because of any deficiency of speed do men act unjustly, but by reason of injustice.

Cal. Very true.

Soc. And he who removes injustice can be in no danger of being treated unjustly: he alone can safely leave the honorarium to his pupils, if he be really able to make them good—am I not right [1]?

Cal. Yes.

Soc. Then we have found the reason why there is no dishonour in a man receiving pay who is called in to advise about building or any other art?

Cal. Yes, we have found the reason.

Soc. But when the point is, how a man may become best himself, and best govern his family and state, then to say that you will give no advice gratis is held to be dishonourable?

Cal. True.

Soc. And why? Because only such benefits call forth a desire to requite them, and there is evidence that a benefit has been conferred when the benefactor receives a return; otherwise not. Is this true?

Cal. It is.

Soc. Then to which service of the State do you invite me? determine for me. Am I to be the physician of the State who will strive and struggle to make the Athenians as good as possible; or am I to be the servant and flatterer of the State? Speak out, my good friend, freely and fairly as you did at first and ought to do again, and tell me your entire mind.

[1] Cp. Protag. 328.

Gorgias

SOCRATES, CALLICLES.

Sophistry is much superior to rhetoric.

He who teaches honesty ought to teach his pupils to pay him for the lesson.

521
Callicles advises Socrates to be the servant of the state, and not

run the
risk of
popular
enmity.

Cal. I say then that you should be the servant of the State.

Soc. The flatterer? well, sir, that is a noble invitation.

Cal. The Mysian, Socrates, or what you please. For if you refuse, the consequences will be—

Soc. Do not repeat the old story—that he who likes will kill me and get my money; for then I shall have to repeat the old answer, that he will be a bad man and will kill the good, and that the money will be of no use to him, but that he will wrongly use that which he wrongly took, and if wrongly, basely, and if basely, hurtfully.

Cal. How confident you are, Socrates, that you will never come to harm! you seem to think that you are living in another country, and can never be brought into a court of justice, as you very likely may be brought by some miserable and mean person.

Socrates
has no
fear of
popular
enmity,
but is
quite
aware
that he
will incur
it, be-
cause he
is the
only true
politician
of his
time,

Soc. Then I must indeed be a fool, Callicles, if I do not know that in the Athenian State any man may suffer anything. And if I am brought to trial and incur the dangers of which you speak, he will be a villain who brings me to trial—of that I am very sure, for no good man would accuse the innocent. Nor shall I be surprised if I am put to death. Shall I tell you why I anticipate this?

Cal. By all means.

Soc. I think that I am the only or almost the only Athenian living who practises the true art of politics; I am the only politician of my time. Now, seeing that when I speak my words are not uttered with any view of gaining favour, and that I look to what is best and not to what is most pleasant, having no mind to use those arts and graces which you recommend, I shall have nothing to say in the justice court. And you might argue with me, as I was arguing with Polus:—I shall be tried just as a physician would be tried in a court of little boys at the indictment of the cook. What would he reply under such circumstances, if some one were to accuse him, saying, 'O my boys, many evil things has this man done to you: he is the death of you, especially of the younger ones among you, cutting

522 and burning and starving and suffocating you, until you know not what to do; he gives you the bitterest potions, and compels you to hunger and thirst. How unlike the variety of meats and sweets on which I feasted you!' What do you suppose that the physician would be able to reply when he found himself in such a predicament? If he told the truth he could only say, 'All these evil things, my boys, I did for your health,' and then would there not just be a clamour among a jury like that? How they would cry out!

Cal. I dare say.

Soc. Would he not be utterly at a loss for a reply?

Cal. He certainly would.

Soc. And I too shall be treated in the same way, as I well know, if I am brought before the court. For I shall not be able to rehearse to the people the pleasures which I have procured for them, and which, although I am not disposed to envy either the procurers or enjoyers of them, are deemed by them to be benefits and advantages. And if any one says that I corrupt young men, and perplex their minds, or that I speak evil of old men, and use bitter words towards them, whether in private or public, it is useless for me to reply, as I truly might:—'All this I do for the sake of justice, and with a view to your interest, my judges, and to nothing else.' And therefore there is no saying what may happen to me.

Cal. And do you think, Socrates, that a man who is thus defenceless is in a good position?

Soc. Yes, Callicles, if he have that defence, which as you have often acknowledged he should have—if he be his own defence, and have never said or done anything wrong, either in respect of gods or men; and this has been repeatedly acknowledged by us to be the best sort of defence. And if any one could convict me of inability to defend myself or others after this sort, I should blush for shame, whether I was convicted before many, or before a few, or by myself alone; and if I died from want of ability to do so, that would indeed grieve me. But if I died because I have no powers of flattery or rhetoric, I am very sure that you would not find me repining at death. For no man who is not an utter fool and coward is afraid of death itself, but he is afraid of doing wrong. For to go to the world below having one's soul full of injustice is the last and worst of all evils. And in proof of what I say, if you have no objection, I should like to tell you a story.

Cal. Very well, proceed; and then we shall have done.

Soc. Listen, then, as story-tellers say, to a very pretty tale, which I dare say that you may be disposed to regard as a fable only, but which, as I believe, is a true tale, for I mean to speak the truth. Homer tells us [1], how Zeus and Poseidon and Pluto divided the empire which they inherited from their father. Now in the days of Cronos there existed a law respecting the destiny of man, which has always been, and still continues to be in Heaven,—that he who has lived all his life in justice and holiness shall go, when he is dead, to the Islands of the Blessed, and dwell there in perfect happiness out of the reach of evil; but that he who has lived unjustly and impiously shall go to the house of vengeance and punishment, which is called Tartarus. And in the time of Cronos, and even quite lately in the reign of Zeus, the judgment was given on the very day on which

[1] Il. xv. 187. foll.

Gorgias

SOCRATES, CALLICLES.

and he has no defence against men such as his opponents:

that is to say, he has the defence of truth, but not such a defence as men ordinarily produce.

523

The philosopher has no reason to dread death, as Socrates will prove by a relation of what happens in the world below.

Gorgias
SOCRATES.

Before
the days
of Zeus,
the judg-
ments of
another
world too
much re-
sembled
the judg-
ments of
this.

Zeus
takes
measures
for the
correction
and im·
prove-
ment of
them.

524

As the
body is,
so is the
soul after
death;
they both
retain the
traces of
what
they
were in
life,

the men were to die; the judges were alive, and the men were alive; and the consequence was that the judgments were not well given. Then Pluto and the authorities from the Islands of the Blessed came to Zeus, and said that the souls found their way to the wrong places. Zeus said: 'I shall put a stop to this; the judgments are not well given, because the persons who are judged have their clothes on, for they are alive; and there are many who, having evil souls, are apparelled in fair bodies, or encased in wealth or rank, and, when the day of judgment arrives, numerous witnesses come forward and testify on their behalf that they have lived righteously. The judges are awed by them, and they themselves too have their clothes on when judging; their eyes and ears and their whole bodies are interposed as a veil before their own souls. All this is a hindrance to them; there are the clothes of the judges and the clothes of the judged.—What is to be done? I will tell you:—In the first place, I will deprive men of the foreknowledge of death, which they possess at present: this power which they have Prometheus has already received my orders to take from them: in the second place, they shall be entirely stripped before they are judged, for they shall be judged when they are dead; and the judge too shall be naked, that is to say, dead—he with his naked soul shall pierce into the other naked souls; and they shall die suddenly and be deprived of all their kindred, and leave their brave attire strewn upon the earth—conducted in this manner, the judgment will be just. I knew all about the matter before any of you, and therefore I have made my sons judges; two from Asia, Minos and Rhadamanthus, and one from Europe, Aeacus. And these, when they are dead, shall give judgment in the meadow at the parting of the ways, whence the two roads lead, one to the Islands of the Blessed, and the other to Tartarus. Rhadamanthus shall judge those who come from Asia, and Aeacus those who come from Europe. And to Minos I shall give the primacy, and he shall hold a court of appeal, in case either of the two others are in any doubt:—then the judgment respecting the last journey of men will be as just as possible.'

From this tale, Callicles, which I have heard and believe, I draw the following inferences:—Death, if I am right, is in the first place the separation from one another of two things, soul and body; nothing else. And after they are separated they retain their several natures, as in life; the body keeps the same habit, and the results of treatment or accident are distinctly visible in it: for example, he who by nature or training or both, was a tall man while he was alive, will remain as he was, after he is dead; and the fat man will remain fat; and so on; and the dead man, who in life had a fancy to

have flowing hair, will have flowing hair. And if he was marked
with the whip and had the prints of the scourge, or of wounds in
him when he was alive, you might see the same in the dead body;
and if his limbs were broken or misshapen when he was alive, the
same appearance would be visible in the dead. And in a word, whatever was the habit of the body during life would be distinguishable
after death, either perfectly, or in a great measure and for a certain
time. And I should imagine that this is equally true of the soul, Callicles; when a man is stripped of the body, all the natural or acquired affections of the soul are laid open to view.—And when they   and they
come to the judge, as those from Asia come to Rhadamanthus, he   are pun-
places them near him and inspects them quite impartially, not   ished ac-
                                                                      cordingly.
knowing whose the soul is: perhaps he may lay hands on the soul of
the great king, or of some other king or potentate, who has no
soundness in him, but his soul is marked with the whip, and is full
of the prints and scars of perjuries and crimes with which each action has stained him, and he is all crooked with falsehood and im-   525
posture, and has no straightness, because he has lived without
truth. Him Rhadamanthus beholds, full of all deformity and dis-
proportion, which is caused by licence and luxury and insolence and
incontinence, and despatches him ignominiously to his prison, and
there he undergoes the punishment which he deserves.

Now the proper office of punishment is twofold: he who is rightly   The pro-
punished ought either to become better and profit by it, or he ought per office
to be made an example to his fellows, that they may see what he   of pun-
suffers, and fear and become better. Those who are improved when   ishment
                                                                      is either
they are punished by gods and men, are those whose sins are cur-   to im-
able; and they are improved, as in this world so also in another, by prove or
pain and suffering; for there is no other way in which they can be   to deter.
delivered from their evil. But they who have been guilty of the
worst crimes, and are incurable by reason of their crimes, are made
examples; for, as they are incurable, the time has passed at which
they can receive any benefit. They get no good themselves, but
others get good when they behold them enduring for ever the most
terrible and painful and fearful sufferings as the penalty of their
sins—there they are, hanging up as examples, in the prison-house
of the world below, a spectacle and a warning to all unrighteous
men who come thither. And among them, as I confidently affirm,
will be found Archelaus, if Polus truly reports of him, and any
other tyrant who is like him. Of these fearful examples, most, as I
believe, are taken from the class of tyrants and kings and potentates and public men, for they are the authors of the greatest and
most impious crimes, because they have the power. And Homer wit-

Gorgias

SOCRATES.

The
meaner
sort of
men are
incapable
of great
[526]
crimes.
Great
men have
some-
times
been good
men; but
power is
apt to
corrupt
them.
The im-
partiality
of the
judges in
another
world.

nesses to the truth of this; for they are always kings and potentates whom he has described as suffering everlasting punishment in
the world below: such were Tantalus and Sisyphus and Tityus. But
no one ever described Thersites, or any private person who was a
villain, as suffering everlasting punishment, or as incurable. For to
commit the worst crimes, as I am inclined to think, was not in his
power, and he was happier than those who had the power. No, Callicles, the very bad men come from the class of those who have
power [1]. And yet in that very class there may arise good men, and
worthy of all admiration they are, for where there is great power to
do wrong, to live and to die justly is a hard thing, and greatly to be
praised, and few there are who attain to this. Such good and true
men, however, there have been, and will be again, at Athens and in
other states, who have fulfilled their trust righteously; and there is
one who is quite famous all over Hellas, Aristeides, the son of Lysi-
machus. But, in general, great men are also bad, my friend.

As I was saying, Rhadamanthus, when he gets a soul of the bad
kind, knows nothing about him, neither who he is, nor who his parents are; he knows only that he has got hold of a villain; and seeing this, he stamps him as curable or incurable, and sends him away
to Tartarus, whither he goes and receives his proper recompense.
Or, again, he looks with admiration on the soul of some just one
who has lived in holiness and truth; he may have been a private
man or not; and I should say, Callicles, that he is most likely to
have been a philosopher who has done his own work, and not trou-
bled himself with the doings of other men in his lifetime; him
Rhadamanthus sends to the Islands of the Blessed. Aeacus does the
same; and they both have sceptres, and judge; but Minos alone has
a golden sceptre and is seated looking on, as Odysseus in Homer [2]
declares that he saw him:

'Holding a sceptre of gold, and giving laws to the dead.'

Now I, Callicles, am persuaded of the truth of these things, and I
consider how I shall present my soul whole and undefiled before the
judge in that day. Renouncing the honours at which the world
aims, I desire only to know the truth, and to live as well as I can,
and, when I die, to die as well as I can. And, to the utmost of my
power, I exhort all other men to do the same. And, in return for
your exhortation of me, I exhort you also to take part in the great
combat, which is the combat of life, and greater than every other
earthly conflict. And I retort your reproach of me, and say, that

[1] Cp. Rep. x. 615 E.
[2] Odyss. xi. 569.

you will not be able to help yourself when the day of trial and judgment, of which I was speaking, comes upon you; you will go before the judge, the son of Aegina, and, when he has got you in his
grip and is carrying you off, you will gape and your head will swim
round, just as mine would in the courts of this world, and very
likely some one will shamefully box you on the ears, and put upon
you any sort of insult.

Perhaps this may appear to you to be only an old wife's tale,
which you will contemn. And there might be reason in your con-
temning such tales, if by searching we could find out anything better or truer: but now you see that you and Polus and Gorgias, who
are the three wisest of the Greeks of our day, are not able to show
that we ought to live any life which does not profit in another world
as well as in this. And of all that has been said, nothing remains
unshaken but the saying, that to do injustice is more to be avoided
than to suffer injustice, and that the reality and not the appearance
of virtue is to be followed above all things, as well in public as in
private life; and that when any one has been wrong in anything, he
is to be chastised, and that the next best thing to a man being just is
that he should become just, and be chastised and punished; also
that he should avoid all flattery of himself as well as of others, of
the few or of the many: and rhetoric and any other art should be
used by him, and all his actions should be done always, with a view
to justice.

Follow me then, and I will lead you where you will be happy in
life and after death, as the argument shows. And never mind if
some one despises you as a fool, and insults you, if he has a mind;
let him strike you, by Zeus, and do you be of good cheer, and do not
mind the insulting blow, for you will never come to any harm in
the practice of virtue, if you are a really good and true man. When
we have practised virtue together, we will apply ourselves to politics, if that seems desirable, or we will advise about whatever else
may seem good to us, for we shall be better able to judge then. In
our present condition we ought not to give ourselves airs, for even
on the most important subjects we are always changing our minds;
so utterly stupid are we! Let us, then, take the argument as our
guide, which has revealed to us that the best way of life is to practise justice and every virtue in life and death. This way let us go;
and in this exhort all men to follow, not in the way to which you
trust and in which you exhort me to follow you; for that way, Callicles, is nothing worth.

GREAT BOOKS IN PHILOSOPHY PAPERBACK SERIES

ETHICS

Aristotle—*The Nicomachean Ethics*	$8.95
Marcus Aurelius—*Meditations*	5.95
Jeremy Bentham—*The Principles of Morals and Legislation*	8.95
John Dewey—*The Moral Writings of John Dewey, Revised Edition* (edited by James Gouinlock)	10.95
Epictetus—*Enchiridion*	3.95
Immanuel Kant—*Fundamental Principles of the Metaphysic of Morals*	4.95
John Stuart Mill—*Utilitarianism*	4.95
George Edward Moore—*Principia Ethica*	8.95
Friedrich Nietzsche—*Beyond Good and Evil*	8.95
Plato—*Protagoras, Philebus,* and *Gorgias*	7.95
Bertrand Russell—*Bertrand Russell On Ethics, Sex, and Marriage* (edited by Al Seckel)	18.95
Arthur Schopenhauer—*The Wisdom of Life* and *Counsels and Maxims*	6.95
Benedict de Spinoza—*Ethics* and *The Improvement of the Understanding*	9.95

SOCIAL AND POLITICAL PHILOSOPHY

Aristotle—*The Politics*	7.95
Francis Bacon—*Essays*	6.95
Mikhail Bakunin—*The Basic Bakunin: Writings, 1869–1871* (translated and edited by Robert M. Cutler)	10.95
Edmund Burke—*Reflections on the Revolution in France*	7.95
John Dewey—*Freedom and Culture*	10.95
G. W. F. Hegel—*The Philosophy of History*	9.95
Thomas Hobbes—*The Leviathan*	7.95
Sidney Hook—*Paradoxes of Freedom*	9.95
Sidney Hook—*Reason, Social Myths, and Democracy*	11.95
John Locke—*Second Treatise on Civil Government*	4.95
Niccolo Machiavelli—*The Prince*	4.95
Karl Marx—*The Poverty of Philosophy*	7.95
Karl Marx/Frederick Engels—*The Economic and Philosophic Manuscripts of 1844* and *The Communist Manifesto*	6.95
John Stuart Mill—*Considerations on Representative Government*	6.95
John Stuart Mill—*On Liberty*	4.95
John Stuart Mill—*On Socialism*	7.95
John Stuart Mill—*The Subjection of Women*	4.95
Friedrich Nietzsche—*Thus Spake Zarathustra*	9.95
Thomas Paine—*Common Sense*	5.95
Thomas Paine—*Rights of Man*	7.95
Plato—*Lysis, Phaedrus,* and *Symposium*	6.95
Plato—*The Republic*	9.95
Jean-Jacques Rousseau—*The Social Contract*	5.95
Mary Wollstonecraft—*A Vindication of the Rights of Women*	6.95

METAPHYSICS/EPISTEMOLOGY

Aristotle—*De Anima*   6.95
Aristotle—*The Metaphysics*   9.95
George Berkeley—*Three Dialogues Between Hylas and Philonous*   4.95
René Descartes—*Discourse on Method* and *The Meditations*   6.95
John Dewey—*How We Think*   10.95
Epicurus—*The Essential Epicurus: Letters,*
    Principal Doctrines, Vatican Sayings, and Fragments
    (translated, and with an introduction, by Eugene O'Connor)   5.95
Sidney Hook—*The Quest for Being*   11.95
David Hume—*An Enquiry Concerning Human Understanding*   4.95
David Hume—*Treatise of Human Nature*   9.95
William James—*Pragmatism*   7.95
Immanuel Kant—*Critique of Practical Reason*   7.95
Immanuel Kant—*Critique of Pure Reason*   9.95
Gottfried Wilhelm Leibniz—*Discourse on Method* and the *Monadology*   6.95
John Locke—*An Essay Concerning Human Understanding*   9.95
Plato—*The Euthyphro, Apology, Crito,* and *Phaedo*   5.95
Bertrand Russell—*The Problems of Philosophy*   8.95
Sextus Empiricus—*Outlines of Pyrrhonism*   8.95

PHILOSOPHY OF RELIGION

Ludwig Feuerbach—*The Essence of Christianity*   8.95
David Hume—*Dialogues Concerning Natural Religion*   5.95
John Locke—*A Letter Concerning Toleration*   4.95
Thomas Paine—*The Age of Reason*   13.95
Bertrand Russell—*Bertrand Russell On God and Religion* (edited by Al Seckel)   18.95

ESTHETICS

Aristotle—*The Poetics*   5.95
Aristotle—*Treatise on Rhetoric*   7.95

GREAT MINDS PAPERBACK SERIES

ECONOMICS

RELIGION

SCIENCE

HISTORY

SOCIOLOGY

LITERATURE

(Prices subject to change without notice.)